About IF...

The Internat...
1975 to iden...
and policies...
basis, with...
groups in th...
objective of...
factors invol...
processes ar...
tute's resea...
and private...
tion and im...
seminated t...
researchers,...
agricultural...

Working Multisectorally in Nutrition

Principles, Practices, and Case Studies

Edited by
James Garrett and Marcela Natalicchio

INTERNATIONAL FOOD POLICY
RESEARCH INSTITUTE
sustainable solutions for ending hunger and poverty

Supported by the CGIAR

International Food Policy Research Institute
2033 K Street, NW
Washington, D.C. 20006-1002, U.S.A.
Telephone +1-202-862-5600
www.ifpri.org

DOI: http://dx.doi.org/10.2499/9780896291812

Library of Congress Cataloging-in-Publication Data

Working multisectorally in nutrition : principles, practices, and case studies / edited by
James Garrett and Marcela Natalicchio.
    p. cm.
  Includes bibliographical references and index.
  ISBN 978-0-89629-181-2 (alk. paper)
    1. Nutrition policy.   2. Nutrition policy—Senegal—Case studies.   3. Nutrition policy—
Colombia—Antioquia—Case studies.   I. Garrett, James L.   II. Natalicchio, Marcela.
  TX359.W66 2011
  363.8'56—dc22

                                               2010038037

Contents

Tables

Figures

Foreword

Combating malnutrition in low-income countries deserves serious attention from governments, the private sector, civil society, and national and international development partners. The negative consequences of malnutrition—particularly maternal and young child malnutrition—for mortality, morbidity, cognitive function, and economic productivity and growth are clear and unchallenged.

Approaches and interventions undertaken by a single sector—such as the agricultural community or health community—have characterized the history of efforts to combat malnutrition. These approaches often reflect different understandings of the causes of and solutions for malnutrition. Nutrition interventions in the 1950s and 1960s, for example, could take the form of home economics extension when led by the agricultural sector, or food technology solutions when led by the health sector. The same tendency toward narrower, more sectoral solutions to nutrition problems exists today in the use of therapeutic feeding in contexts of chronic rather than acute malnutrition (often at the expense of necessary preventive action) and in a lingering insistence by some to equate increased agricultural foodgrains production with nutrition security.

Multisectoral approaches, which emerged as a key planning tool for nutrition in the 1970s, provide a sharp contrast to these more narrowly conceived interventions. Despite some criticisms that multisectoral programs are too complex to effectively implement, many practitioners believe such approaches still hold the greatest promise for reducing malnutrition since nutrition insecurity is multicausal. In fact, despite limited support from the international community, multisectoral approaches continue to function today in various forms at the country level.

The need to know more about multisectoral nutrition approaches, and the preconditions and principles for their success, has increased significantly in the past few years with the emergence of several broadly supported programs. Scaling Up Nutrition and REACH initiatives and the United States–supported Feed the Future program all urge the integration of nutrition into related sectors.

These broader-based and potentially more effective multisectoral efforts are the focus of this important new book edited by James Garrett and Marcela

Natalicchio. The book traces the development of these initiatives and seeks to understand the contexts in which they are likely to succeed. Based on both theory and evidence, it provides guidance for practitioners on how such approaches can best be implemented.

Readers will find a cogent history of multisectoral nutrition efforts, a conceptual model based on a range of relevant disciplines, specific hypotheses on contexts likely to be conducive to cooperative efforts among diverse groups of stakeholders, and two valuable case studies to test the model and hypotheses in practice.

This book will be valuable not only to those interested in reducing malnutrition, but also to those seeking to address other similar development problems that call for multisectoral approaches.

Shenggen Fan
Director General, International Food Policy Research Institute

Acknowledgments

This volume represents the result of a collaboration between the World Bank and the International Food Policy Research Institute (IFPRI). From 2005 to 2007, I worked as a senior economist for nutrition in the Health, Nutrition, and Population Division of the World Bank, under the Staff Exchange Program. The primary purpose of my assignment to the World Bank was to support the Bank's efforts to improve political commitment and institutional arrangements for nutrition. That concern, about how to mainstream nutrition into sectors outside health, was the genesis of this report.

The book itself emerges from an environment where a number of supportive or related initiatives were taking place. Most importantly was the study on working multisectorally in nutrition developed by Lucy Bassett, Jim Levinson, and myself, which served as a background paper for this volume. We are grateful to the World Bank's Development Grant Facility for supporting that work. The case study in Colombia, which I carried out, was a complementary study, with the fieldwork being financed directly by the Health, Nutrition, and Population Division of the World Bank.

In Colombia, I thank especially Dora Cecilia Gutiérrez Hernández, Angela Molina, and Patricia Monsalve as well as the other core staff of the Food and Nutrition Improvement Plan of Antioquia (Plan de Mejoramiento Alimentario y Nutricional de Antioquia, or MANA), the program studied here. They graciously facilitated all my requests for documentation and helped to determine whom to invite and how to structure the interviews most effectively. They kindly set up the individual and group interviews, providing transport and venues when necessary, and they spent hours of their own time with me, answering my questions and telling the story of MANA. Of course, I am also grateful to all those who participated in focus groups or gave individual interviews, especially Marta Celia, Alírio García, and Mauricio Hernández.

At the World Bank, Kei Kawabata, Meera Shekar, and Menno Mulder-Sibanda were instrumental in their support. At IFPRI, Lynette Aspillera, Ramela Morales, Nelly Tioco, and Jay Willis provided administrative as well as moral support and good cheer throughout the process, and Anuja Saurkar provided timely research assistance down the final stretch. We also extend our sincere appreciation to the editorial staff at IFPRI, particularly John Whitehead; the staff of the Publications Review Committee; and three anonymous reviewers whose insights contributed greatly to improving the manuscript. Finally, this book is truly the result of the collective contributions of all the authors. I extend my sincere appreciation to my coeditor Marcela Natalicchio and my coauthors Lucy Bassett and James Levinson for their friendship, collaboration, insights, and, most of all, hard work and patience as we put the manuscript together.

James Garrett

In 2007, I started working for the World Bank as part of a collaborative project involving three of its units: Poverty Reduction and Economic Management (PREM); Health, Nutrition and Population (HNP) Africa; and HNP Network. The units' common goal was to understand the political economy of nutrition policies. In particular, they wanted to figure out why—despite the evidence that malnutrition hampered development at the individual and societal levels and the existence of known, cost-effective responses to it—most African governments had traditionally made this policy domain a low priority. This project marked the beginning of a long-term collaboration with James Garrett, who was working in the HNP Network at the time.

The project's first activity was organizing a workshop including experts from different fields (political economy, politics of nutrition, change management) and nutrition practitioners from Africa. The workshop participants tried to develop a framework for understanding the main reasons why African governments do or do not commit to nutrition policies. This led to the February 2009 joint publication, by the World Bank and IFPRI, of an HNP Discussion Paper titled *Carrots and Sticks: The Political Economy of Nutrition Policy Reforms,* which I coedited with James Garrett, Menno Mulder-Sibanda, Steve Ndegwa, and Doris Voorbraak.

The workshop also informed the design of a World Bank regional research project in Africa, which I led and coordinated from 2007 to 2009, and of which Menno Mulder-Sibanda of the HNP Africa unit was the Task Team Leader (TTL). The research project compared case studies of eight countries (Benin, Burkina Faso, Ethiopia, The Gambia, Ghana, Madagascar, Senegal, and Tanzania), some of which had more success than others in convincing their governments to commit to fighting malnutrition. The workshop's final objective was to tease out the factors that explained how countries got trapped in what I termed the "low-priority cycle" and determine how they could break out of it. The first case study we carried out, when we began in 2007, was of Senegal, one of the successful countries.

At the same time, in December 2007, I started collaborating with James Garrett while he was still working for the World Bank on a project for IFPRI on multisectoral cooperation in nutrition. Many of the drivers of nutritional commitment that the World Bank's Africa project identified resembled the factors necessary for a successful multisectoral collaboration. Further, it became apparent that Senegal was not only a successful case of government commitment to nutrition but also an interesting case of multisectoral collaboration. Using a study developed by Lucy Bassett, Jim Levinson, and James Garrett on working multisectorally in nutrition as a point of departure, we started to establish the intellectual underpinnings of this volume, comparing our case studies of Colombia and Senegal in order to test the theories and hypothesis developed for it.

For the Senegal case, I drew on the case study that I had designed, directed, and supervised, and for which I had conducted part of the field research, between September and October 2007. As the case study was originally conducted to answer a different set of questions, I had to look at it through the lens of multisectoral cooperation and complement it with archival research and additional interviews. For the case study, I thank all the people in Senegal who generously gave their time to answer questions. In particular, I thank Biram Ndiaye, the program coordinator for the Programme de Renforcement Nutritionnel (Nutrition Enhancement Program, or NEP) in Senegal, who not only facilitated contacts and interviews but also devoted several hours to discussing his role in NEP and his views on why multisectoral collaboration had worked there. I also thank Alfred Ndiaye, the World Bank consultant who carried out most of the fieldwork in Senegal and wrote a final report for the political economy study, and who has undoubtedly contributed to my understanding of the case.

I am very grateful to Menno Mulder-Sibanda, senior nutrition specialist at the World Bank and TTL for NEP in Senegal, with whom I have been coordinating an eight-country study on the political economy of nutrition in Africa. He has always been very supportive of the publication of this volume. He has provided insightful comments and essential pieces of information and has always responded gracefully to our numerous requests for updates. Claudia Rokx, a former TTL for NEP in Senegal, has also enthusiastically contributed her views on and insights into the process of creating the program in which she played a pivotal role.

Finally, I thank the Italian Trust Fund for Children and Youth in Africa for providing funds for several case studies in Africa on the political economy of nutrition, including the one for Senegal.

Marcela Natalicchio

Acronyms and Abbreviations

AED	Academy for Educational Development
AGETIP	Executing Agency for Works of Public Interest against Unemployment
APL	Adaptable Program Loan
BEN	National Executive Bureau
BER	Regional Executive Bureau
CFA	African Financial Community
CLM	Coordination Unit for the Reduction of Malnutrition
CNLM	National Commission for the Fight against Malnutrition
COMPOS	Social Policy Committee
DHS	Demographic and Health Survey
FAO	Food and Agriculture Organization of the United Nations
FARC	Revolutionary Armed Forces of Colombia
GDP	gross domestic product
GMP	growth monitoring and promotion
HNP	Health, Nutrition and Population (World Bank)
ICBF	Colombian Institute for Family Welfare
IEC	Information-Education-Communication
IFPRI	International Food Policy Research Institute
IMCI	Integrated Management of Childhood Illness
IRD	integrated rural development
MANA	Food and Nutrition Improvement Plan of Antioquia
MDG	Millennium Development Goal

MIC   microenterprise

MNP   multisectoral nutrition planning

NCHS   National Center for Health Statistics

NEP   Nutrition Enhancement Program

NFNP   National Food and Nutrition Plan

NGO   nongovernmental organization

PES   Situational Strategic Planning

PIU   Project Implementation Unit

PNC   Community Nutrition Program

PRSC   Poverty Reduction Strategy Credit

PRSP   Poverty Reduction Strategy Paper

ReSA   Food Security Network

SWAp   sectorwide approach

TTL   Task Team Leader

USAID   United States Agency for International Development

WFP   World Food Programme

Summary

A multisectoral approach is arguably the most effective way to reduce malnutrition, but there is little evidence about how to implement it, and that evidence is not well known. Common beliefs about the difficulty of multisectoral collaboration inhibit action. Among these are that institutional defensiveness and jealousies doom attempts at collaboration; nutrition activities get lost in a dominant sector, especially health; nutrition is not prioritized because policymakers see it as an outcome, not an input into human development; and nutritionists are technical and narrowly trained, so they fail to incorporate or value insights from other sectors.

Although these beliefs are still common in the international nutrition community, the most vigorous examination of multisectoral approaches was conducted more than 20 years ago. Even then the arguments had more to do with the challenges of national planning than with the validity or possibility of implementing a multisectoral program. Other analysts have since stated their beliefs in the usefulness of multisectoral approaches, but mostly these are general statements that, although likely true, have undergone limited empirical scrutiny. Available country studies and project documents are largely descriptive rather than analytical. None has explicitly examined the design or mechanics of operation of multisectoral approaches in depth. The result is that these beliefs fail to fully reflect ground truths in countries. Many governments are in fact pursuing multisectoral strategies and in some cases multisectoral programs to combat malnutrition.

This volume is an initial foray into the in-depth research necessary to develop that evidence base and answer questions about whether it is possible to work multisectorally in nutrition. The main question is how to facilitate collaboration vertically and horizontally across interrelated sectors, ministries, and actors inside and outside government. The two case studies described in this book, from Senegal and Colombia, provide intriguing evidence that challenges the stated presumptions and suggest how and when to work multisectorally. More specifically, this book goes beyond statements about the importance of multisectoral action or the logic behind such collaboration to consider the following:

- How do initiatives to work multisectorally get started? What are the triggers?
- How does the collaboration work? How does it evolve over time? What are the dynamics and mechanisms of the collaboration process?

- What are the issues surrounding the sustainability of collaboration?
- What characterizes the broader environment in which the collaboration takes place? How does it affect the collaboration?

Our analyses seek to shed light on motivations for collaboration and the expected dynamics inherent in multisectoral strategies. This volume does not attempt to address another important question: even if a multisectoral approach can be made successful, are multisectoral projects more effective than standard approaches in combating malnutrition? Principally the aim here is to establish that multisectoral approaches are indeed viable.

In the end, we are able to decipher associations among several factors (or approaches) and the operational success of our case studies. Our comparative analyses, along with a review of literature, allow us to suggest elements of successful approaches to the design and implementation of the integrative processes that are the essence of multisectoral programs.

Because of the general nature of the approaches that emerge from these case studies, we believe these lessons can be used to educate and orient policy-makers, practitioners, and advocates involved in working multisectorally not only in nutrition but also in other cross-sectoral and interagency endeavors.

Chapter 2 provides a succinct narrative history of the multisectorality in the field of international nutrition. Chapter 3 reviews the relevant literature from public management, political science, and sociology, among other fields, to devise a tentative conceptual model and analytical framework. Chapter 4 develops this model to produce specific research questions and hypotheses; it also describes our methods and approach. The country studies in Chapter 5 (Senegal) and Chapter 6 (Colombia) then apply this framework to two cases of multisectoral action in nutrition in diverse circumstances. Chapter 7 concludes by comparing findings from the case studies with hypotheses posited in Chapter 4 and placing the discussion in the overall context of where we are today.

Conceptual Model and Hypotheses

The case studies examine and test the internal and external factors that affect the success of collaboration as well as the nature of the mechanisms that link organizations.

Among the factors in the internal context (internal characteristics of the organization) that affect collaboration are leadership; vision; technical, financial, and managerial capacity; organizational structures, values, culture, and experience; and incentives for collaboration. The factors associated with the external environment surrounding the partnership include having nutrition as a development priority; the urgency of action; and the economic, social, cultural, political, and legal environments. Some factors that seem to help lubricate the mechanisms of coordination include shared understanding and genuine participation and ownership among participants and stakeholders; having clear roles, responsibility, and accountability mechanisms; and having flexibility that allows creation of appropriate mechanisms and partnership types.

From the conceptual model and the literature we develop a set of statements that could potentially provide explanations for successfully working multisectorally in nutrition. These statements are grouped by internal context, external context, and institutional links and are summarized here.

Internal Context

- Nutrition is a chosen issue. Champions are needed to put it on the policy agenda. Leaders must develop vision and structures to support action.
- Advocates work to build a shared vision, through developing a shared language, understanding, and sense of purpose.
- Partner organizations have relatively strong technical, financial, administrative, and managerial capacities, so they can carry out their defined responsibilities.
- Organizations have values that promote collaboration, including respect for the organizational routines and missions of others, an openness to learning from them, and an orientation toward results. These values encourage participation, transparency, accountability, and institutional flexibility.
- Organizations provide incentives for action, including personal and financial incentives, and have established accountability structures.
- Partner organizations perceive that the benefits of participation outweigh the costs.

External Context

- Promoting nutrition as a development priority among a wide range of stakeholders creates openings for action and sustained attention to nutrition.
- Advocates create a sense of urgency to promote action.
- General economic, political, and social conditions do not bring attention to nutrition, although specific events may.

Institutional Links

- Multisectoral collaboration requires institutional change, in budgeting structures or modalities of implementation, for example.
- Successful multisectoral collaboration involves establishing linking structures that
  - promote shared understanding;
  - are inclusive and participatory;

○ promote accountability to the public and stakeholders, including partners and program management;

○ value the contributions of all partners; and

○ make the roles and responsibilities of all partners clear.

The Case Studies: Testing the Hypotheses

This volume uses case studies from two countries to examine these hypotheses.

Senegal

Senegal is on track to be one of the few countries in Sub-Saharan Africa to reach the Millennium Development Goals (MDGs) for nutrition. One of the main programs Senegal has to reach this goal is the Programme de Renforce-ment Nutritionnel (Nutrition Enhancement Program, or NEP). The first phase of NEP ran from 2002 to 2006. It is now in its second phase (2007-11).

NEP uses a multisectoral and multiactor approach, coordinating actions across ministries, donors, and nongovernmental organizations (NGOs). NEP operates under the supervision of the Coordination Unit for the Reduction of Malnutrition (Cellule de Lutte contre la Malnutrition, or CLM). CLM, attached to the Prime Minister's Office, coordinates programs and actions undertaken by both the public and private sectors to reduce malnutrition.

Colombia

The Food and Nutrition Improvement Plan of Antioquia (Plan de Mejoramiento Alimentario y Nutricional de Antioquia, or MANA) began in 2001. Over about three years, MANA has expanded to all 125 municipalities in the depart-ment of Antioquia, Colombia. MANA comprises six axes of action: comple-mentary feeding, health services, and children's rights; a nutrition and food security surveillance system; agricultural production projects; and educa-tional projects.

The program is coordinated through an office in the Ministry of Health but has only one staff member of its own. The other members come from the par-ticipating ministries of Health, Agriculture, and Education. It has implement-ing agreements with NGOs, universities, producer and regional development associations, and private-sector firms.

Comparing and Contrasting Experiences: Summary Findings

• Leadership of a particular type is essential for success. Indeed, the leader-ship exhibited in Senegal and Colombia shared specific characteristics. Succeeding in working in a complex system may owe much to personal—not just institutional—factors.

The main actors in Senegal and Colombia shared elements of a common approach to collaboration, an approach with a people-oriented perspective, rather than just a focus on institutional relations and coordinating mechanisms. The approach suggests a strategy, with a bundle of elements working together, rather than the presence or absence of specific factors. Specifically, the approach involves an inclusive process of bringing potential partners together to build consensus around the problem and its solutions. It respects their institutional mission and procedures, helping them see how they can contribute to achieving the common vision, providing incentives, and using evidence and reason to support the discussion in designing and implementing the program.

- In both case studies, an external catalyst chose to put nutrition on the policy agenda. In Senegal, it was interest by political authorities plus the World Bank. In Colombia, it was the governor. These authorities created the policy space, but then senior staff and others (including the donor in Senegal) were responsible for filling that space and developing a multisectoral program. The locus of leadership may change over time in the dynamic environment surrounding nutrition.

- Logic suggests that coordination and implementation are more difficult when agencies are institutionally weak and not prepared to carry out their responsibilities as part of the partnership. Although the case studies support the general thrust of this hypothesis, institutional strength did not in fact guarantee success. In fact, the possession of such strengths can mean that ministries have less incentive to collaborate, because they can implement programs and policies on their own. Collaboration may, in fact, prove easier at the local level, because that level often lacks a multi-institutional structure and has less capacity. The case studies also showed that collaboration can work even when partners are weak. MANA, for example, established a separate team specifically to strengthen the ability of municipalities to work with the program. In both countries, implementation depended to a large extent on NGOs, which had the necessary implementation capacity and could assist weaker partners at the local level.

- The organizations in both countries exhibited values that promoted collaboration, including institutional flexibility and an ability to value the contributions of others. Program management worked hard to be inclusive, involving a wide range of stakeholders and potential partners in creating vision and strategy for the program. In Colombia, they built on existing programs and largely respected institutional missions and routines. This approach reduced the level of threat from change that the partner institutions might feel. As a result, MANA seems to have been able to form a functioning umbrella coordinating unit. In contrast, NEP was much stronger at working vertically than at working horizontally. The lead council largely implemented the program through NGOs in collaboration with local governments. Operational integration among ministries at the national level was still weak.

Both programs thus exhibited substantial operational flexibility internally and in contracting implementing partners. Such an approach is not as random in its outputs as one might think, as both programs conveyed clear principles of operation to partners, especially implementing organizations, and agreed on expected results.

- MANA and NEP provided incentives for cooperation, which helped partners to recognize that the benefits of their participation exceeded the costs. But these incentives were not only financial. Instead, managers pursued organizational incentives by offering assistance or arrangements that would help partner organizations achieve their own goals. In both cases, personal interests and passions tended to be the initial forces that brought people together (once a higher authority had established a space for the initiative to develop).
- The role of information turned out to be more influential than expected. Survey data in Antioquia helped establish the severity of the problem of hunger and malnutrition. Staff used the conceptual model of nutrition from UNICEF and a particular technique to develop strategy among multiple stakeholders. Information was used not only for tracking operational performance but also for making the issue of nutrition politically viable, promoting widespread understanding and ownership, creating calls for action, and keeping nutrition on the development agenda.
- Achieving multisectorality can take years. To succeed at working multisectorally requires a long, multiactivity process, not a one-off workshop. In Colombia and Senegal, it required extensive consultation, particularly with other mid- and upper-level civil servants and the entire range of operating partners, to develop understanding, vision, and strategy, not simply agreement at the ministerial level. Participants in both countries said the process was difficult and littered with contention. But in the end they succeeded and are now reaping the benefits.

Conclusions

These case studies exhibit two examples of approaches taken to working multisectorally in nutrition that reflect new understanding about how to solve complex social problems. Despite different country conditions and operational contexts, close analysis shows that the initiators, creators, and managers of these programs shared certain values and methods. We do not argue that these are the only ways of achieving multisectoral success in nutrition. Nor do we argue we have identified causal links between these factors and guaranteed success. But we have shown an association between the nature of these approaches and operational success. The case studies confirm that working multisectorally in nutrition is possible, although it may mean changes to the usual ways of working and thinking. It may also involve a process that develops a strategy for action that is more reflective of partner needs, conditions, and context than is traditionally the case. These examples strongly suggest that addressing complex social problems, like nutrition, will need to go beyond sector-bound and single agencies. Because of the need to coordinate action among multiple agencies, arriving at a solution will require an inclusive process (of institutions and actors) and lateral, rather than top-down, leadership.

The focus on process emerges from an understanding that many of these problems, such as nutrition, result from the operation of complex systems. Understanding how to devise and manage dynamic, multiagent, multi-institutional processes is an emerging facet of modern management. These case studies can help us begin to understand how we might better manage the dimensions of complexity, including possible strategies and the conditions needed to support them, such as the importance of shared vision, the need for institutional incentives, and an understanding of how others gauge costs and benefits of participation.

CHAPTER 1

Introduction

JAMES GARRETT, LUCY BASSETT, F. JAMES LEVINSON,
AND MARCELA NATALICCHIO

According to Richard Heaver, "multisectoral programs are the most effective way to tackle malnutrition" (2005a, 20). Still, despite general agreement that multisectoral actions (if not programs per se) are the best way to reduce malnutrition, many observers believe that multisectoral planning and coordination are simply too difficult to carry out:

> Doing more and doing it systematically has appeal when most of what is done [in regard to interventions for nutrition] is so limited and inadequate. The dilemma is that comprehensive understanding (a virtue) often leads to highly complex interventions with lots of interdependencies; and these overwhelm the capacities of weak institutions and make action reliant on coordinated efforts by lots of different actors who don't particularly appreciate being harnessed to and subordinated by the requirements of a comprehensive plan. (Field 2006)

The ostensible consensus: even if policies and strategies are conceived multisectorally, operationally programs must be run vertically or at least along sectoral lines.

Part of the problem of promoting a large-scale multisectoral approach to nutrition is that many attempts do seem to have failed or have not been sustained. However, analysis of such attempts has been relatively rare, and so the evidence base supporting this perception is limited. So are we sure that we know what we say we know?

Time for a New Look

Perhaps not, for while the international nutrition research community's consensus largely continues to reflect that of 20 years ago—that multisectoral programming cannot work—some country experiences, although not well documented and largely anecdotal, are providing intriguing evidence that challenges that presumption. The program literature continues to document numerous interventions, projects, and programs that have multi- or intersectoral activities. At the country level, policymakers and programmers, building on the fledgling efforts of the 1970s, continue to design and implement nutrition programs in multisectoral ways. And so, although the international nutrition research community has largely abandoned support for a multisectoral approach to nutrition, policymakers, programmers, and donors have not.

Interest in multisectoral collaboration thus remains strong, and the continuing high levels of malnutrition and a sympathetic development environment encourage reconsideration of multisectoral approaches. The belief remains that to reduce malnutrition, comprehensive integrated strategies may sometimes bring about more substantial advances than strategies that rely on separate, uncoordinated interventions.

The main question is how to facilitate collaboration vertically and horizontally across interrelated sectors, ministries, and actors inside and outside government. Commonly cited obstacles to such cooperation include the following:

- Each agency seeks to preserve its autonomy and independence, which can be compromised through cooperation with other agencies.
- Agencies have different visions, goals, routines, and procedures. Agencies and individuals may conflict in terms of technical understanding of the problem and appropriate solutions.
- Organizational capacities and power may be uneven across the partners in a collaboration, affecting abilities to make and implement decisions. They may also face different timelines for action. Organizational coordination, alignment, and synchronization can become difficult.
- Agencies have different political constituencies to which they respond and, often, different structures for accountability. Different constituencies can bring different expectations and pressures to bear on each agency. The various pressures for action can actually pull agencies in different directions.
- Working multisectorally may not be a guiding principle for government or for outside interest groups, including potential beneficiaries. Thus incentives (political, organizational, and personal) for multisectoral action may be weak, as perceived benefits do not overcome the costs of coordination. This factor seems to be particularly relevant in the case of nutrition.

Need for New Evidence

Unfortunately, the evidence base for guiding actions is weak. Even the most vigorous examination of multisectoral approaches[1] had more to do with the chal-

---

[1] This examination was reflected in a contentious point-counterpoint between Alan Berg and John

lenges of national planning rather than with the operation of a multisectoral program—although observations on the planning aspects quickly morphed into judgments on operational feasibility as the bottom-line conclusion.

Other analysts have stated their belief in the usefulness of multisectoral approaches (Gillespie, McLachlan, and Shrimpton 2003; Heaver 2005b). But these have tended to be general statements that, although likely true, have had limited empirical scrutiny. The few country case studies that have been published (for example, Dolan and Levinson 2000; Heaver 2002a) provide an overview of nutrition policy and programs rather than detailed analyses of how to work multisectorally. Many unpublished project documents exist, but they are more often descriptive than analytical. None has explicitly examined the processes involved in the design or operation of multisectoral approaches in depth, despite urgings from analysts and the good intentions of donors (Heaver 2002b).

Significant questions thus remain about how a multisectoral approach to help reduce malnutrition might work. Improving coordination across sectors is clearly an imperative understood by many of those working in nutrition at the national and international levels, but one for which policymakers and programmers have little documented country experience or detailed analysis to guide them. Missing has been in-depth research focused on the relevant concepts and experiences associated with such multisectoral action.

Aims of the Study

This volume is an initial, more systematic foray into the topic, to begin to answer questions about how to work multisectorally. Research at these interorganizational boundaries is not easy, and is likely more difficult than a study of operations within a single organization (Agranoff and McGuire 2003). Indeed, scholars sometimes avoid such research because of a lack of concreteness; a need for interpretation; and, due to variation in context, ambiguity in findings and an inability to provide guidance applicable to all situations. These problems have informed our approach to this study and are further explored in Chapter 4.

Building on insights from the case studies and literature from other fields, this book goes beyond statements about the importance or rationale for multisectoral action. Although the findings certainly require further study, the book presents a new analytical framework and some principles to help guide analysis and action. It provides a checklist of factors that will likely inhibit

Field more than 20 years ago about whether such approaches had made substantial contributions to nutrition initiatives or had been spectacular failures (Berg 1987; Field 1987).

or promote successful multisectoral action in nutrition. The volume suggests answers to such questions as the following:

- How do initiatives to work multisectorally get started? What are the triggers?
- How does the collaboration work? How does it evolve over time? What are the dynamics and mechanisms of the collaboration process?
- What are the issues surrounding the sustainability of collaboration?
- What characterizes the broader environment in which the collaboration takes place? How does it affect the collaboration?

The resulting analyses seek to shed light on the motivations for collaboration and the expected dynamics inherent in multisectoral strategies. In the end, our findings suggest that a wide array of elements makes up successful multisectoral approaches to reducing malnutrition. These factors have to do with all stages of the process, from inception to design to implementation. The case studies suggest that collaborative and integrative processes following certain general stages are essential to establishment and sustainability. Because of the general nature of the approaches that emerge from these case studies, we believe these lessons can be used to educate and orient policymakers, practitioners, and advocates involved in working multisectorally, not only in nutrition but also in other cross-sectoral and interagency endeavors.

Note that this work revolves around questions of program initiation and implementation. We look at how collaborations can be created successfully and what conditions sustain them. In understanding "success," we are using primarily the prism of operations and management—of workable institutional arrangements—and not the impact on malnutrition per se. We examine particular programs as examples of operationally successful multisectoral collaborations based on three factors: they have operated for a number of years, they have been externally reviewed, and they have demonstrated at least some ability to reduce malnutrition. Our volume focuses on the factors or approaches that underlie the multisectoral aspects of these programs.

Whether a multisectoral program will work at all is a key empirical question for policymakers, programmers, and donors, who, following the accepted wisdom, would generally assume that it will not. This assumption endures despite their affinity for a multisectoral approach, based on conceptual models and much research that confirms the multisectoral nature of nutrition.

Neither of the programs examined in our case studies have undergone rigorous, randomized trials to measure whether they have quantifiably reduced malnutrition, although both programs have other evidence at hand that suggests they do. For our purposes, we largely assume that logically structured programs, such as these, based on principles of programming and on what we know so far about effective intervention strategies, can reasonably be expected to reduce malnutrition.

At the same time, we are not trying to compare these programs either in terms of impacts or costs with alternative interventions that might attempt to achieve the same goal. Addressing those issues would require comparative analysis of multisectoral and single-sector programs with similar objectives and comparable settings, a situation that is rarely available in the real world. This volume therefore does not address the important question of whether—supposing that a multisectoral approach can be made successful—multisectoral or single-sector projects are more effective in combating malnutrition.

The aim here is principally to establish that multisectoral approaches are indeed viable. The purpose is not to argue that multisectoral programs, such as those analyzed here, are the answer to reducing malnutrition in every case. In fact, we would argue that each country simply needs to understand context and strategically structure its interventions to have the greatest impact. We are simply putting a multisectoral program approach back on the table as an option. Based on the examination of these relatively successful country programs, we argue that working multisectorally can be part of that array of choices in programs and policies. A complete strategy would likely involve sectoral interventions as well as less complex programs that link across sectors.

This operational focus may initially seem of somewhat limited interest. But as explained below, it is not. The accepted wisdom is that, in nutrition, although we can conceive multisectorally, we must work sectorally. This study challenges that basic assumption.

The analytical framework and case studies, as well as literature from nutrition and other fields, will help reveal the factors that appear to inhibit or promote successful multisectoral action in nutrition. The main questions of inquiry are then about what makes working multisectorally an operationally viable option, not what conditions lead to success in terms of having optimal impact on nutrition.

John Field noted in 1985 how critical these sorts of questions were. Self-referencing an earlier paper from 1977, in discussing the difficulties and apparent failure of multisectoral nutrition planning, he wrote the following:

> In sum, implementation is the true "soft underbelly" of nutrition planning as it is, in varying degrees, of other social sector efforts where the process affects the outcome. In nutrition, the plan and control model based on the machine theory of implementation is a proven failure. . . . The danger is that, unless work on implementation is encouraged, the capacity of evaluation to detect failure is likely to outpace the ability of implementation to cause success.
>
> Nutrition planning is well positioned to enrich the implementation literature in turn, benefitting both theory and practice. There is obvi-

ous merit in examining nutrition programs in action. . . . We need to learn a great deal more about how different nutrition programs function in their environment; that is, how a given system mobilizes energies and resources; how it packages and operationalizes interventions; how it generates consensus and either deflects or resolves conflict; how it structures participation; how it monitors performance and directs accountability; how it seeks to institutionalize new capabilities; and whether and how it builds self-reliance or creates vertical linkages to enduring sources of support. (Field 1985, 169)

More than 30 years later, we have advanced little in our knowledge of the implementation of nutrition programs, although various voices have recently decried this lacuna once again (Garrett 2008; Leroy and Menon 2008; Shekar et al. 2008). Field's (1985) questions remain largely unanswered and unexplored in any systematic way, so that over time we are failing to build a base for evidence and action, despite the promises of working multisectorally.

Much still remains to be done, but our book does provide substantial insights into many of the questions Field (1985) raises. Based on the literature and our case studies, we look closely at how to work operationally across sectors in nutrition. Thirty years later, with more knowledge, experience, examples, frameworks, even epistemologies, and examples, we hope to provide well-considered guidance for action so that we can, in Field's words, "cause success."

Organization of the Study

Based on renewed attention to programming issues at the international level and some further examples of successful multisectoral programs (such as those we discuss and Seecaline in Madagascar), multisectoral approaches for addressing nutrition may be getting a second chance.[2] We hope that this study proves useful both for those actors already undertaking multisectoral approaches (but who may be unaware of those earlier experiences and are therefore in danger of repeating past failures) and those who have not updated their notions in light of today's contexts (and are therefore in danger of missing an opportunity to work more effectively in nutrition).[3] Our findings show that, indeed, working multisectorally can be done successfully, but they also show how much success depends on having solid strategies that make sense in a given context.

---

[2] Seecaline is Madagascar's community-based nutrition program for children zero to three years of age. For further information, see Galasso and Umapathi (2009).
[3] We thank one of our anonymous reviewers for this observation.

Chapter 2 provides a justification and motivation for looking at this issue. It describes the conceptual and empirical rationale for working multisectorally in nutrition but also provides a short narrative about past experiences with multisectoral approaches, history that colors perceptions today.

Chapter 3 reviews relevant literature from nutrition and beyond, including public management, political science, and sociology. This broad review is especially important, as it shows that programmers and policymakers in other sectors have faced similar challenges and have also come up with some solutions. Chapter 3 also describes factors that, based on the evidence from practice, appear to encourage success when working across sectors or agencies. These factors then form the basis for the conceptual model and analytical framework, which, in turn, given a temporal overlay, guides development of questions for our inquiry.

Chapter 4 outlines the specific research questions and hypotheses that we explored. The volume looks at two case studies, in Senegal and Colombia, so these questions are examined as part of a narrative of the development of multisectoral nutrition programs in each country. This chapter also describes the methodologies used for data collection, analysis, and interpretation. It also explains the epistemological approach we have taken and notes how the work draws on classical approaches (such as positivism) but also on new ideas from such fields as complexity theory and systems thinking.

The country studies in Chapters 5 and 6 then apply this framework to allow a close analysis of multisectoral nutrition programs in Senegal and Colombia, respectively. The origins, design, and implementation of these programs occurred under diverse circumstances, providing a rich context from which to draw out contrasts and similarities in the programs. The in-depth analysis allows us to break each program apart into its elements and examine what they are, how the program came to be, what has happened to it over time, and where it might be going. Lessons drawn from the cases individually, as well as comparisons between the two, suggest how to initiate and manage a successful multisectoral process and how to determine the circumstances under which interorganizational collaboration or integration might make sense. Findings from the cases then also suggest where to modify the framework to increase its operational usefulness and its explanatory power.

Multisectoral Approaches to Nutrition: Rationale and Historical Perspectives

JAMES GARRETT, LUCY BASSETT, AND F. JAMES LEVINSON

Why Involve Multiple Sectors?

Multisectoral thinking has long been attractive in the field of development, especially in the social sector, because social problems and their determinants are so complex and multifaceted. For nutrition, UNICEF's (1990) conceptual framework of the causality of child malnutrition illustrates the multisectoral nature of the problem (Figure 2.1). It shows the immediate determinants of malnutrition at the individual level (inadequate dietary intake and disease) as products of underlying causes at the family or household level (insufficient access to food, inadequate maternal and child practices, poor water and sanitation, and inadequate access to quality health services). These, in turn, are influenced by basic causes at a societal level, including the quality and quantity of human, economic, and organizational resources and the way (or by whom) they are controlled. More fundamentally, these factors operate within a given—although dynamic—economic, political, cultural, and social structure, where each actor has specific resources. Figure 2.1 emphasizes the importance of this sociopolitical environment.

Figure 2.2 is an alternative representation, which presents the more immediate determinants of child malnutrition in greater detail. This figure makes clear the diversity of actions needed across sectors, levels, actors, and environments to address the problem of child malnutrition. Specifically, for example, actions are needed to provide market infrastructure, education, and healthcare, as well as to support equitable economic growth. Actions are needed at the national level and also among subnational governments and communities. Government, the private sector, civil society organizations, and households all have roles, and recommendations for actions must adapt to specific situations, such as predominantly rural or urban areas and those areas in between.

Figure 2.1   Determinants of nutrition security, by causal level

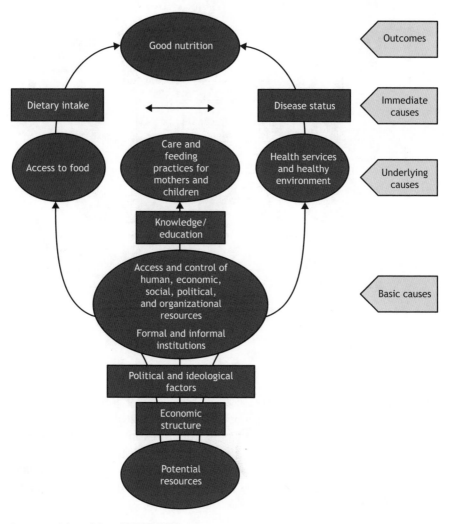

Source: Adapted from UNICEF (1990).

The framework captures the substantial empirical evidence demonstrating that economic growth or action in a single sector cannot solve the problem of malnutrition. Even fairly narrow interventions, such as those for micronutrient supplementation, cross sectoral boundaries, because their effective implementation and impact often depend on inputs not directly focused on nutrition and certainly outside a single sector (Rokx 2000). And in terms of reliance on income growth, Haddad et al. (2003) use a cross-country

Figure 2.2   Determinants of food, nutrition, and health security, by actor level

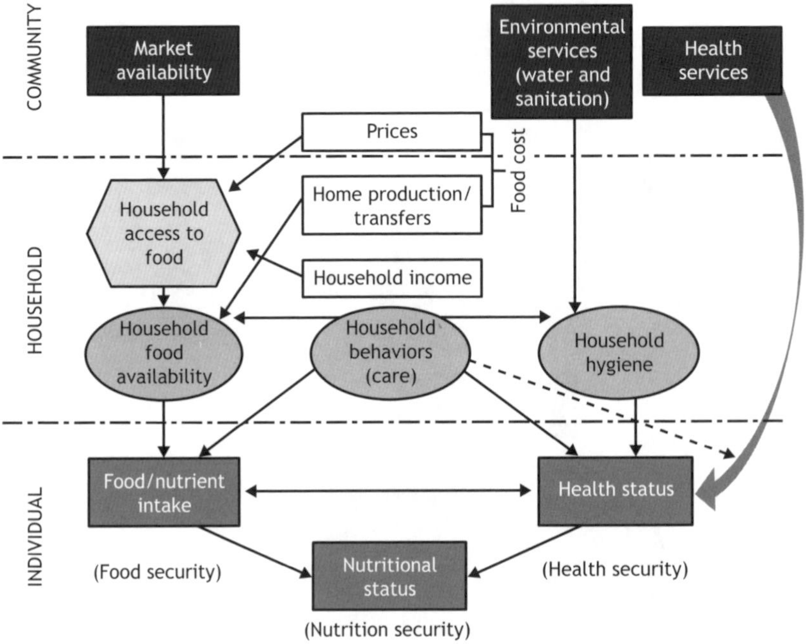

Source: Adapted from Ruel et al. (1998).

regression to estimate that a stable 2.5 percent annual growth rate in gross domestic product (GDP) per capita between 1995 and 2015 would reduce the malnutrition rate by 8 percentage points from rates in the 1990s. This estimate is significant but still optimistic. In only one-fourth of a more limited sample did economic growth exceed 2.5 percent annually during the 1990s. At this rate, waiting for economic growth to solve nutrition problems will take many decades.

Historical Context: Multisectoral Approaches in Nutrition

An abbreviated annotated history of multisectoral approaches in nutrition can help to set the context for the discussions of today.[1] Up until the 1970s, the health sector functioned as the traditional home for nutrition.[2] The under-

---

[1] This section and the following one build on Levinson (1995) and Bassett, Levinson, and Garrett (2007).
[2] The health sector was not the only home for nutrition even then, however. Agricultural extension services in the United States and in developing countries already employed home extension agents. The job of these agents, usually women, paralleled that of the agricultural extension agent. Instead of focusing on the producer and the production side of agriculture, these agents

standing of nutrition largely followed a disease model, with a presumption that infection or poor diet led to undernutrition. The response was tightly focused along medical and technological lines: treat the illness or improve the diet. Interventions tended to be supply oriented and focused on the malnourished individual and the proximate causes of malnutrition (diet and health status).

Developing-country realities made the insufficiencies of this model clear. Decisionmakers and researchers began to recognize that malnutrition was not simply a health problem but was also inextricably linked to actions and conditions across many sectors, including food and agriculture, education, economics, and environment. They also realized that reducing malnutrition required not only dealing with proximate causes but with underlying causes as well. Over time, researchers incorporated a constellation of socioeconomic, behavioral, and environmental determinants into new causal models. Ideas about how to address malnutrition then also had to change. A multisectoral understanding of the causes of malnutrition seemed to lay bare the need for a multisectoral institutional response. This new thinking was often referred to as "multisectoral nutrition planning," and it emphasized the applications of systems analysis to nutrition and the need to develop techniques and organizational models for multisectoral work (Pines 1982; Levinson 1995).

Workshops and conferences began to organize around the theme, with the 1971 Massachusetts Institute of Technology's Conference on Nutrition, National Development, and Planning (Berg, Scrimshaw, and Call 1975) being particularly influential. Programs in several universities began to address the approach, and international development agencies also revamped their strategies to take this shift in thinking into account. Berg's (1973) book, *The Nutrition Factor in National Development,* as well as works by others, gave major impetus to the idea of a multisectoral response. Of more importance, governments in several developing countries established units, councils, and committees to carry out explicitly multisectoral nutrition planning (Pines 1982; Levinson 1995).

The idea was that systematic multidisciplinary planning would produce a combination of policy or project interventions in several development sectors. If well operated and coordinated, these initiatives could be effective in reducing malnutrition, because they treated the problem holistically, with a more unified multisectoral approach. Specific tools for multisectoral nutrition planning (MNP) emerged. Techniques and approaches from the field of

---

focused on the homemaker to enhance the consumption side of the food and agricultural system and take advantage of own-production. They provided information on food production, food preparation, hygiene, and diet for the rural family.

planning provided ways to assess the entire system and consider not only the immediate causes of malnutrition found in poor health and diets but also the broader causes beyond health, including markets, education, environmental conditions, and social and economic relations.

This new approach raised awareness about the range of causes and the importance of disaggregating analysis to more local levels. The new perspective further implied that strategies to address malnutrition had to shift from curative to preventive approaches. The approach—argued to be comprehensive, systematic, and cost effective—seemed to promise far greater national and international impact than previous isolated initiatives in such sectors as agriculture, health, and education (Field 1987).

This systems perspective was also present in other aspects of development discourse at the time and coincided with the rise of integrated rural development (IRD) programs (Loevinsohn and Gillespie 2003). That approach similarly used a holistic framework, attempted to address multiple constraints simultaneously, and emphasized elements of planning. Likewise, despite theoretical attractiveness, operational complexities made implementation of IRD very difficult, and few IRD projects were able to achieve sustained success.

The complex causality of nutrition was being rightfully acknowledged, but the resulting demands for data across sectors and even down to local levels (to be able to better understand causality and improve targeting there) overwhelmed institutions for planning and implementation and systems for data collection and analysis. National nutrition planners presented other actors with long lists of demands for data that were hardly taken seriously by anyone except the nutrition advocates themselves (Field 1985; Levinson 1995).

Such complexity made more difficult what was, in general, an already weak institutional response. For example, IRD had relatively strong institutional backing. Agriculture was a key economic sector in most developing countries; most of their populations lived in rural areas and depended on agriculture for livelihoods; and IRD programs could find a stable home in the Ministry of Agriculture. In contrast, responsibility for the promotion of multisectoral nutrition planning, or even for integration of nutrition into sectoral programs, usually fell to a small number of people with a limited budget in a nutrition-planning cell. This cell was generally located centrally in a planning commission or the Office of the President and was charged with coordinating nutrition planning efforts for the government.

These units were an initial response in the 1970s to try to raise awareness of nutrition in sectors outside health and to promote genuine cross-sectoral planning and intersectoral activities. Despite their potential, these units were largely unsuccessful. Although policymakers and technicians began to recognize the multiple causalities of malnutrition, the prescription of a single nutrition planning unit, with a mandate to somehow orchestrate coordination among multiple sectors using top-down, highly planned actions, was generally a failure (Loevinsohn and Gillespie 2003).

The units were generally small, and their mission was often seen as being at odds with the main purpose of their host ministries (promoting nutrition instead of agricultural production within the agricultural ministry, for example). The nutrition cells lacked the presence or the political or financial clout to force other sectors to incorporate nutrition into their projects or programs. As planners, they usually had no budget to fund operations, even pilots, that could demonstrate to others how to integrate nutrition into their activities and the value of doing so.

Given their small scale, the multisectoral programs that did develop often suffered from a lack of scope (and perhaps appropriate focus), and the potential impact of the approach remained limited. A multisectoral program in Sri Lanka, for instance, remained largely sectoral, albeit this time the sector was agriculture, as it intervened in wage rates and attempted to stabilize agricultural prices and generate employment in the subsidiary crops sector. In the Philippines, resource allocation and coordination were placed in the hands of local nutrition committees headed by governors or mayors. This action was an attempt to elicit local political support and raise money. It sensitized local leaders to the importance of the malnutrition problem, but the result was often showcase projects with minimal reach and effectiveness (Levinson 1995).

Instead of increasing visibility and resources for nutrition, existing ministries often thought of these units as trespassing on their turfs (Levinson 2000). In Sri Lanka, the Food and Nutrition Policy Planning Division, frustrated by its inability to be taken seriously by other ministries (particularly Health), sought to assume operational control for food supplementation and community nutrition activities. In so doing, it generated even greater antagonisms with needed partner ministries (Levinson 1995).

In addition, at the time, nutrition itself was not considered a national priority, so even in the planning ministries the nutrition cells had little influence. The priority given to the cells' work was highly contingent on specific political support. The focus on traditional priority sectors—such as health (disease), agriculture (crop production), and education—could quickly resume its former dominance, if the political winds changed. In Colombia, for instance, an early multisectoral food-and-nutrition program, which involved agricultural cooperatives, agro-industry, and food coupons, met its demise with a change of government. The administration following the López government, which had initiated the program, dropped major components in an effort to put its own stamp on the program. The following government, frustrated by a fragmented effort, dismantled the program altogether. In Sri Lanka, the Ministry of Plan Implementation that housed the division responsible for multisectoral nutrition was merged into the Ministry of Finance and Planning, which, in turn, responded to a governmentwide call for a reduction in the number of government units by abolishing the division altogether. In both of these countries, the programs, targeted primarily to the politically powerless rural poor, were largely devoid of an effective political constituency and were disbanded with hardly a whimper of dissent (Levinson 1995).

Following the derailing of MNP in the late 1970s and early 1980s, an era of "nutrition isolationism," or stand-alone nutrition programs, set in. The pendulum swung back to direct, nutrition-specific interventions, although with a greater emphasis on contextual understanding, as partly expressed through community ownership. In this phase, nutrition activists, who had felt marginalized and perhaps overstretched by the MNP process, chose to focus on things that the nutrition community could do alone and do well (Levinson 2000).

As with MNP, these community-based nutrition programs held promise and made much programmatic sense. However, in practice, true community-based programs were difficult to carry out, as they, too, required a holistic vision and, often, organizational capacities at the regional and local levels that were practically nonexistent. These efforts may have been community based, but they tended not to be community driven, were often not sustainable, and appeared to be difficult to scale up to the national level (capacity building and intensive program management seemed much easier at a local level).

Even these community-based nutrition programs tended to become more narrowly focused than originally intended and less holistic and multisectoral. They increasingly promoted micronutrients, primarily vitamin A capsules and iron supplements. National-level programs also narrowed their goals, focusing on salt iodization and occasionally other food-fortification initiatives. The broader and deeper problem of basic energy malnutrition—manifested as stunting and wasting in children, particularly in South Asia and Sub-Saharan Africa—was largely ignored as being too complex (Loevinsohn and Gillespie 2003). The poster children of nutrition became breastfeeding and micronutrients (Levinson 2000), and these continued to be the primary focal points of nutrition programs internationally for the next 20 years.

The Legacy of Multisectoral Thinking

This brief history illustrates some of the jousting with and within the international nutrition community during recent decades. Regardless of outcome, the discourse demonstrates the existence of a community of knowledge that was at least concerned about these issues and had begun to appreciate working and thinking multisectorally. The history also demonstrates some uneasy fault lines not only of this community with other sectors but also of this community with the health sector, with research-oriented nutritionists who spent more time in the lab, and with those who worked on policy and program issues (the international nutritionists).

According to Field (1987, 19), multisectoral nutrition planning experienced a "meteoric rise and an equally meteoric fall," initially implying that little was left for the effort. What was elegant in thought was too cumbersome in practice (Field 2006). Yet in reply to Field's (1987) critique, "Multisectoral Nutrition Planning: A Post-Mortem," Berg argued that "nutrition planning is alive and well, thank you." Berg argued that MNP was not "holistic daydreaming" and nowhere near the "debacle" or "hapless odyssey" that Field described (McLaren 1977, 742; Berg 1987, 365–66). Acknowledging the weaknesses of early multisectoral nutrition planning—overblown assumptions about the primacy of nutrition within national structures and poor implementation strategies—Berg pointed to MNP's positive legacy: demand-oriented thinking, interventions extending beyond food-based approaches, and the use of economic and management tools in targeting and in project monitoring and evaluation (Berg 1987).

With MNP, holistic systems thinking and the concept of planning as responses took on a new forcefulness. Program staff began to communicate about interdependent relationships and the influence of sectors outside health. They brought in tools from the field of planning as they considered how to integrate actions across sectors. Nutrition began to penetrate development thinking as a legitimate subject of discussion for national policy, as a presence in national development planning, and in the design of projects outside the health sector, particularly agriculture.

Even during the period of nutrition isolationism, debate continued over the institutional positioning of nutrition. Did nutrition belong in the realm of health or in ministries of food or agriculture? Should nutrition be organized and institutionalized based on its technical aspects (for example, the type of malnutrition) or its practice (for example, methods of combating malnutrition) (Levinson 2000)?

Countries continued to attempt to operationalize multisectoral understanding and implement plans (or at least portions of them) in multi- or intersectoral ways during this period. In Thailand, for example, the first National Food and Nutrition Plan (NFNP) in 1976 formally adopted a multisectoral approach to improving nutrition, with activities in agriculture, health, education, and poverty reduction (Heaver and Kachondam 2002). Even as the international nutrition community drew back from multisectoral programs, Thailand's second NFNP, financed under the fifth national development plan (1982-86), confirmed this approach and integrated nutrition activities into national plans for poverty reduction and rural development. This NFNP even expanded attention to water supply, sanitation, and community development.

The sixth national development plan (1987–91) emphasized primary healthcare, rural development, and poverty alleviation. This plan employed a Basic Minimum Needs approach at the community level, of which nutrition was an integral part. The result of mainstreaming nutrition into multiple sectors over time is that now national policymakers as well as village residents understand nutrition as being at the heart of development (Heaver and Kachondam 2002).

In another example, in Madagascar, Seecaline, which began in 1993 as a limited community-based nutrition project, became a national-level intersectoral project drawing largely on collaboration between the Ministry of Health and the Ministry of Agriculture (Natalicchio et al. 2009). Relying largely on community mobilization, Seecaline's components include traditional elements of community nutrition (such as growth monitoring and promotion); connection with health services; and support of community activities to improve nutrition, hygiene, and sanitation. But beyond these efforts, Seecaline links with schools to distribute micronutrient supplements, carries out deworming, and promotes nutrition education; it also links with the agriculture sector to disseminate technical guidelines on improved crop diversification and home storage (World Bank 2006a).

The use of a more holistic conceptual framework received an important sustained push from the 1992 International Conference on Nutrition and widespread dissemination beginning in the early 1990s of the UNICEF (1990) model of nutrition, an explicitly multisectoral understanding of the causes of malnutrition. This model, which emphasizes malnutrition as a problem of development rather than of disease, has become the favored framework for understanding determinants of and action for nutrition (Pelletier 2002). The livelihoods framework that emerged during the mid-1990s further supported a holistic approach to development analysis and interventions (Carney et al. 1999).

So despite an international focus on rather isolated interventions, by 1996 a large number of countries (139) were preparing national plans of action for nutrition. Interestingly, regardless of the previous experience with MNP, these plans largely took as given the need for multisectoral action in nutrition. The analytical frameworks underlying these plans were clearly based on a multisectoral understanding of nutrition; strategies were seldom criticized as weak or incomplete. However, these plans, strategies, or national policies, frequently sponsored by donors or external partners, often failed to specify priority interventions or provide the resources and mechanisms necessary for implementation (Rokx 2000). Again, what seemed a good idea in theory was not well executed in practice. In effect, the understanding of nutrition as a development problem with multisectoral causes far exceeded an understanding of how to respond institutionally. The holistic understanding of nutrition, strong on an understanding of the breadth of determinants, was again proving less helpful in providing guidance to operationalize responses.

Why Reconsider Working Multisectorally?

Given this history, why reconsider attempts to work multisectorally in nutrition? In the more than 20 years since the vigorous exchange between Field and Berg (Berg 1987; Field 1987), the conceptual, planning, and operational environment has changed, making continued consideration of the idea sensible. Several factors have altered the operational environment so it is more encouraging for multisectoral approaches in nutrition. Program managers and policymakers now often have a more explicit goal-oriented or results-based approach, paying greater attention to capacity for implementation and, often, community involvement. Increasing pressure by donors and from national governments to demonstrate the impact of investment also supports the idea of a reorientation toward results.

In addition, developing countries have more resources than before, which may ameliorate the challenges of implementation. Although often still quite limited, in almost every country more human resources—technical experts and analysts, managers, and academics across a range of disciplines—do exist. Increased attention and funding has gone to support data collection and analysis and planning for social sectors, including health and nutrition. Surveys on nutrition are more systematic, broader, deeper, and more frequent than before. Knowledge about country context, determinants, and what works and what does not is more advanced.

Greater emphasis by governments and donors on stakeholder analysis and country-level ownership has made nutrition advocates more aware of the political landscape (and its effects on their success) than was the case for the initial attempts at multisectoral nutrition planning. Specific tools for social, political, and institutional analysis developed in recent years now provide these actors with the means to understand the political context and what to do about it.

In a similar vein, knowledge about institutions and program operation, implementation, and change is vastly greater now. Management science, along with other social sciences (such as political science, psychology, and sociology) now has two more decades of insight into individual behavior and institutional and organizational processes and arrangements. Literature and experience with change processes and knowledge management provide paradigms and tools for improving implementation in complex organizations (McLachlan and Garrett 2008).

Social and technological advances also encourage institutional change. With more experience in cross-sectoral management, capacity, and newer technologies, transactions costs (those related to operation as well as to the costs of gaining needed data for analysis, planning, coordination, and monitoring) are likely much lower than before. Thus the benefit–cost calculation of multisectoral actions may now be much more favorable than before.

In addition, the development community at large is also much more supportive of, and familiar with, multisectoral development approaches than before. They usually use UNICEF's (1990) nutrition framework, which emphasizes multiple causalities and connections among the determinants of nutrition. More integrated, nutrition-friendly development tools exist at the international level, such as the World Bank's Comprehensive Development Framework and Poverty Reduction Strategy Paper and the United Nations Development Programme's Human Development Index.

International and national commitment to the Millennium Development Goals (MDGs) has further galvanized support for social and economic development. The MDGs include nutrition as an indicator, and many of them are interrelated and so encourage multisectoral analysis and action (Gillespie and Haddad 2003). Some observers have predicted that a collective initiative like the MDGs that explicitly recognizes the cross-sectoral and synergistic causalities will motivate increased interaction among sectors and ministries to treat problems as a set rather than individually (Gentilini and Webb 2008).

In addition, at the level of development of national strategies, many of the prevailing development tools, such as the World Bank's PRSCs (Poverty Reduction Strategy Credits), use a cross-sectoral focus. Even donors' sector-wide approaches, or SWAps, require significant coordination among programs and agencies, giving countries more experience in managing complex programs, an element that proved a major constraint to the success of MNP.

Other social initiatives are also pushing to better understand how to work multisectorally. Increasingly popular conditional cash-transfer programs, for example, are usually located in ministries of social welfare or social development or are operated by independent agencies. They frequently use nutritional status as an indicator and require coordination across other sectors, particularly health and education. More holistic, open-ended thinking is also infiltrating local and national programs and planning. Flexible but more holistic community-driven development initiatives are increasingly replacing isolated, single-sector, top-down projects.

In this environment, donors and international lenders, already pushing hard for aid harmonization, can urge the examination of ways to link and align sectors to improve efficiency. Now aware of the multisectoral nature of malnutrition, they may easily inquire whether a multipronged attack on the causes of malnutrition is less costly and more effective than uncoordinated independent projects. Governments, now more aware of the importance of nutrition to economic growth and labor productivity and facing tight budgets, are likely to ask the same questions. Instead of small nutrition-planning cells with minimal clout and influence being responsible for identifying and generating multisectoral action, governments themselves may now take on this accountability (Levinson 2006).

The institutional and operational environment for working multisectorally seems to be more promising than before. One might argue, then, that success in working multisectorally in nutrition now depends more on creating a vision and managing innovatively and on changing ways of thinking and acting across a complex institutional landscape than on not having the basics in terms of human, financial, technical, or even conceptual resources.

Rigorous analysis of existing evidence and new cases can provide useful insights for such a reconsideration and contribute to its success. (Alternatively, it could suggest that the environment is not yet friendly enough or that the approach itself is flawed.) Such a review could also provide framework and principles for analysis and action.

This sort of analysis is badly needed. Some of the most effective nutrition advocates have been individuals who conquered the challenges of compartmentalized organizational structures and processes to work in a truly multisectoral way—but we have little documentation or analysis of what they did or how they did it (Gillespie, McLachlan, and Shrimpton 2003). The goal of this book is to provide concrete suggestions, based on an examination of experiences, on how to work multisectorally. Such work involves forging partnerships at different levels and promoting integration and intersectoral convergence of relevant programs to address the multiple causes and consequences of malnutrition.

CHAPTER 3

Principles and a Conceptual Model for Working Multisectorally

JAMES GARRETT, LUCY BASSETT,
AND F. JAMES LEVINSON

T he motivation for a multisectoral approach to nutrition applies whether we are talking about complex multicomponent programs or more straightforward integration of nutrition activities into programs being undertaken by sectors outside health. Adding a nutrition education component to a home-gardening project being promoted by the Ministry of Agriculture, for instance, is one example of straightforward integration.

The focus of this volume, however, is on programs that address the more complex institutional challenge of working across sectors. By this we mean programs that attempt to integrate activities or components across ministries, institutions, or agencies that have fundamentally different missions, such as agriculture, education, or health. So here we are looking beyond cross- or intersectoral programs in which nutrition activities might simply span or link two or more sectors. Rather, our case studies are of programs that comprehensively involve multiple institutions (ministries or agencies) in systematic efforts to address problems of malnutrition.

In general, particularly because we are focusing on government action, these different institutions do correspond to different sectors in government. In practice, however, they need not. To inform our study, then, we can draw from a more expansive literature on collaboration and cooperation, on partnerships, networks, and interagency coordination that provides frameworks and insights about how to work interorganizationally. Literature from political science, public policy, management and administration, and innovation and change provides particularly relevant theories and models for how to build effective interorganizational collaborations.

The general concern is how those from different agencies and institutions can work together. What does it take to align, coordinate, or integrate efforts across organizational boundaries? This question applies not only to people working in nutrition but also to those working across levels of government, or on issues that clearly involve tasks that cross agency and sector boundaries, including disaster management, national security, food safety, and health issues (such as HIV/AIDS). The question also applies to those who are interested in promoting action on particular issues, such as gender. The insights we gather from the literature and from our case studies are therefore broadly applicable to others outside nutrition who are interested in promoting multisectoral or interagency collaboration.

In our case, the focus is not so much on how to mainstream nutrition into a multiplicity of programs (regardless of sector) or how to promote the uptake of nutrition by other actors. Rather, the study considers organizational issues more broadly. That is, assuming we want to undertake a multisectoral approach to nutrition, what are the challenges faced in program design, operation, and sustainability? And how might we design, develop, and manage the program to overcome them? A general overview of current understanding surrounding the issue of working multisectorally, and in particular of collaboration, can be useful for suggesting answers to some of these questions and suggesting how to structure the study and analysis.

Why Work Multisectorally?

Although many factors are likely to contribute to the success of multisectoral programs, effective collaboration is likely to be central among them. Collaboration is not a natural state of affairs for organizations. Government ministries and development organizations rarely place high premiums on collaboration outside of the sectors in which they work, and incentives for individuals in these organizations to step outside their sectors are unusual.

Collaboration requires adaptation of one's own way of doing things as well as understanding how to motivate others to participate in joint action. To take advantage of opportunities to work multisectorally, policymakers and programmers must clearly understand the motives, conditions, mechanisms, and processes that trigger and sustain multisectoral activities. None of this is easy to achieve.

Collaboration implies the existence of a partner, one who is interested in participating because of the potential to receive some benefit. An essential and useful question to ask about any multisectoral action, then, is Why? Why would any of the participants want to work together? This question quickly reminds us that these are not inanimate institutions collaborating but separate organizations led and staffed by individuals, each with their own reasons (goals and incentives) for promoting or hindering (or ignoring) collaboration.

Although the mechanisms to sustain collaboration are certainly important for framing analysis and action, it is even more important to understand the motives that individuals have for pursuing collaboration in the first place. The initiation and survival of alliances depend heavily on the ability of these alliances to create and command value (Cropper 1996). If they cannot, then potential partners have little reason to support the collaboration, and it will fail.

But emphasizing motivation as an underlying question raises others: What does each individual (and his or her organization) gain from working together? What factors increase the value of gains to collaboration or facilitate their achievement? What factors increase the costs of collaboration or provide additional disincentives?

Often experts in nutrition who try to work across sectors or organizations seem to have forgotten the role of incentives and motivation, of demonstrating the benefits of collaboration to potential partners. Instead of understanding the needs of others, they use a nutrition- (or nutritionist-) centric view. The question becomes less about how to promote collaboration between agencies and more about how to force uptake of one's own nutrition interests or perspectives into existing organizations, policies, projects, or programs.

Many past efforts seem to have presumed that such collaboration would emerge from an understanding (held mostly by nutrition advocates) that nutrition had multisectoral causes, and so working together across sectors would help efforts to reduce malnutrition. The concrete operational gap between concept and result, however, was wide. Advocates do not seem to have made a concerted or sustained effort to persuade the actual participants in these endeavors of any operational and hence political benefits that would accrue to them from adopting a more multisectoral approach. The simple knowledge that cross-sectoral collaboration might help reduce malnutrition more rapidly, perhaps in a less expensive way, seems to have been the main element of persuasion. Because operational, individual, or institutional benefits were not clear and actors could apparently achieve reductions in malnutrition even without collaborating, individuals and institutions had little reason to vigorously pursue multisectoral efforts.

This lack of motivation may have much to do with the institutional culture and professional preparation or perspectives of those involved. Nutrition programmers or advocates often have backgrounds in science or research. The usual process is to conduct the research and then produce and present the evidence to decisionmakers. The approach is almost to say, "Here is the evidence. Now use it." There is limited planning or implementation of strategic communications that might help convince potential partners to cooperate, especially those in fields largely unfamiliar with nutrition who have different institutional missions and interests.

This circumstance is unfortunate, because, assuming collaboration functions acceptably well, the benefits can be high. Collaboration can increase program impact and lower program costs (Jennings and Krane 1994; Bardach 1998). Multisectoral activities can capitalize on combined strengths (access to resources, opportunities, skills, and knowledge) for framing and solving problems. The benefits can flow into other aspects of programming and policy-making as well: working together on one issue provides an example for how to work together on another. Cropper (1996, 80) calls this effect "collaborative advantage," or "greater whole system effectiveness": the creation of synergy among collaborating organizations such that what is achieved through partnership could not have been achieved by each party alone.

Given the cross-sectoral causes of malnutrition, the operational benefits, with commensurate individual or institutional benefits, are potentially significant. Particularly in nutrition, agencies in different sectors not only control and compartmentalize information because of bureaucratic structures but also because the staff in different organizations have disparate ways of thinking about both problems and solutions. Multisectoral work can provide the chance to exchange evidence and views.

Using cooperation, agencies may be able to employ the same institutional channels to deliver or monitor services. Organizations can reduce transaction costs by avoiding redundant activities or creating dedicated mechanisms for cooperation. For example, cross-sectoral delivery systems between Ministries of Education and Health could complement one another in school feeding programs. In conditional cash-transfer programs with nutrition-related conditionalities (such as requiring attendance at scheduled prenatal care visits), or when implementing a system for health and nutrition information-management and planning, different agencies may work together to avoid duplication of effort. Well-functioning multisectoral planning boards or task forces can improve information exchange, and illuminate and act on these potential areas of cooperation.

Collaboration itself can foster empowerment. Organizing in support of a collaborative purpose can help participants understand how to work together (including through the integration of outside resources) to reach their agreed-on goals (Himmelman 1996). Rapid Results Initiatives have taken this tack in addressing micronutrient malnutrition in several African countries, using time-bound, results-focused efforts to help normally rather disparate players come together and work to quickly achieve a common goal (see, for example, Rapid Results Institute and Micronutrient Initiative 2009).

Participatory analytical work can help create common understanding. Workshops, seminars, and training can become tools for changing perspectives,

identifying common agendas, building partnerships, and transferring knowledge and skills across involving multiple sectors, with their many and sometimes contradictory points of view. Sharing and debating the evidence base
can give individuals and organizations knowledge that helps them understand
the whole picture. Knowledge about interrelated causes and solutions clari-
fies the roles of various partners in the system, the ways in which they contribute to both problem and solution, what to do, with whom, and how. The
Maharashtra Change Lab is one example of applying this sort of systematic
transformative process to nutrition (McLachlan and Garrett 2008).

For higher level management and for ministries with a broader mandate
(such as Ministries of Economy or Finance), more strategic use of information
and appropriate financing and management arrangements (such as national
nutrition investment plans) can be helpful and in themselves can lead logically to the integration of nutrition into programs in many sectors. Cooperative work to integrate nutrition into Poverty Reduction Strategy Papers (PRSPs)
and Poverty Reduction Strategy Credits (PRSCs), using the Millennium Development Goals (MDGs) as a lever, can highlight the interconnectedness of
nutrition and other development goals and suggest ways to improve the efficiency of government expenditures.

Institutionalization of cooperation can also increase the chances for longer-
term presence and impact. For example, mechanisms that support bureaucratic interactions or advocacy networks may take time to develop, but ultimately they can smooth and support operations. Making things work and
achieving visible, successful outcomes can help the work in nutrition gain
legitimacy and prestige (Benson 2008).

The Collaboration Continuum:
Definition and Modalities of Collaboration

The potential gains from collaborating across sectors in nutrition seem high,
but what exactly do we mean?[1] A brief consideration of the term "collaboration" can convey a bit more formally how we understand and use the term
for this study. The Merriam-Webster dictionary defines "collaboration" as when
one (1) works jointly with others or together, especially in an intellectual
endeavor; (2) cooperates with an agency or instrumentality with which one is
not immediately connected (<http://www.m-w.com/dictionary/collaboration>).

This rather dry definition usefully points out again that collaboration implies
working with others with whom there is no immediate connection. But its

---

[1] This section and those following it build on Serrano-Berthet (2003) and Bassett, Levinson, and
Garrett (2007).

conciseness obscures the fact that collaboration comes in many flavors. These permutations arise largely because, as emphasized above, "collaboration" refers to actions carried out by independent entities. It "implies a positive, purposive relationship between organizations that retain autonomy, integrity and distinct identity, and thus, the potential to withdraw from the relationship" (Huxham 1996).

The costs and benefits perceived by each actor are the primary factors that will influence the decision to collaborate. Basically, the individual or organization will ask: What modality maximizes benefits in relation to costs in order to achieve my objective? The answer may differ for each actor. Consequently, the nature of optimal collaboration for each actor, as well as for each issue or intervention, will be different. The connections are also dynamic: the optimal structure changes over time, as do knowledge and the internal and external environments.

In principle, such action should help to address those problems that are multifaceted and that have multiple causes by bringing the most appropriate organization to bear on a particular aspect of a problem in accord with its comparative advantage. But as a consequence, the modality of collaboration may differ in each case and may even differ within the same program, depending on the organizations involved and the task at hand.

Several ideas describe the potential multiplicity of modalities of collaboration. Networking, coordination, cooperation, collaboration, and partnerships are some of them, and together these ideas create a collaboration continuum.

Himmelman (2002) presents a collaboration continuum that takes these different potential modalities into account. He provides an overall definition for multisectoral organizational collaboration, calling it "a process in which organizations exchange information, alter activities, share resources, and enhance each other's capacity for mutual benefit and a common purpose by sharing risks, responsibilities, and rewards" (Himmelman 2002, 3).

As described here, each type of interaction in the continuum builds on the previous one, reflecting the definition above and following the definition of terms found in Himmelman (1996) (we have put characteristics added at each stage in italics):

- Networking: exchanging information for mutual benefit
- Coordination: exchanging information and *altering activities* for mutual benefit and *to achieve a common purpose*
- Cooperation: exchanging information, altering activities, and *sharing resources* for mutual benefit and to achieve a common purpose
- Collaboration: exchanging information, altering activities, sharing resources, and *enhancing one another's capacity* for mutual benefit and to achieve a common purpose

These definitional distinctions can be quite useful for analysis and discussion, but the distinctions among these terms still remain somewhat intuitive. All imply working or acting together jointly. Still, most actors would probably agree with Himmelman's ordering of the terms, as they move from less to more integration of activities and shared use of resources.

Thus, at bottom, it is most important to note that the term "collaboration" can refer to a range of interactions, but all revolve around mutually beneficial interactions among independent entities. For the types of organizational interactions studied here, we mean activities that go beyond networking or somewhat infrequent sharing of information and concerns, as well as beyond periodic, usually voluntary, cooperation on specific tasks.

Within Himmelman's continuum, the multisectoral collaborations that interest us are those in which organizations are involved in more formal and integrated actions that imply specific obligations and institutional arrangements for decisionmaking and coordination of implementation. Thus, for example, we are interested in moves from sharing information (as in networking) or using task forces, councils, or committees to address a specific issue (as in cooperation) to more formal joint ventures or partnerships that have binding obligations for action and are organized around common outputs and results (Kamensky, Burlin, and Abramson 2004). Using Himmelman's definitions, we mean cross-organizational collaboration and cooperation when working multisectorally, and this book uses those terms almost interchangeably.

Just as modalities can vary, many kinds of organizational relationships can also exist. Another characteristic to consider when characterizing a collaboration is the types of actor involved. Formally, these include (1) intersectoral, or horizontal, coordination that involves the joint action of agencies from different sectors at more or less the same government level (such as the Ministry of Health and Ministry of Agriculture); (2) intergovernmental, or vertical, coordination that involves joint action of agencies at different government levels (such as between a federal and a state level); and (3) public-private coordination. In nutrition, some combination of all three is not uncommon.

These relationships can be different among different organizations in the collaboration and may even change over time. Such relationships (modified from Ranson and Stewart 1994) include the following:

- Competitive relations—more than one agency is responsible for a similar task and acts largely independently of others in carrying it out.
- Trading relations—one agency sells or barters its services to another.
- Supervisory relations—one agency has oversight responsibility over another.
- Coercive relations—one agency can lay down rules directing another's actions.

- Planning relations—one agency operates under a plan generated by another.
- Consultative relations—agencies discuss shared problems, solutions, and actions.
- Joint working relations—agencies agree to work together on a shared task.
- Financial relations—one agency provides, manages, or controls funding for another.

Structural characteristics can also help categorize these associations. For example, one might consider the degree of interdependence of participants (intensity or degree of coupling) and type of interaction (formal or informal) (Berger 1996). Formal mechanisms include organizational structures, definitions of roles and responsibilities, managerial instruments (such as plans, agreements, contracts, and budgets), and managerial mechanisms (such as an inter-organizational group or coordinating unit). Informal coordination mechanisms include interpersonal contacts and informal channels of communication. Informal interactions can be appropriate for some tasks, but they can also complement or compensate for failures of more formal coordination mechanisms.

Formal networks or informal communities of practice can help practitioners to connect to solve problems, share ideas, set standards, build tools, and develop relationships with peers and stakeholders (Snyder and Briggs 2004). Knowing what structures and ways of working are most likely to achieve success would be of great use to programmers and policymakers. Analysts have examined this question, correlating a few characteristics with some outcomes. Agranoff and McGuire (2003) developed an activity-strategy continuum that focused on the relationship between activity level and purpose of the collaborative effort. But available evidence does not appear to indicate that there is any one optimal coordination structure (Alexander 1995).

In any case, the evidence thus far indicates that the factors more closely examined below are more relevant to success than the specific structure that governs the collaboration. Success can also depend more on the environment for collaboration than on the structure per se. Indeed, one of the goals of the process of developing collaboration should be to identify the structure that is best for the problem, given a particular environment.

We should consider this hypothesis as tentative, however. The literature on this issue is not so recent, and it has not been examined in the context of nutrition. Our case studies examine whether any particular characteristics of the interaction appear to be related to the success of the effort.

Facilitating Collaboration

Factors affecting the success of a collaboration have to do with the internal and external context (Bassett, Levinson, and Garrett 2007) and with the nature of the mechanisms that link organizations. The internal context encompasses those characteristics of the organizations and individuals participating in the partnership. The existence or lack of these factors can help or hinder the collaboration, as in the presence or lack of leadership.

Although analyses tend to focus on problems among agencies, these internal—or intraagency—factors also condition success. Conflicting interests, perspectives, and capacities can exist within as well as among partner institutions. We often speak of government as a unit, for instance, but government is not monolithic, and factors within each agency may affect its ability to collaborate across sectors and its internal capacity to support such collaboration. For instance, although it is important for partners to share a vision of the issue and potential solutions, it is also important for an organization's own staff to do so.

The external context is the cultural, economic, and political environment in which these organizations and individuals operate. They particularly influence success. For example, interagency coordination does not normally spring from regular bureaucratic lines and so can depend heavily on political support. Thus it is particularly sensitive to changes in the political environment (Benson 2008).

We must also remember that collaboration does not involve just one organization or agency, but several. The main question is how to facilitate vertical and horizontal collaboration among them. In such collaborations, each agency faces a different internal context and perhaps operates under different external pressures.

Thus the evidence also strongly suggests we should pay special attention to two additional elements: incentives and enabling institutional links. These seem critically important to success. To reiterate, individuals and organizations have to have convincing reasons for working together, reasons that make sense in terms of their own personal and institutional goals. And linking mechanisms among institutions have to exist to allow, or even encourage, these different actors and organizations to work together, with a level of effort that each judges to be acceptable. Some sort of mechanism must exist to permit coordination of planning and action. These mechanisms allow organizations to share information about problems, solutions, and strategies. These mechanisms have to reflect and will be affected by both the internal and external contexts.

An example may help to illustrate these ideas. In one southern African country, an international development agency funding a health/nutrition/population project through the Ministry of Health discovered that malnutrition in outlying districts was related to the absence of local maize-milling facilities. Accordingly, with token assistance of the Ministry of Food and Agriculture and the Agricultural Development Bank as well as the Health Ministry, a multisectoral mechanism was put in place, with moderate amounts of funding for the participating entities. This mechanism was to facilitate the establishment of hammer mills in these districts by establishing cooperatives of low-income women.

The mechanism was sound in principle. But none of the participating government entities had a convincing reason, in terms of their own institutional purposes, to deploy staff and senior-level attention for this multisectoral undertaking. Additionally, staff in these organizations, often subject to an unyielding bureaucratic culture, had no incentive to become actively involved. (Low-income households, and particularly women from those households in the outlying districts who stood to benefit from the project, were unsurprisingly not involved in such activities at the national level.) Thus, although the institutional mechanism for multisectoral cooperation existed, there was in fact little active coordination across these sectors in planning and implementation, and the project failed to materialize.

The following sections highlight and describe what, from the literature, appear to be the main factors that influence the ability to work successfully in a multisectoral way. In effect, these conclusions should be seen as tentative; we examine them more closely for the case of nutrition using the case studies for Senegal and Colombia.

Internal Context

Among the internal organizational characteristics that shape the collaboration are the following:

- Leadership. Is there a champion or champions to take the lead in initiating or implementing the collaboration, including the creation of political space? What behaviors and characteristics are associated with their leadership and guidance?
- Vision. Do organizations have a common sense of purpose, a vision of the problem, solutions, and collective goals? Do they share objectives, priorities, an understanding of the issues, and definitions of success?
- Capacity. Does the organization have adequate technical and managerial capacities (including human resource management, negotiation, and mediation), experience, and financial resources, separately or in partnership with others, to carry out design, implementation, and evaluation?
- Organizational structures, values, culture, and experience. Do organizational and individual attitudes, behaviors, and methods of acting or sharing knowledge encourage collaboration? Is there a history of working with others in other sectors and being open to new ideas? Are decisionmaking structures appropriate to needs, capacities, authority, legal frameworks, and

values? Do they encourage participation and ownership, such as transparency in decisionmaking processes and the existence of some authority to make decisions? Does decisionmaking align with organizational deadlines (or other considerations of timing) and resources? Are institutional structures and decisionmaking arrangements flexible enough to adapt to differences in needs, capabilities, and structures within and across partners?

- Incentives. Are there tangible or intangible economic, financial, political, and personal incentives that encourage working together?

Leadership

The literature on leadership is vast and runs from academic treatises to practical and popular guides for managers. These studies tend to focus on how to lead an organization (especially one in the private sector) or a social or political movement (Tucker 1995; Yukl 2001; Kouzes and Posner 2007; Bennis 2009). Although they may distinguish themselves by developing different typologies of leadership, these studies and guides generally look at leadership from a dyadic point of view, developing principles of how to lead within a hierarchy or to have productive relationships between leaders and followers.

Much more limited is the literature on the characteristics of those who must lead across sectors and who are dealing with organizations over which they have little direct control. Nevertheless, this research mostly draws conclusions similar to the general literature. How leading multisectorally differs from leading within a sector or organization is not particularly clear. Jennings and Krane (1994) and Bardach (1998), for example, unsurprisingly state that effective, visionary leadership is a key ingredient of successful cooperation. They do expand on this observation and note that leadership need not be limited to the most senior decisionmakers but can include upper- and middle-level managers (program or unit directors), advisers and other technical staff, frontline workers (operational staff), politicians, and community advocates. In this view, the role of leadership is to put forth the vision and devote the effort, energy, and creativity that is necessary to get partners to work together.

Berger (1996) pays attention to leadership in multisectoral collaborations. She develops typologies as well. But it does not clearly emerge which of the approaches examined works best, and ultimately she judges that the outcome is conditional on the inputs. Procedures, information, goals, and standards, she notes, are associated with structure, and to some extent with more autocratic or directive styles of leadership. Group interaction and participation are more relationship oriented and are more strongly associated with democratic or participative leadership. Professional preparation and experience, professional and personal connections, and skills, combined with power and position, affect the outcomes of leadership efforts, such as the development of consensus, quality of products, and satisfaction of participants.

This lack of attention to leadership in studies of multisectoral collaboration may be partly because much of the analysis centers on collaboration, which can then favor a focus on the mechanics of collaboration. Agranoff and McGuire (2003) focus on interagency collaboration at the local level, for example, but their in-depth analysis of what public managers do finds answers in institutional mechanisms, such as committees, councils, and contracts, rather than in leadership alone.

In nutrition, leadership does not emerge as a principal element of analysis, likely for similar reasons and perhaps because of so much attention to determining "what went wrong." Failures of multisectoral nutrition planning, for instance, are mostly attributed to bureaucratic politics, institutional jealousies, or organizational capacities, areas where different leadership might have made a difference but issues for which leadership is not central to the paradigm of analysis (Field 1985; Levinson 1995). The issue of leadership remains latent, present in discussions of political commitment, coordination authority, or stakeholders' understanding of the issue.

Another set of literature, perhaps more pertinent to our work in the public sector, looks at the role of political leadership in promoting policy change (Grindle and Thomas 1991). Although this literature has to do with policy rather the program operations, such studies have much in common with the questions we are asking here. Working multisectorally, like generating broad policy change, generally requires bringing together disparate actors over which a policymaker has only limited control. Like our investigation, these studies consider how the issue comes to the attention of the decisionmaker and what factors influence how reforms are pursued and sustained (Grindle and Thomas 1991).

Leadership of change processes also seem pertinent, as much of multisectoral collaboration is working to change how partners think and the way they do things (Kotter 1996; Waddell 2005). Scholars of these processes tend to identify similar pathways, arguing that leaders must establish a sense of urgency, create an inclusive coalition of those who are part of the problem as well as the solution, develop a vision, communicate it consistently and repeatedly, and generate results that partners can feel a part of and others can see (Kotter 1996; Waddell 2005; McLachlan and Garrett 2008).

The concept of lateral leadership (Fisher and Sharp 2004; Kühl, Schnelle, and Tillmann 2005) probably comes closest to providing a paradigm for understanding effective leadership in multisectoral operations. Lateral leadership represents a change from hierarchical leadership (in the case of multisectoral collaboration, a forced change, not simply because hierarchy is considered old-fashioned). Lateral leadership is one answer to leading and achieving results in situations where no well-defined power structure exists, as when employees from different sections of the firm must cooperate on a project or, as in our case, on multisectoral collaborations (Kühl, Schnelle, and Tillmann 2005).

The core concepts share much with change management, as similarly a primary objective is to decrease the threatening aspects of change. But lateral leadership goes beyond this effort to explicitly encourage cooperation. In lateral leadership, leaders employ processes of creating shared understanding (a common framework to replace otherwise rigid points of view), changing power games (forming viable connections among participants' divergent interests), and generating trust (making concessions in hopes of receiving concessions in return) (Kühl, Schnelle, and Tillmann 2005).

Vision

Building a common sense of purpose is crucial to effective and more efficient coordination (Seidman and Gilmour 1986; Alexander 1995; Bardach 1998). It creates a common language for discussion, an understanding of the points of view of other partners, shared interpretations of the evidence, and, often, trust among professionals from different agencies. Working relationships at all levels are improved by staff from collaborating agencies who understand the worldviews of one another's agencies and professions. This task is often not easy and takes time.

These cognitive barriers to cooperation arise from differences in perspective associated with training, institutional mission, and institutional culture. They can lead participants to focus on different aspects of a problem and push for divergent interpretations of the situation and solutions. Different perceptions of the problem and its causes may lead to different ways of framing the issue, which then suggest different, and often only partial, policy responses. Differences in the use of language, again tied to specific disciplines or institutional cultures, can grow "into a lethal source of misunderstanding and frustration" (Bardach 1998, 131). Participants may talk past one another, as they perceive different priorities for action or do not see the contribution others can make; or they may disagree vehemently on an issue only to discover belatedly that they agree on the underlying premise; or language may lead them to believe they agree on an issue, only to find out later that they most fundamentally do not.

As two examples, classifying malnutrition as only a household-level problem would suggest to some that it does not merit public attention and political action. Others may perceive malnutrition as a medical problem rather than a social policy problem, so that limited, technical solutions are considered adequate (Benson 2008).

This lack of a shared vision can also apply to the nutrition community. Despite consensus on the causes of malnutrition, nutritionists still disagree about specific technical responses and the prioritization, design, and implementation of interventions. Coupled with gaps in information about costs and benefits of various interventions, this lack of agreement frustrates opportunities for advocacy and action.

Capacity

Coordination is more difficult when the agencies themselves are institutionally weak. Financially and administratively, for instance, each partner should be able to carry out its own activities and be able to implement effective controls for monitoring, evaluating, and reporting (internally and to others). Technically, staff should be sound, with a focus on results and an ability to work creatively and effectively in an environment that is changing (introducing the needs and structures of partners) and challenging (to current mental constructs and ways of doing things). Institutional design should follow the rule of the lowest common denominator, striving to use the minimum complexity necessary to achieve a satisfactory level of coordination (Chisholm 1989).

Limited capacity in nutrition on the part of development policymakers and practitioners imposes certain barriers. Without a holistic understanding of the determinants of malnutrition, the potential for well-designed complementary activities is weakened. Lack of capacity in implementation, monitoring, and evaluation can further undermine efforts. Poor leadership in cross-sectoral bodies can lead to ineffectual outcomes and weak commitment (Benson 2008).

Along with technical and financial capacity, managerial or administrative capacity may be among the most elusive to define but the most critical in practice. Management involves strategic decisionmaking on the best way to achieve given objectives. It necessarily shapes the way situations are interpreted and actions implemented. Among the tasks of management are policy planning, including strategic choices and systems and capacity for policy analysis; selection, motivation, and training of staff; internal and external communications; organizational development, including organization of work and decisionmaking, division and definition of roles and responsibilities, accountability, and feedback for change; public, partner, client, and donor relations; and review and evaluation.

Management must also manage group processes, including those outside the home organization. For example, managers must engender trust, deal with conflict, and determine the frequency and format of group interactions. For successful interagency collaboration, management must have the flexibility to work with, or around, rules and structures of partner bureaucracies and other stakeholders. Likewise, partners in the collaboration, most especially the leaders, must be skilled in negotiation, as they will need to persuade others to share their vision and join the collaborative effort. Organizations will likely have to incorporate new ways of seeing things and alter their ways of doing things. They will also likely need to be convinced to contribute some of their own resources (financial and human), and a good negotiator will help them feel that they are getting value for the money.

The history of multisectoral nutrition planning reveals that program management is critical to translating good but abstract ideas into effective action on the ground. This observation was made abundantly clear in multisectoral nutrition planning (MNP), in which the premium was placed on the planning process and not on program stewardship (Field 2006).

Organizational Structures, Values, Culture, and Experience

Leadership does not operate in a vacuum. In addition to the factors already noted, organizational structures, values, culture, and past experience with collaboration can also affect the ease with which leaders can take the effort forward.

The training and experience of nutrition workers differ considerably from the training and experience of workers in other disciplines, and even from that of other workers within the health sector. Program structures are often designed to follow a usual, more sectorally restricted understanding of an issue, resulting in traditional interventions that target traditional groups and needs. In a Ministry of Health, for example, the institutional focus and professional frame of discourse center on disease. Nutrition activities tend to be relatively small as a proportion of the budget and are usually not perceived to be part of the Ministry's core focus.

For multisectoral action on nutrition to be effective, then, organizational structures may need to be redesigned to allow for a focus on nutrition in line with this multisectoral understanding of its causes. Strictly vertical or top-down approaches will likely not work well in a situation in which the organizations need to reach across sectoral boundaries and integrate their actions—but the partner organizations may have exactly that kind of modality of operation.

Faced with the need to work with partners outside the organization, a high premium needs to be placed on operational flexibility (and on allowing supervisors and managers to facilitate such flexibility). Staff may need to work around often rigid rules of bureaucracies. Highly bureaucratic cultures, with multiple levels of approvals or rules that provide only for restricted ways of doing things, make interagency collaboration more difficult. Making sure decisionmakers understand the multisectoral causality of nutrition and are aware of how each agency contributes to the problem and its solution—a genuine focus on achieving results rather than defending institutional or bureaucratic prerogatives—may support attempts to build a more flexible structure.

Of course, organizational culture may undermine an appropriate structure. Working multisectorally is often new to most partners, and staff will likely bring their own perceptions of the problems and solutions to the table. Participating organizations must be open to look at and understand problems and solutions from different perspectives. They must be willing to find solutions to the challenges of working with others, even integrating the ideas or interventions of others into their own program designs. In the southern Africa maize-milling example cited earlier, the staff of the sectors involved had no incentive to overcome institutional barriers and become active in the multisectoral pursuit, much less seek to understand the challenges facing their partners.

Organizations will likely not be able to draw from established routines. Variations in the organizational and decisionmaking structures of partners, as well as their different needs and capacities, must be accommodated. New approaches (from ways to communicate and coordinate, to decisionmaking processes, to design, implementation, and evaluation of interventions) must be tried and evaluated. Decisionmakers and managers have to accept that supporting multisectoral activities means their organization must be a learning organization. Mistakes will be made, and so participants must share a vision of and be comfortable with working on a trial-and-error basis. As noted above, interagency collaboration needs to nurture a results orientation among all staff, so that the objective dictates structure and culture instead of the other way around.

Experience in working with other sectors or agencies outside government can provide helpful guides to working on nutrition multisectorally. Such experiences may have already broken down institutional structures that inhibit collaboration, opened staff members' minds to other ways of working, and presented them with lessons about how to work together. Values, culture, and experience can also add up to a somewhat intangible commitment by the organization to the collaboration. An organization may demonstrate that commitment to making the issue a priority by being willing to work through difficult moments and dedicating the time and resources to it that are needed to achieve success.

Incentives

Institutional arrangements support interactions, but personal and organizational incentives must provide initial and sustaining motivations. The nature of incentives can vary. They include advancing organizational goals (financial gain, agency prestige or power, reducing risk, and enhancing gain, for example) or personal and professional values and goals.

Legal provisions can mandate that organizations act together, which can initiate some forms of cooperation. However, legal impositions are rarely enough to sustain cooperation, particularly in countries where law enforcement and institutional capacity are weak. Nevertheless, legal recognition of operational structures and mechanisms can be useful as leverage and guidance, if other factors are in place to support the interactions.

Financial Incentives

Obtaining extra resources, especially financial resources and staff, can be a strong incentive to coordinate. Some advocates of integrated programs in the United States have said "nothing coordinates like cash" (Bardach 1998, 191). But, as illustrated in the maize-milling example earlier in this chapter, even financial incentives are unlikely to sustain cooperation in the long term, and indeed, on their own, may violate the ability of collaboration to generate greater efficiency and to reduce costs. Only if the costs are associated with expanding the program or enhancing outcomes (in ways that the marginal benefit outweighs the marginal cost) would financial incentives be economically defensible.

Even then, financial incentives are often not sufficient to promote multisectoral collaboration. Extra financial resources may not compensate for the effort of coordination, for example. Those who provide the funds must be sure that they incorporate appropriate incentives for synergistic actions so that they do not merely provide additional funds for agencies to do what they were already doing. Reliance on financial incentives may also mean that continuity of multisectoral efforts becomes dependent on the constant flow of funds. Financial incentives (that is, an expanded budget) may be instrumental in sparking interagency cooperation and assisting with initiation, but other factors having to do with personal and organizational motivations are probably necessary to ensure sustainability of cooperation.

Organizational Advantage

Public administrators try to accumulate advantages for themselves or their organizations. Interagency cooperation may help an organization gain prestige or power; increase its budget; or improve its performance through increasing synergies, reducing costs, or reducing uncertainties.

Personal and Professional Values

Some agencies may cooperate because leaders and staff support the idea and goals of collaboration. They may believe that cooperation across agencies will help them achieve personal or institutional goals, such as providing better services or more effectively reducing malnutrition. They may also enjoy working together and sharing experiences, ideas, and information.

Oliver (1990) gives some specific motivations (incentives) for the formation of partnerships, which can function alone or in combination. These include a mandate from a higher authority (necessity); requirement from another organization (asymmetry of power); mutual interests (reciprocity); reducing costs or increasing returns (efficiency); reducing instability or uncertainty, especially from lack of information (stability); and justification of activities and outputs (legitimacy).

External Context

The factors associated with the political, social, cultural, and economic climate surrounding the partnership include the following:

- Development priorities. Do actors believe and agree that the issue is a priority for national economic and political development?
- Urgency. Does the problem lead the different actors to believe there is a need for urgent action? What priority does the issue have for society or influential stakeholders? Is there an urgent need for action resulting from, say, a natural, economic, or political crisis or from donor pressure that might encourage joint action? Are there windows of opportunity that can be taken advantage of? Are there considerations of timing or issue development that may encourage or discourage action?
- Economic, social, cultural, political, and legal environment. How does the broader socioeconomic, cultural, or politico-legal environment in which organizations operate affect the collaboration?

Development Priorities

Creating an understanding across all influential actors of why the issue is important to them can promote a sustained focus on nutrition regardless of political or organizational change. In this case, one of the most important goals is to persuade actors of the importance of nutrition to development. Providing an evidence-based narrative to these actors, which persuades them of the need for policy attention, the efficacy of policy solutions, and the benefits to society of taking public action is important for the creation of widespread support for action on nutrition across sectoral and political divides.

Broad acceptance of such a policy narrative allows attention to nutrition to continue regardless of political shifts or changes in organizational structures or sectoral priorities, as all key actors would agree on its importance (Benson 2008). This understanding would support the efforts of a variety of players to integrate nutrition into multisectoral development efforts (inside as well as outside the government and under conditions that change over time).

Urgency of the Issue
Some issues find their way onto the policy agenda because of external pressures, such as an economic crisis that compels policymakers to act. Others end up there only because policymakers have chosen to take up the issue. Hirschman (1975) distinguishes between these as pressing and chosen issues.

In a pressing issue, powerful groups inside or outside government, including donors and advocacy groups, demand action, greater accountability, and results. Political and economic circumstances provide a strong impetus for institutions to overcome their resistance to collaboration and act. Of course, when pressures cease, organizations may lose their incentive for further cooperation (Kotter 1996).

Unfortunately, policymakers, donors, and local communities rarely consider nutrition to be an urgent need and seldom press for action. Nutrition primarily has characteristics of a chosen issue. With a chosen issue, advocates have to make the case for action to policymakers, donors, or other advocacy groups, so those groups will choose to do something about it. The evidence would need to underscore the importance of nutrition to development and of coordinated action across sectors (operational alignment). Advocates would need to promote widespread awareness among policymakers as well as broad social mobilization to create and maintain a sense of urgency.

Economic, Social, Cultural, Political, and Legal Environment
The broad context in which the organizations operate can also affect the success of the collaboration. That is, beyond the specifics of each partner organization, the larger environment may influence how individuals or institutions relate to one another. Macroeconomic crisis might launch food and nutrition issues onto the policy agenda, or they might force budget cuts even in a successful program. A donor agency might switch funding priorities and so highlight or undermine attention to nutrition. Organizations outside the core operational group,[2] such as the Ministry of Economics and Finance, could affect

---

[2] The agencies that most often implement nutrition programs are the Ministries of Health, Agriculture, and Education. These ministries exist in almost every country. In some countries, there are ministries with broad social protection portfolios (Ministry of Social Welfare) or with responsibility for vulnerable groups (Ministry of Women and Children) that also undertake nutrition programming. Ministries responsible for water and sanitation (such as a Ministry of Infrastructure

the design of a program or the investment allocation a program receives. New legal mandates, such as decentralization or results-based budgeting, could also affect how collaborations play out.

Institutional Links

As noted earlier, for collaboration to work, a mechanism to link and integrate agencies must exist. Yet discussions of multisectoral collaboration in nutrition generally pay little attention to the nature of these links, beyond noting basic staffing plans (for example, nutritionist cells) or a program's organizational placement (for example, in the Prime Minister's Office). Yet how these mechanisms work will significantly affect whether the collaboration works at all, and so they merit closer and more critical analysis. Review of experience also makes clear the dynamism and variation in institutional connections. That partnerships can vary over time and with circumstances, especially in terms of needs and capacities, casts doubt on searching for some unique optimal and largely static modality.

For nutrition, structuring work across sectoral boundaries is among the greatest challenges. The multisectoral conceptualization of nutrition itself complicates matters. Lacking a common language or framework can make intersectoral discussions and program and policy alignment more difficult. Yet the conceptual understanding of nutrition requires staff to reach beyond sectoral boundaries, an effort that others in the sector may not understand or know how to support when, to a large extent, they can remain within their respective sectors for operations.

Structurally, organizations need to develop mechanisms to support interactions and reach mutual agreement on what defines success. Benson (2008) notes that organizations following their own traditional markers to guide action can miss a potential impetus for collaboration. Mechanisms should promote collaboration, but they must account for the intraorganizational factors—the internal conditions faced by every partner. They should provide a forum for discussion of different viewpoints and of ways to adapt to the different capacities and decisionmaking structures of each partner. Roles and responsibilities must be clear, and the linking mechanisms should reinforce, rather than resist, collaboration. Transparent decisionmaking, especially on budget allocations, is likely a critical factor for continued cooperation. Participatory approaches are more likely to promote sustained collaboration, because institutional links and decisionmaking hierarchies are generally weak

---

or of Local Government), the environment and natural resources, and finance and planning generally do not take direct responsibility for nutrition interventions, but their actions do affect nutrition through other causal links or decisions they make about program design and budgeting.

across agencies. Making sure the needs and wants of partner organizations are heard and incorporated into action can promote the sense of ownership needed for success.

Some analysts argue that one of the most important constraints to effective implementation of nutrition programs is the lack of an institutional home (Levinson 2000; Rokx 2000). Conceptually and structurally, nutrition fails to fit comfortably into existing national sectoral and policymaking institutions. There is no Ministry of Nutrition as there is a Ministry of Agriculture or Health, for instance.[3]

Since nutrition does not fit neatly or completely into the worldviews of any of the core sectors of government concerned—agriculture, health, education, and so on—it is easily neglected in the formulation of government policies and strategies, in the definition of government programs, and in the allocations of government resources (Benson 2008).

Still, ministries of health and agriculture have indeed frequently claimed to be the institutional home for nutrition. The problem is that nutrition is often marginalized even within these organizations. For example, there has been an increasing tendency to subsume nutrition into the pre-existing confines of health systems. And even the creation of new national nutrition programs or nutrition plans of action often rests on the clear understanding that existing regimens of service delivery (often facility based) and of service-related monitoring will not be disturbed.

Even within a home sector, then, nutrition already may operate as if it were undertaking an intersectoral effort: crossing disciplinary boundaries and coordinating among a variety of professional perspectives to obtain appropriate attention and investment. The weak base nutrition has even within its traditional sectoral homes makes reaching out to other sectors or agencies as part of interagency collaboration even more difficult.

Clearly, then, interagency coordination lacks the solid foundation that would spring from agency-based bureaucratic lines. The success or sustainability of such coordination will depend to a large degree on continuing political support. A cross-sectoral body housing nutrition (even a revamped nutrition planning body), for example, does not easily fit sectoral patterns of resource allocation, thus depriving it of a usual element of support. Thus nutrition is particularly sensitive to changes in the political environment (Benson 2008). These changes can range from new governments to personnel turnover in

---

[3] Consideration was briefly given to the inclusion of the word "nutrition" in the name of the Ministry of Health and Family Welfare in Bangladesh in 2001.

leadership positions or the emergence of a new political agenda that draws the attention of the people involved in the interagency cooperation. Despite advantages gained from being close to demand and from reducing some of the rigidity in central government bureaucracies, decentralization can complicate efforts if responsibilities are not clear and capacities are relatively weak.

Given the usual fragility of the collaboration, some measures need to be taken to make sure turbulence is minimized. One measure is to initiate collaborative arrangements early in the political cycle to have time to build them. Another is to create a broader alliance from among interest groups (including donors or parliamentarians) inside and outside government to support the core coordination effort through change.

Some principles that seem to help lubricate the mechanisms of coordination include the following:

- Shared understanding. As in the case of vision (presented above), do members share a common understanding of the problem, and where they fit in the solution?
- Roles, responsibility, and accountability. Are organizational and individual roles and responsibilities clearly defined? Do organizations share a mutual responsibility and obligation—an ownership—for activities, results, and success? Are these roles in line with institutional missions, capabilities, and timelines? Are there lines of accountability, both within and outside the agency, both upward and downward? Do organizations and individuals have a shared interest in seeing the venture succeed, because all parties have something at risk or because of mutual interdependencies?
- Participation and partner and stakeholder relations. Are decisionmaking and action inclusive? Do mechanisms support participation by operational partners and other stakeholders to build consensus and trust around goals and actions? How do differences in power, resources, and capabilities among the organizations affect collaboration?
- Partnership types. What are the types of partnership? What are their characteristics, and how do they vary among partners, in terms of intensity, structure, size, level of autonomy, decisionmaking processes, and implementation?

Shared Understanding

Stakeholders need to share a common understanding of the problem, including how to frame it, what is known about it, and possible solutions to it. Although each stakeholder may be directly involved in only a part of the problem, understanding the overall picture is important if they are to understand what is at stake and either why they should or how they can coordinate their actions with others. Frequently, if actors try to move forward when not everyone is operating from the same basis of understanding, energy is wasted and operational alignment is lost. Creating this understanding involves bringing all key actors to the table and presenting them with evidence for review and assessment. This evidence can include personal experiences as well as research. Creating this understanding likely requires constant communication, to continually remind stakeholders of what is known, to update them as new information becomes available, and to educate new members of the group as individual actors come and go.

Roles, Responsibility, and Accountability

Although having a common understanding of the problem is important, each institution and individual must also understand their specific roles and responsibilities and be prepared to carry them out. These ideas could be developed over time, as the collaboration develops, or they could be part of a structure imposed from the beginning. In either case, it would seem important for all actors to be clear on what they need to do and how to coordinate with one another.

Measurable goals (Berger 1996) and a system to hold actors accountable for their obligations also contribute to success. Kabeer (2003) suggests that accountability may involve three levers: an awareness lever that raises awareness of the formal and informal norms, rules, and attitudes that can govern behavior within organizations; a communications lever to ensure the timely flow of information and analysis across the system; and an incentives lever that institutionalizes performance-based appraisal systems with incentives and penalties. Accountability systems can also provide positive reinforcement by allowing actors to concretely verify their progress and achievements and maintain a sense of urgency.

Partnership and Stakeholder Relations

Stakeholder participation in identifying problems or providing information on conditions and potential solutions can benefit coordination in several ways. Participation forces agencies to focus on stakeholders' needs. Given the right structure, this pressure can also make them more accountable and so encourage better coordination that facilitates a focus on results.

Participation also enhances a feeling of ownership in the program. Participation in putting together the program can also help make sure that program design and operation meet partner needs and capabilities. Increasing a sense of ownership and helping participants to feel the program is useful to them enhances the probability of success.

The idea of partnership may also need to expand beyond the operational core to include those who can influence the environment in which the collaboration operates (parliamentarians, for example) or who could be important supporters (private-sector industries or nongovernmental organization [NGO] umbrella groups, for instance).

Partnership Type

Earlier in this chapter we described various types of collaborations, but it is unclear whether any one type of partnership, in terms of corporative structure, intensity, size, or autonomy, is better than another. Of course, as with any task that requires coordination among multiple participants, management, especially decisionmaking and follow-up of implementation, becomes more difficult as the number of partner organizations increases. Cooperation is likely easier when it involves the smallest number of stakeholders possible (although participation and ownership remain core values).

Conceptual Model and Analytical Framework

The discussion above highlights various factors that emerge from the literature as influences on the success or failure of multisectoral collaborations. The literature itself, often consisting of qualitative case studies of institutional, managerial, or policy experiences, gives little indication of the operational hierarchy, magnitude of influence, or necessary sequencing of these factors. Indeed, our approach would suggest that there is no single answer to such questions, and which factors are primary will depend largely on context.

Given the formative nature of this research, our aim in reviewing the literature across a wide range of experiences and disciplines was to develop a checklist of factors, not to predetermine which would be most influential in our case studies. However, in analyzing the case studies, we are interested in finding out, if possible, which factors generally matter most. By using a qualitative, case-study approach, we are not able to quantify the influence of a particular factor (variable), holding all other factors (variables) constant. But we can employ some techniques that suggest which factors may be most important or which approaches may be most effective in working multisectorally. First, we allow those narrating the history to tell us what things they did that mattered. We also use triangulation (including documentation) to obtain further insights and confirmation. Second, we can compare our results to findings from other situations, which helps build the case for which factors tend to be more or less important in different contexts.

We have few preconceptions about which factors will emerge as most dominant for nutrition or how factors might interact to constrain or energize one another, and we do not want to orient our analysis from the beginning with hypotheses that, in fact, have little empirical support. Our approach at this stage is to provide a relatively complete list of possibilities based on the literature and then see how these factors (or others) may have played out in the program experiences in Senegal and Colombia. This research helps answer those questions about the factors that influence the ability to work multisectorally in nutrition (a case that remains largely unexamined).

Our reading indicates that two elements deserve rather greater attention than they often receive: incentives and institutional links. The intrinsic requirement that collaboration be mutual seems to give primacy to incentives: What reasons do the organizations and individuals have for working together? And the requirement of coordinated activities between the organizations means that the linking mechanisms are critical. Without some sort of feasible, functional structure that links organizations and promotes (or at least facilitates) their interaction, the collaboration must fail. In our analysis, we explore whether further primary or critical factors emerge or whether other conditions, such as sequencing, play a role.

And although it is true that the list of potential factors is long, we can organize it in a relatively succinct way. We can group the actions and activities that can support multisectoral work into a few broad categories. Frameworks by their nature are schemata. We have developed this one to highlight connections and influences in working multisectorally and to diagram our complex system. As shown by its visual representation (Figure 3.1), our conceptual model aims not to provide complicated descriptions of these connections or determinants but rather to "direct the attention of the analyst to critical features of the social and physical landscape. [It provides] a foundation for inquiry by specifying classes of variables loosely fit together into a coherent structure" (Schlager 1999, 234).

This framework, or conceptual model, will be used to underpin the development of ideas about multisectoral collaboration that can be studied in the field and can structure our inquiry. Based on the framework, we have developed a more complete matrix, or adaptable checklist, of categorized crosscutting questions, which we use to guide the empirical studies.

Figure 3.1 structures the list of factors, providing a visual representation of how these categories of factors relate to one another spatially and dynamically and how they shape the operation of strategic collaboration. The figure summarizes the above discussion on internal and external contexts and linking mechanisms.

Figure 3.1a represents the internal organizational factors affecting multisectoral collaboration. Figure 3.1b represents those factors in the environment outside these organizations. And Figure 3.1c illustrates what happens when

Figure 3.1   Conceptual framework: Working multisectorally

a. Internal context

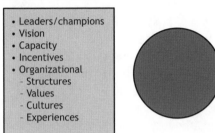

- Leaders/champions
- Vision
- Capacity
- Incentives
- Organizational
  - Structures
  - Values
  - Cultures
  - Experiences

b. External context

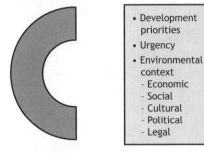

- Development priorities
- Urgency
- Environmental context
  - Economic
  - Social
  - Cultural
  - Political
  - Legal

c. Institutional links

- Shared understanding
- Roles and accountability
- Participation and partner relations
- Partnership types

Source: Authors.

the internal and external environments are combined. Activities and interests of different organizations overlap, and all are affected by the external environment. At the same time, mechanisms link these organizations both hierarchically (vertically) and across their structures.

Developmental Stages of Collaboration

The analytical checklist for internal and external factors and institutional linking mechanisms developed above does not incorporate the contemporaneous dynamics that occur among these factors. Nor does it reflect the dynamics of the collaboration over time. Although progression will not be precisely linear—nor will it occur at the same time for all partners—we can distinguish some plausible developmental stages in collaboration (Austin 2000; Agranoff and McGuire 2003). Three such stages are as follows:

- Exploratory stage. In the beginning, there is little cooperation or coordination among the potential partners. With rising awareness of the problem and the potential for cooperative, cross-sectoral solutions, partners may hold meetings to seek more information on the problem, solutions, and ways to work together. Operationally, discussions begin to identify preconditions for cooperation, including identifying sources of funding, outlining processes and procedures (to work together and also internal standard operating procedures that may influence the nature of the collaboration), collecting information on existing policies and programs, and identifying institutional focal points and adjustments that may be needed in or among the organizations.
- Transactional stage. Partners have determined that they value working together and have developed the main outlines of such a collaboration (objectives, core organizations, main activities, and responsibilities). Interactions become more formal as partners set directions and undertake planning and make decisions regarding strategy and implementation of plans.
- Integrative stage. Partners implement action strategies, institutionalize mechanisms for decisionmaking and coordination, and incorporate necessary institutional changes. Institutional boundaries blur as organizations implement activities. Agencies seek to plan for, acquire, and use resources (human and financial) jointly.

The dimension of time and the issue of incentives sharpen the questions and add dynamics to the analysis of these stages. For example, how did the collaboration start, how did it develop, and what has sustained it? Understanding what is happening in each of these temporal phases is important, as each is essential for continued successful collaboration and impact.

Considering time, context, and institutions, we can ask: What incentives led to the initiation of the collaboration, its operation, and its continuation or sustainability? Within each internal or external context, what organizational and individual incentives influenced the collaboration? Which factors inhibited the partnership, and which supported it? Some factors may contribute more to the initiation of the collaboration (motivation), some to its operation, and still others to its sustainability. Initiating coordination is not enough to sustain it, and making coordination work over time requires that organizations acquire a certain set of enabling managerial behaviors and conditions.

In the next chapter we build on this review of knowledge and the tentative conceptual model we have developed to specify the research questions that guide our analysis and some hypotheses we wish to explore in the context of our specific country cases. We also describe more fully the research approach and research methods that guide our work and our interpretation of findings.

CHAPTER 4

Research Questions, Methods, and Approach

JAMES GARRETT, LUCY BASSETT, F. JAMES LEVINSON,
AND MARCELA NATALICCHIO

D rawing on the key issues illustrated by the framework (internal and external contexts, linking mechanisms, and dynamics) developed in Chapter 3, we have developed four primary sets of questions, following a rough chronology, to guide the empirical studies:

- How do initiatives to work multisectorally get started? What are the triggers?
- How does the collaboration work? How does it evolve over time? What are the dynamics and mechanisms of the collaboration process?
- What are the issues surrounding the sustainability of collaboration?
- What characterizes the broader environment in which the collaboration takes place? How does it affect the collaboration?

Constructing a narrative around these questions should give us an idea of the key factors, or approaches, that affect how multisectoral collaboration comes about, how it operates, and how it might be sustained.

Hypotheses and Research Questions

An explicit, well-developed theory of working multisectorally does not exist, certainly not for nutrition. But researchers in other fields have begun to develop models and stylized facts about what seems to affect operational success. In addition we can draw on statements about what went wrong in previous efforts to work multisectorally in nutrition (and so identify what was lacking) in order to suggest hypotheses about what factors should be present for things to go right.

Ultimately our hypotheses are more about identifying elements of an approach that the literature suggests facilitates collaboration, rather than about examining individual factors. This approach involves making sure all partners share a common vision of the collaboration and understand their role and responsibilities, that they sense ownership and feel they are participating and making valued contributions, and that institutional and operational capacity exists to allow all partners to do their jobs.

Given the limits of knowledge at this point, our necessary reliance on a limited number of studies, and our own research perspective (explored in more detail below), this volume is much more about exploration of context, development of models, and hypothesis seeking than about hypothesis testing. In some cases, we have hypotheses that are fairly well defined; in other cases, too little, or mixed, evidence exists to make a confident claim. Based on the literature review and our model, for example, it would be difficult to formulate sensible hypotheses about which factors are essential or how they might work synergistically or sequentially. To begin to build this knowledge base, we will examine the ideas presented as hypotheses more explicitly in the case studies of programs in Senegal and Colombia.

For now we present the following statements, associated with the different elements in our analytical framework, as hypotheses to be explored.

Internal Context

Hypothesis 1: Nutrition is a chosen issue. Champions are needed to put it on the policy agenda. Leaders must develop vision and structures to support action.

Hypothesis 2: Advocates work to build a shared vision through developing a shared language, understanding, and sense of purpose.

Hypothesis 3: Partner organizations have relatively strong technical, financial, administrative, and managerial capacities, so they can carry out their defined responsibilities.

Hypothesis 4: Organizations have values that promote collaboration, including respect for the organizational routines and missions of others, an openness to learning from them, and an orientation toward results. These values encourage participation, transparency, accountability, and institutional flexibility.

Hypothesis 5: Organizations provide incentives for action, including personal and financial incentives, and have established accountability structures.

Hypothesis 6: Partner organizations perceive that the benefits of participation outweigh the costs.

External Context

Hypothesis 7: Promoting nutrition as a development priority across a wide range of stakeholders creates openings for action and sustained attention to nutrition.

Hypothesis 8: Advocates create a sense of urgency for action.

Hypothesis 9: General economic, political, and social conditions do not bring attention to nutrition, although specific events may.

Institutional Links

Hypothesis 10: Multisectoral collaboration requires institutional change, in budgeting structures or modalities of implementation, for example.

Hypothesis 11: Successful multisectoral collaboration involves establishing linking structures that

- promote shared understanding;
- are inclusive and participatory;
- promote accountability to the public and stakeholders, including partners and program management;
- value the contributions of all partners; and
- make the roles and responsibilities of all partners clear.

The Nature of Factors and Hypotheses

These hypotheses represent a reduction or refinement of the long list of potentially influential factors described in Chapter 3. It is true that even this long list of factors may not include every potentially influential one in the policy system, and we could have identified an even larger set of hypotheses. This is true for any research project. But compression of the possibilities of some sort is necessary for analysis to be feasible.

This compression is done in two ways: one conceptual, the other merely practical. Both are supported by empirical as well as personal observation. First, we have narrowed the scope of inquiry by identifying those particular aspects of the system (the programs) that have to do with operating multisectorally. We are not examining the individual program components, for example. So we are not attempting to consider the influence of every factor in the policy or program system. Second, we have synthesized the factors into more descriptive statements that symbolize an approach to working multisectorally. This synthesis makes holistic examination of the general elements of the approach more tractable than if we tried to separate out and test each factor individually. It is also a more realistic appreciation of how the factors may work together to affect multisectoral operations.

This approach does imply some limitations, however. Because by implication these hypotheses only relate to a portion of the system (the programs), they also represent an abstract, compressed representation of that system. The resulting knowledge is also still approximate and provisional (Richardson 2008).

Still, these hypotheses are drawn from the literature of several fields and from our experiences and professional discussions. We are thus confident that our hypotheses identify the main essential elements and so represent a reasonable compression of the system that still allows us to develop insight and understanding.

Thus these statements represent our own synthetic, holistic interpretation of that information in hypothesis form. Other researchers may have developed other hypotheses, but to us the above points are reasonable summary statements that also reflect questions from policymakers and programmers about how to work multisectorally. That these are questions posed by decisionmakers and other development practitioners is another indication of the utility of our compression.

In sum, we have attempted to compress the approach yet keep it holistic and not lose essential complexity. We are presenting hypotheses as they relate to the workings of the system (program), as a whole, yet formulating them so that data collection and analysis will still be tractable.

We also emphasize that these explanations are tentative. One of the main aims of the study is to see which factors may have been left out (especially regarding work in nutrition), or which ones (such as the internal workings of ministries or leadership) might need to be investigated further in future studies. Seeing how these potential explanations play out in the case studies allows us to sharpen hypotheses for future examination.

However, in our hypotheses we are positing that certain ways of operating or thinking (not just specific individual variables or factors) matter to success. These approaches are, by their nature, somewhat amorphous. A reductionist strategy might suggest a single indicator, which we might then test, to conceptually represent a multifaceted process. But to do so would be unnecessarily reductionist at this exploratory stage, and we also do not have the data to test the validity or strength of the proposed association between the indicator and our more general description. Thus we prefer to frame these hypotheses about factors as general descriptive statements of what (we initially posit) is required to be able to work successfully multisectorally, rather than to identify a specific variable to test, either on its own or as a representative indicator.

Relating Hypotheses to Fieldwork

Table 4.1 juxtaposes the conceptual framework and the loose chronology inherent in the field research questions. Answers to these questions will shed light on the ideas about working multisectorally contained in the hypotheses. At the same time, the framework and hypotheses guide the interactions in the field and the analysis. More specifically, as we conduct the interviews, review the documents, or analyze the statements, we can use the analytical framework and the hypotheses as mental models to inform our questions and

Table 4.1   Research questions: Factors affecting multisectoral collaboration

General questions	Specific questions
1. How do initiatives to work multisectorally get started? What are the triggers?	• What are the initial motivations for collaboration? • Who are the principal movers? • What are their interests and incentives? • What internal and external factors affect initiation—either promoting or inhibiting it? • Is the collaboration new or did it develop within the existing institutional context?
2. How does the collaboration work? How does it evolve over time? What are the dynamics and mechanisms of the collaboration process?	• How does the collaboration develop over time? • Who are the stakeholders/participants, and what are their roles and responsibilities? • What is the nature and content of the partnerships? • What specific structures are in place to guide the interaction? • What internal and external factors have affected the evolution of the collaboration and the structures for collaboration? How have they helped or hindered the collaboration?
3. What issues surround the sustainability of collaboration?	• What is the potential for sustainability? • What internal and external factors support or hinder its sustainability?
4. What characterizes the broader environment in which collaboration takes place? How does this environment affect the collaboration?	• How have the economic, political, and social contexts affected the development of collaboration and its sustainability?

interpretations. Thus these hypotheses serve mostly as signposts for key relationships we should be looking for. Rather than explicitly testing them, we
are seeing whether these factors—these relationships—emerge as expected in
the narratives told by the participants.

Use of Case Study Methodology

Our research uses a case study approach. (The details of how each country
case study was conducted are given in Chapters 5 and 6.) The case study
method is often used in such fields as political science, management, and
administration, because alternative experimental or rigorous statistical
analyses are often difficult to carry out in real-world conditions. Conducting
an experiment in real time and in the real world of politics or management
is difficult, and statistical methods require more cases than are normally
available, especially in the initial stages of exploration. Such quantitative
approaches are also not optimal where a qualitative explanation of what is

happening and why is of primary interest, as in this study. Case studies are, in fact, the best methodological choice when one wants to investigate a contemporary phenomenon within its real-life context, especially when one is asking questions of "how" and "why" (Yin 2009).

In this study, we are primarily concerned with investigation and description, not causal analysis. For theorists, this focus contributes to further development of models and hypotheses. For those concerned with practical implications for administration and management, it provides important guidance for working multisectorally, even if we do not make causal claims about specific elements of those approaches. With this understanding, case study selection may proceed somewhat differently than if we were aspiring to test causal explanations based on some well-developed existing model (Seawright and Gerring 2008).

We understand the limitations imposed by the use of only two case studies that have furthermore been deemed success stories (Geddes 1990; Seawright and Gerring 2008). We appreciate that selection of such relatively successful cases certainly affects the answers obtained (Geddes 1990), but we believe they are useful answers. Even with such criticisms, our selection and analytical approach appear to hold up well against accepted methodological criteria for selection, sharing elements of known case-selection methods that look at both typical and diverse cases (Seawright and Gerring 2008).

Based on our own professional assessment, the country conditions in Senegal and Colombia are fairly typical of what policymakers, programmers, and development practitioners might find if they are interested in the sorts of approaches described here. The conditions are fairly representative along several key vectors: in terms of the socioeconomic and political context from which the programs emerge, the elements included in the programs themselves, and the sectors that they try to bring together. At the same time, although typical of developing countries, the conditions in Senegal and Colombia also represent a range of human, technical, and financial capacities.

The country conditions in which these programs developed and operate, then, are thus typical yet diverse. They are, fortunately, then reasonably representative of the population at large in which we are interested: developing countries where decisionmakers or programmers might wish to include multisectoral nutrition programs in their strategies to reduce malnutrition. These conditions help ensure that our analysis will have meaning and utility (Seawright and Gerring 2008).

In case studies that are selected on the basis of being diverse, analysts focus on a range of values that characterize X (or a range of Xs), the explanatory variable, but not on a particular single-variable relationship between X and Y, the outcome of interest. In our selection, we have perhaps not achieved the maximum variation across all relevant dimensions of X (that is, across all potential causal factors), because we have not examined all possible multisectoral programs, but we are confident that the diversity of initial conditions (the sociopolitical, economic, and institutional contexts) is significant across the cases.

Part of this exercise is to see what sort of development paths emerge from our analysis of these typical yet diverse experiences. We can ask questions such as: Are the pathways similar or dissimilar? Did leaders pursue similar or different strategies? Did partners come together or fall apart in similar or different ways? The pathways do not at all have to be similar, so the emergence of different typologies could guide future research. However, if pathways tend to be similar, it could strengthen our presumption that there are some general facets of successful approaches to working multisectorally that apply across contexts.

Without more complete development of a causal model and additional studies for causal analysis, we cannot claim with certainty which of the factors (or ways of operating) are critical. We can move toward that sort of understanding, however, because of the diversity in our cases. Depending on the analysis, we may be able to reasonably produce conclusions about: What are the common elements of success despite variations in context? What factors or approaches seem to make less of a difference?

Over time, with additional studies chosen for their ability to respond to particular inquiries, researchers should be better able to answer: What factors do not seem to matter (by choosing cases that show success even without having those factors)? Which factors do matter (by choosing cases for which the outcomes were different, even when the hypothesized fundamental factors and conditions were the same)? Without additional studies, we may also uncover whether there are implications for sequencing, that is, that programs can advance only so far without removing another limiting constraint, as in a linear programming problem.

Given our purposes and the research context, we believe the case study method has significant merits and can produce methodologically valid and useful results. For many researchers, case studies such as we present here can also be the first step in a more positivist method of inquiry. Over time we and others can add additional cases (both successes and failures) to gain even more insight. By comparing and contrasting experiences, we deepen understanding, test hypotheses, and develop typologies.[1]

---

[1] For other researchers with a more postmodern approach, the cases are not more than what they are: rich contextual experiences. For these researchers, the cases represent some possible ways of working multisectorally but cannot fully represent all aspects of reality or all ways of

More specifically, regarding the usefulness and validity of using a case study methodology for this particular volume:

1. None of the previous studies on this topic of which we are aware develop an analytical framework (as expressed particularly in the research questions in Table 4.1) or hypotheses about working multisectorally to test against the case studies themselves, as we do here. Some studies of multisectoral nutrition programs do exist, but most are neither in-depth nor rigorous, and they do not look specifically at the operational nature of the collaboration as these case studies do.

2. Our approach not only permits testing these two country cases but also provides a comparative analytical framework to guide future studies. The advantage of adding future cases would be largely lost if we had not developed a more rigorous framework and set of hypotheses that provides a foundation for future comparative work.

3. We developed and applied the framework prior to and independently of case or country selection. Researchers conducting the two cases were also different. Although the researchers used the same framework for analysis and considered the same hypotheses, they conducted their fieldwork and analysis independently. In fact, the Senegal case study is based on data initially collected for a separate study of the political economy of nutrition (Ndiaye 2007). The Senegal case study described in Chapter 5 emerged from additional work that used a multisectoral prism on that experience and complemented the original data with additional documentation and analysis.

4. Having two researchers work independently to conduct two case studies using the same framework, we would argue, strengthens the findings. This approach recognizes not only the importance of context but also the fact that the researchers bring different perspectives to their analyses. Finding similarities, for example, suggests a relatively strong result, as it means that the two researchers, each with different perspectives and professional preparations, have arrived at similar conclusions about the validity of the hypothesis. A continuing process of mutual critique allowed for the emergence of new ideas and interpretations over time.

5. The diversity of conditions in the case studies also allowed for increased confidence in the results. Although the main focus of analysis (that is, multisectoral collaboration in nutrition) was the same, the political and economic conditions under which the programs were implemented were very different. The diversity in the cases thus allows us to detect what

working. The findings reflect the context of the cases as well as the perspectives of the investigators themselves.

difference variation in these contextual factors (such as institutional capacity and governance) might make and helps identify key common or differentiating factors that affect outcomes. Such variation provides an interesting test of whether our hypotheses extend beyond the specific contexts of individual programs.

6. Although we selected cases known as successful attempts to work multisectorally in nutrition, we did not explore the programs in depth. Thus one could argue that both programs represented operational successes at working multisectorally, and a possible next step would be to choose failures and see how they match up against these studies and the hypotheses. Nevertheless, this observation does not have much effect on our findings for the purposes of this study. The hypotheses were developed as factors we would expect to find in successful cases of working multisectorally, and so the hypotheses and their testing against these successful cases still hold.

7. Both researchers involved in the country studies were careful to address the research questions using several primary and secondary sources. In both countries, researchers conducted interviews with the primary movers behind the collaboration but supported these data with extensive secondary documentation, including evaluation reports, presentations, and planning documents. The final draft cases were also shared and discussed with those who assisted with the case studies, providing a further check on validity. Such triangulation through documentation, interviews, and sharing ensures that the evidence supports our history and analyses.

In conclusion, we use a case study approach, but we have also developed a particular analytical framework and employed rigorous methods of data collection, analysis, and verification to test hypotheses and support our findings. In this sense, the work we have done here is more than exploratory. Our findings are also explanatory, as we seek to explain why collaboration happens and which conditions sustain it.

Our Research Approach

We do not feel researchers must view reality (or their data) through only one lens. Significant disagreements exist among researchers about what is a valid approach to knowing (Ambert et al. 1995; Fischer 1998). Even within qualitative approaches, there are multiple divergent, and acceptable, epistemologies. Some researchers prefer more classically positivistic approaches, others tend to be more postmodern. The strict divides are often left to academic practitioners, whereas in practice researchers employ multiple methods that suggest various underlying epistemologies and ontologies (Ambert et al. 1995).

In fact, drawing from distinct epistemologies can actually strengthen a study and in some sense reflects the underlying ethos of a postmodern approach that recognizes the validity of multiple viewpoints.

Although we did not strictly adhere to any one epistemological construct in our work, we do not believe our approach creates any more difficulties than if we had chosen to address the question from just one viewpoint. Indeed, if we had done so, those from alternate camps would be just as likely to criticize us for choosing one perspective over another.

Theoretical and Methodological Considerations

All researchers ask the basic question, "how can we best understand the phenomena we are dealing with?" (Byrne 1998). Our own framework for generating knowledge is reflected in our methodologies. Although we find a mix of approaches works best, the methods, tools, and processes we use are quite common to those used in comparative politics, public administration, and management.

A soft or flexible version of positivism has a long history in the policy-oriented social sciences, and we acknowledge building on that history here (Porter and Ross 2003; Gubser 2006). But we also find bringing elements of complexity theory and systems thinking into the analysis is helpful. This multi-perspective approach avoids a reductionist positivism that unwisely attempts to identify and isolate deterministic relationships that remain immutable across different contexts. We also use the concept of double fitting, introducing an element of dialectic between theory, model, and reality.

Although an event is historical, it is often difficult to know the determinate truth of an event or its exact causes or effects in some perfectly objective sense. The narrative that emerges will depend on the perspectives of participants and observers, as well as the documentation surrounding it and the methods, tools, and perspectives of the investigators.

Nevertheless, we can provide an approximate truth of the event. We can observe, describe, and perhaps even quantitatively measure some aspects of it. Based on previous experiences, we can identify reasonable causal relationships and hypotheses about these determinants and mechanisms. We can use rigorous research methods to test these hypotheses. In that sense, our approach has elements of positivism. Yet we adopt elements of the post-positivist perspective by emphasizing that such measurement occurs within the limitations of observation and interpretation described above.

This perspective does not mean we cannot discern the general outlines and fundamental principles about the events of interest (or similar ones). It just means that the magnitudes of effects of causal factors, or even the causal factors themselves, are not the same in each case (even when the cases are similar), and that context matters. We still employ methods widely accepted by the research community as being valid but use them in ways that permit a holistic view of the event, with an emphasis on triangulating information from a range of observers, participants, and documents. We still search for general principles, similarities, and differences, but we also recognize the divergence of conditions. This push for generalization rescues this approach from hopeless relativism (Byrne 1998), but it does require an appreciation for general rather than specific truths, an understanding that there is a diverse array of causes, and a tolerance for open-endedness in analysis.

This sort of understanding shares much with complexity theory (Richardson 2008). Complexity theory would acknowledge that the social world is tricky for scientific investigation precisely because the world is complex, whereas the methods and forms of understanding generally employed in science are highly dependent on things being sorted out in simple absolutist terms, usually quantitatively (Byrne 1998). Consequently, complexity theory emphasizes the importance of knowledge within context; of nonlinearity in causal relationships and the impact of feedback among elements of the system (which then disrupt attempts to identify fixed, linear relationships). It also emphasizes the fundamental incompressibility of a complex system to a few variables. Recognition of these aspects of the world (or object of study) does not mean we cannot compress the system for analysis, or that analysis is futile, but it does mean we have limits to what we know and what we can achieve in a predetermined, planned way, an especially relevant insight for managers and policymakers (Fischer 1998; Richardson 2008).

We also bring systems thinking to the discussion. Systems thinking recognizes that, in its attempt to quantify relationships and effects, positivism too often looks at potential causal elements in isolation. Instead, we take a more holistic approach. There are different pieces of a system that we are trying to understand. This holistic approach seems especially fruitful and, in fact, inevitable when studying multisectoral collaboration.

Our approach presents a more realistic account of the world by recognizing that there is complex and contingent causation. It embraces the complexity of the social world and does not try to reduce it to simple linear relationships. But by recognizing the structure of a system, our approach acknowledges that the world is not completely indeterminate (Byrne 1998).

The very nature of our inquiry—looking at interactions among and within organizations—practically requires this approach. Complexity theory and systems thinking are natural counterparts for our investigations. We understand that "a system is complex, in the sense that a great many independent agents are interacting with each other in a great many ways" (Waldrop 1993, 11). In addition, "the complexity arises because you have a great many of these simple components interacting simultaneously. The complexity is actually in the organization—the myriad possible ways that the components of the system can interact" (Stephen Wolfram cited in Waldrop 1993, 86). Complexity theory then would argue that certain interactions matter more in different situations, and that, in fact, unknown or unusual factors outside our mental model may at times play the crucial roles. We agree, and although the data itself do not always allow it, we try to incorporate discussion of this sort of uncertainty into our analysis.

A final aspect of our approach is the concept of double-fitting, or adaptation through an interchange between theory and evidence (Katz 1982; Partington 2002). Although this concept fits comfortably inside the framework of complexity theory (paralleling ideas of the use of fuzzy sets), it is a primary element of qualitative research regardless of epistemology (Ambert et al. 1995). This fundamental and accepted element of qualitative research implicitly acknowledges the indeterminacy suggested by complexity theory. The iterations between model and reality and the changing insights over time are part of the process of discovery through research. They are part of the dialectic, the dialogue that surrounds such research. In practice, these iterations are evident in our approach: we initially generated conceptual images of factors affecting multisectoral collaborations (as noted in Chapter 3) and shaped and reshaped them to fashion conclusions according to our observations, collegial dialogues, further readings, and comparative analysis of the cases.

What We Did in Practice

The above description is important for understanding our approach to the generation of knowledge. But how is this mindset reflected in the course of undertaking these country studies? Two of the hallmarks of complexity theory (and a less rigidly positivist perspective) are an appreciation of two ideas: (1) multiple valid representations (perspectives) exist of the same complex system, so that it is difficult to find a single objective truth and (2) context matters, so that it is unrealistic to claim that relationships among the variables remain fixed under all conditions, or that the model includes all variables of interest (Richardson 2008).[2] By paying attention to these concerns, we hope to get at the approximate, if not the determinate, truth.

---

[2] A strict postpositivist perspective even somewhat combines these concerns about perspective and context. This paradigm would argue that the empirical object of study is not only rooted in the time and place in which it occurs but also dependent on the researcher's individual perspective and understanding (his or her constructs). Thus there is no complete factual description independent of the social circumstances in which the event occurred. So instead of the object itself, we get an interpretation of the object (Fischer 1998).

Econometric theory even explicitly recognizes these problems, allowing for varying-parameter

Multiple Perspectives

We responded to the need for understanding multiple perspectives in several ways at different points in the research process. First, in the preparatory stage, we began with a review of knowledge on multisectoral collaborations. But we did not just search the literature on nutrition. We searched across fields of study for theory, concepts, experiences, and lessons. This review gave us a trove of ideas about how to frame the study and what the principal elements of successful collaboration were, as well as general lessons.

We went further than might be usual for studies in political science by intentionally crossing disciplinary boundaries to draw on ideas not only from studies in government (especially in terms of local and national government) but also from studies on management and on cooperation in agriculture and nutrition. This work unearthed new ideas and led to the development of an initial analytical framework.

In the fieldwork, we interviewed individuals who participated in the programs and those who were observers or researchers. The roles of these individuals varied by how they interacted with the program (as colleagues, implementers, observers, and so forth), and also varied over time. These interviews provided us with multiple points of view.

We also employed flexible interview methods that allowed for variation in causal explanations. For example, instead of asking direct questions about hypotheses, we conducted more general interviews about processes and pathways. As part of the investigation, we followed up on explanations of events or causal factors. This approach is in line with standard practice for qualitative research but also with an epistemological approach that leaves investigation open for surprises and the pursuit of new directions (the concepts of uncertainty and indeterminacy as expressed in complexity theory, for example).

And, finally, it is important to recognize that as a group, the authors of this study already represent a range of epistemological and ontological orientations. We ourselves thus bring multiple perspectives to bear on all aspects of the research, from preparation to fieldwork, analysis, orientations that derive from our own disciplinary backgrounds in economics, sociology, political science, public administration, and nutrition. This diversity ensures that our own individual biases have a positive effect on the work, even as our potential disciplinary blinders or excesses are somewhat checked by the other members of the group.

---

models or developing procedures to overcome bias stemming from omitted influential variables. At the same time, econometric results depend greatly on having variation in the data, so that much of what is interesting remains captured in the error term, thus illustrating why econometricians also spend so much energy worrying about the fit (or explanatory power) of their models.

Context

The importance of context means that we did not try to establish fixed hypotheses to test quantitatively but rather identified potential explanations (what we call "hypotheses") that might in the end provide principles for working multisectorally. Thus we were searching for principles or checklists that policymakers could apply and adapt across contexts, rather than predetermined, invariant procedures to create certain conditions or do things in a certain way.

The expression of those principles and the influence of the factors vary by context—not only by geography (different countries) but also by history, culture, personalities, economic situation (more versus less developed), political structures (national versus state), and time.

As noted above, the methods we use have much in common with analyses in management and public administration. We made a concerted effort to focus on the practical, aiming to provide policymakers and development practitioners with useful general models and checklists to guide their actions in different contexts. The case studies illustrate how the factors on the checklist may interact in certain situations to affect outcomes.[3] This flexible and dialectical approach is particularly apt in this initial stage of inquiry, where the literature and truths are not yet well established. It is also especially appropriate for providing operational principles to managers working in a variety of contexts.

---

[3] Neustadt and May (1986) take a similar approach in their academic, but practitioner-oriented, study on the uses of comparative history for policymaking.

CHAPTER 5

Senegal's Fight against Malnutrition:
The Nutrition Enhancement Program

MARCELA NATALICCHIO

Malnutrition in Sub-Saharan Africa is increasing—but Senegal shines as an exception to this rule. According to data from Demographic and Health Surveys, between 1992 and 2005, stunting (low height for age) in children under five years of age in Senegal declined from 22 to 16 percent, and the prevalence of underweight for the same age group went from 20 to 17 percent (Republic of Senegal 2006). Senegal is on track to be one of the few countries in the region that will reach the Millennium Development Goal (MDG) for nutrition.

The implementation of the Nutrition Enhancement Program (Programme de Renforcement Nutritionnel, or NEP) has undoubtedly contributed to these achievements. During the first phase of NEP, from 2002 to 2006, malnutrition in NEP zones decreased by 42 percent. More than 200,000 mother-child pairs benefited from the program, some 20 percent of children five years of age or younger (Republic of Senegal 2006).

NEP is the principal nutrition program in Senegal and is an element of the poverty reduction strategy of the government, part of its investment in human development aimed at improving the nutritional status of women and children. Now in its second phase (2007-11), NEP is scaling up, so that by the end of the second phase NEP will cover all of the country's 11 regions, with a focus on rural areas and regions with the highest prevalence of malnutrition. By the end of the second phase, NEP should have reached 700,000 children under five years of age, more than 50,000 pregnant women, 65,000 lactating women, and 177,000 teenagers (Republic of Senegal 2006).

NEP represents the Government of Senegal's strong belief in using a multisectoral approach to reduce malnutrition. NEP works using a multisectoral and multiactor approach, coordinating actions across ministries, donors, and nongovernmental organizations (NGOs). As such, NEP operates under the supervision of the Coordination Unit for the Reduction of Malnutrition (Cellule de Lutte contre la Malnutrition, or CLM). CLM, attached to the Prime Minister's Office, coordinates programs and actions to reduce malnutrition by means of both the public and private sectors.

This chapter examines NEP using the framework established and testing the hypotheses developed in Chapters 3 and 4. As a multisectoral program operating under a multisectoral coordinating committee and based in a non-sectoral home (the Prime Minister's Office), NEP provides an important case for study of how to work multisectorally in nutrition, even in resource-limited conditions.

In this chapter I first present country characteristics for Senegal, describe the methods used to collect and analyze the data for this case, and then follow with an in-depth analysis of the initiation and evolution of NEP. The case is organized around three main questions in rough chronological order:

- How and why did the collaboration begin?
- How have factors internal to the participating organizations and the program itself influenced the development of the collaboration over time? How have factors in the external environment influenced the collaboration?
- How have internal and external factors affected the sustainability or fragility of the collaboration over time?

By answering these questions, which cover different phases of collaboration, I explore how internal and external contexts and the design of institutional links, presented in Chapter 3, have affected NEP's ability to work multisectorally.

Country Description

Senegal is a Sahelian country, located at the western extremity of the African continent, with an area of 196,722 square kilometers (Figure 5.1). It is subdivided into 11 regions, 34 departments, 67 communes, 103 *arrondissements*, and 324 rural communities (Republic of Senegal 2006). In 2007 Senegal had an estimated population of 12,521,851, about 75 percent of whom lived in rural areas (U.S. Department of State 2008). Population density varies from about 77 inhabitants per square kilometer in the west-central region to 2 per square kilometer in the arid eastern section. The Senegalese landscape consists mainly of the rolling sandy plains of the western Sahel, which rise to foothills in the southeast. Senegal's highest point of 584 meters (1,926 feet) is found here, an otherwise unnamed feature near Nepen Diakha. The northern border is formed by the Senegal River, and other important waterways include the Gambia and Casamance rivers. The capital, Dakar, lies on the Cap-Vert peninsula, the westernmost point of continental Africa (Britannica 2009).

Figure 5.1   Physical and topographical maps of Senegal

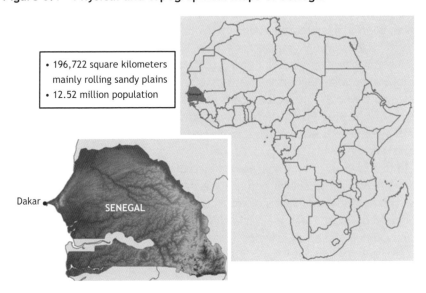

- 196,722 square kilometers
  mainly rolling sandy plains
- 12.52 million population

Dakar

SENEGAL

Sources: GADM (2010), Jarvis et al. (2008).

Senegal is a democracy. It has several competitive political parties and a free press. A process of decentralization has been launched with the transfer of central-government responsibilities to local governments, but difficulties with resource transfers still exist.

Senegal's main industries include food processing, mining, cement, artificial fertilizer, chemicals, textiles, imported petroleum refining, and tourism (EIU 2005; UNECA 2009). Agriculture is the largest economic sector, representing 18 percent of gross domestic product (GDP). Of the workforce of 4 million, 70 percent are employed in agriculture. Exports include fish, chemicals, cotton, fabrics, groundnuts, and calcium phosphate. Major foreign markets include France, other European Union members, and West Africa (U.S. Department of State 2008).

By historical and regional standards, Senegal has achieved good economic results over the past decade, although its performance weakened in 2006. GDP growth has recently averaged almost 5 percent per year. As a member of the West African Economic and Monetary Union, Senegal is working toward greater regional integration and a unified external tariff (Boogaerde and Tsangarides 2005; UNECA 2009). The World Bank considers, despite a relatively good political environment, that the enabling environment for growth remains limited. It notes continued weaknesses in governance, obstacles for the private sector to doing business, and lagging technology development along with substantial deficiencies in infrastructure and human development, all of which are crucial for a country that cannot rely on significant natural resources (World Bank 2006b).

With a 2.2 percent annual population growth rate and a crude birthrate of 37 per 1,000, 43 percent of the population is under 15 years of age. Life expectancy at birth is 59 years (61 for women and 57 for men) (UNFPA 2006). The adult mortality rate for those between 15 and 60 years of age is still high at 271 per 1,000. The infant mortality rate is 53 per 1,000 live births (WHO 2008). The main causes of child mortality are diarrheal diseases, malaria, acute respiratory infections, and diseases that can be prevented by immunization.

The large majority of the Senegalese population is Muslim (94 percent) (CIA 2005). The adult literacy rate is estimated at 42 percent, with 53 percent of men and only 32 percent of women being literate (UNESCO 2008).

Despite economic and political progress, Senegal remains a poor country, with a GDP per capita of US$710 in 2005. Fifty-seven percent of the population is poor, but this percentage is higher among women (Republic of Senegal 2004). Vulnerability is even more widespread, as studies find that 65 percent of households consider themselves poor (WHO 2006).

The probability of being poor in Senegal is highly correlated with access to basic infrastructure services. The regions with the highest levels of poverty (Diourbel, Kaoloack, Kolda, and Ziguinchor) are those with the lowest access to water and sanitation and electricity. For the rural population, and for the poor in both the urban and rural areas, gaps in terms of access to services are large and simply reinforce their vulnerability (World Bank 2006b). The sum of these conditions can be found in Senegal's rank as 156 out of 177 countries, according to the *Human Development Report* (UNDP 2008).

Senegal has made substantial progress in reducing malnutrition, although 16 percent of children under five in Senegal remain stunted. Even more worrisome is that micronutrient deficiencies remain high. Anemia (iron deficiency) prevails among 84 percent of children under five years of age and among 61 percent of women. Goiter (iodine deficiency) is endemic in the southeastern part of the country, with a prevalence of 34 percent and reaching 51 percent in some places (Republic of Senegal 2000). Sixty-one percent of children six years of age and younger are vitamin A deficient. Micronutrient deficiencies are the underlying cause of 30 percent of child mortalities (Republic of Senegal 2006).

Senegal must import food to cover its needs, especially cereals. National cereal production covered only 35 percent of the needs for 2002/03. For 2004/05, internal availability, including net national production and stocks, was estimated at 1,007,004 metric tons and covered only 44 percent of human consumption needs. The average daily per capita availability of calories and proteins was satisfactory at 2,861 kcal (adequacy is considered to be 2,400 kcal), but this average hides a tremendous disparity in terms of individual consumption and access to food.

Methods and Data for the Case Study

This case study is based on primary and secondary data. For the primary data, the principal researcher conducted interviews in Senegal during October and November 2007 with key players in the nutrition field. The information was primarily collected for a comparative investigation of the political economy of nutrition in Africa (Ndiaye 2007), which overlapped in content and focus with this institutional study.

The interviews carried out for that investigation and subsequently used for this case study were 36 in total and included (1) three advisers to the Prime Minister's Office who had participated in the negotiations of NEP I and II with the World Bank; (2) two public officials from the Ministry of Health who work on nutrition; (3) two public officials from the Ministry of Education; (4) one public official from the Ministry of Industry; (5) 14 representatives of the local communities, civil society, and NGOs; (6) eight representatives of international agencies and donors; (7) three academics; (8) three staff members of NEP and the Community Nutrition Program (Programme de Nutrition Communautaire, or PNC); and (9) two nutritionists who had participated in the field of nutrition in the past 30 years. Additional interviews and personal communications were conducted in Washington, D.C., with two World Bank staff associated with NEP during its launch and development.

All interviewees consented to participate in the research and to be quoted, except when explicitly requested to remain anonymous if discussing a sensitive issue. Note-taking was used during the interviews. Follow-up with interviewees was agreed on during the first interview and was done when information was lacking or needed clarification. Note-taking was preferred to tape recording, as the researcher finds that interviewees feel more at ease and are more open in their testimonies without a tape recorder. The veracity of the testimonies was tested by triangulation with other informants and documentation. In addition, the researcher made extensive use of secondary data, including documents from the Government of Senegal and the World Bank, as well as the study of the political economy of nutrition in Senegal carried out by Alfred Ndiaye under supervision of the primary researcher (Ndiaye 2007).

Getting Started

The origins of NEP owe much to PNC, a previous nutrition project. Because Senegal's experience with PNC provided a significant opening for NEP and useful lessons on how to work multisectorally in nutrition, I describe this program in some detail.

PNC functioned from 1995 to 2001, and NEP, which began in 2002, is in a real sense its follow up. PNC was really the first program in Senegal to promote collaboration on nutrition among national agencies. This collaboration did not include the participation of NGOs, as NEP would. According to some views, PNC did not work very well, but it did bring the notion of the importance of multisectoral cooperation in nutrition to the forefront of the government agenda. Professor Galaye Sall, the director of the Nutrition Unit in the Ministry of Health at the time and a national leader in nutrition, said, "One of the advantages of PNC was that it considered other environmental aspects related to nutrition, such as the distribution of potable water, although the program still revolved a lot around the idea of food distribution" (GS).[1]

The Government of Senegal started PNC in 1995 with funding from the World Bank. The program officially ended on June 30, 2001. The project was aligned with the objectives of the five-year National Nutrition Program, but its design fundamentally represented a response to concerns about urban unrest after the devaluation of the African Financial Community (Communauté Financière d'Afrique, or CFA) franc in 1994. The PNC targeted poor urban areas where economic conditions and food and nutrition security had been deteriorating. Underweight in urban areas, for example, had increased from 14.1 percent to 16.5 percent between 1992 and 1996 (World Bank 2006b).

At the time of preparation of the project, the Government of Senegal was particularly concerned about the high unemployment rate among young urban professionals. It was thought that economic and social conditions would deteriorate even faster and further following a currency devaluation (which could quickly and dramatically increase the cost of living), perhaps sparking protests and a challenge to political stability and to plans for longer-term economic adjustment. As part of the government's response to this situation, PNC attempted to provide an employment safety net for some of these urban youths. From the beginning, then, PNC was an employment scheme as well as a nutrition program.

By 2000, economic conditions had improved, and PNC was coming to a close. The Government of Senegal began to engage in renegotiation of the PNC project with the World Bank. As described in more detail later in this chapter, several factors came together to provide an opportunity to alter the nature of Senegal's fight against malnutrition. In some ways, these factors represent exactly the types of changes and opportunities—particularly in terms of shifting perceptions across a range of stakeholders—that have occurred throughout the world and now enable implementing a more multisectoral approach to reducing malnutrition. In Senegal, among the most impor-

---

[1] The codes for the interviews are listed in the references.

tant factors that provided such an environment for change included a change in government administration, findings of corruption in the initial program, and the arrival of a new Task Team Leader (TTL) for the World Bank. These changes occurred as PNC was coming to a close, and thus as discussions and renegotiations about how the government and the World Bank would deal with malnutrition were beginning.

Although perhaps limited from the perspective of nutrition, in general PNC was very popular and quite successful. PNC provided nutritional services and employment in the urban areas at a time of economic and social hardship. PNC was also very effective in providing potable water, again an important achievement in urban areas, where safe water and good sanitation are often scarce and their lack is a significant contributor to poor health and nutrition. PNC also had a community focus. Over time, it managed to mobilize communities to take responsibility for their nutritional and other needs.

In devising the management for PNC, the Government of Senegal and the World Bank arrived at a rather innovative arrangement for the time. Although a nutrition program would often be placed under the aegis of the Ministry of Health, in this case the government and the World Bank did not believe that the Ministry of Health had sufficiently strong implementation capacity, management structures, or practices to deliver good results for the project. As a result, they turned to the Executing Agency for Works of Public Interest against Unemployment (Agence d'Exécution des Travaux d'Intéret Public Contre le Sous-Emploi, or AGETIP).

AGETIP was an uncommon organization. Although a state agency, it had managerial autonomy from the government bureaucracy and a private-sector orientation. That is, it was not officially or hierarchically part of the bureaucracy, but it was responsible for executing government programs. It worked under private-sector management principles and offered salaries that were more competitive with the private sector than was typical of public agencies. AGETIP had previously managed projects for the World Bank and demonstrated institutional and absorptive capacity, essentially meaning it could disburse money effectively. The placement of PNC under the management of AGETIP represented stronger confidence in AGETIP's implementing capacities than in those of the Ministry of Health, an affinity for its private-sector management qualities, and a perception of PNC as a program to address unemployment and not only malnutrition.

AGETIP had more experience in managing infrastructure projects than in implementing social interventions, although it had managed the construction of rural community health centers run by local women's organizations. Because the agency did not have any specific expertise in nutrition, it recruited nutrition experts with backgrounds in implementing social programs at the community level. In addition, a Technical Advisory Committee was created to support AGETIP on technical matters during implementation. The Technical Advisory Committee was composed of leading professionals from Senegalese universities and medical schools and representatives from international technical agencies. In addition, several microenterprises (MICs) were created to provide services in the community nutrition centers. Per the conceptualization of PNC, these MICs hired young professionals who had previously been unemployed.

PNC consisted of three major components: (1) a nutrition program, (2) a water program, and (3) a food-security program. The nutrition program was the main component of the project and targeted children under three years of age and pregnant and lactating women in poor urban areas. AGETIP contracted MICs to manage the program's activities, which were based in urban community nutrition centers. Each MIC was made up of four young people approved by the local steering committee representing the community.

The community nutrition activities included (1) growth monitoring of children under three; (2) provision of a weekly take-home food supplement during six months for children whose weight-for-age was more than 2 standard deviations of the mean Z-score (a standard indicator of malnutrition using underweight); (3) Information-Education-Communication (IEC) sessions for pregnant and lactating women; and (4) provision of a weekly take-home food supplement for three months for pregnant women during the last trimester of their first pregnancy and for six months for lactating women with a child in the program or with an infant less than six months old. Participants received nutrition services for six months. Severely malnourished and sick children were referred to nearby health centers. Thus some coordination between the community nutrition centers and the health system was necessary.

The water program installed drinking-water standpipes and waterpipe networks in the urban areas targeted by the nutrition program. The food-security program provided food and nutrition information, advice, and food supplements to beneficiaries. PNC also supported improved food and nutrition security by providing employment in labor-intensive infrastructure works or supporting other income-generating activities through cash- or food-for-work schemes. However, as this component was delayed in start-up, much of its funds were reallocated to the nutrition component.

Problems with PNC

The project became very popular and achieved many of its objectives, although it had shortcomings. By the time of renegotiation, the Ministry of Health and the World Bank had become quite critical of it and were moving to take these concerns into account in the renegotiation. These criticisms revolved around costs, targeting, and, of particular interest for our study, interagency coordination. Specifically, some of the main criticisms were that (1) PNC focused on the urban areas, whereas the rate of malnutrition was higher in rural areas; (2) the interventions were based in the nutrition centers, making them expensive compared to other alternatives that might make more intensive use of community agents; (3) the interventions themselves were also more expensive, as they relied heavily on food distribution; (4) coordination with the Ministry of Health, meant to be a main partner, did not work; (5) line ministries were not substantially involved, and there was therefore little capacity building at the state level.

Interagency coordination was a particular problem. In 1994, just after the devaluation of the CFA franc, a presidential decree had created a national commission, the National Commission for the Fight against Malnutrition (Commission Nationale de Lutte Contre la Malnutrition, or CNLM). The mandate of CNLM was to provide a safety net for the poor. In particular, CNLM was tasked with coordinating and guiding activities that would prevent malnutrition from increasing in Senegal. Before the establishment of CNLM, there were no multisectoral coordination mechanisms in Senegal. CNLM was set up following recommendations that, because of the multisectoral nature of nutrition, no one line ministry or institution could, or should, be solely responsible for nutrition.

As explained in Chapter 2, by the 1990s, at least the idea of a multisectoral conceptualization of nutrition was changing the way policymakers, programmers, and advocates were thinking about nutrition, even if they did not yet have a viable implementation structure. Following this idea, CNLM was placed in the President's Office. It was composed of representatives from the Prime Minister's Office; the Ministries of Economy, Planning and Finance, Health and Social Action, Women's, Children's and Family Affairs; AGETIP; and NGOs and civil society organizations.

A technical subcommission of CNLM was actively involved in the design and preparation of PNC and provided general policy guidance. At the time, Senegal did not have a country-level strategy or policy, and CNLM did not produce one. Rather, throughout PNC, CNLM simply met and offered tactical rather than strategic guidance. In its mandate for coordination and its composition, CNLM was not so different from myriad other failed attempts to work multisectorally in nutrition. And indeed, CNLM did not function very well either.

After initial involvement in design of PNC, CNLM participated only to a certain degree in monitoring and evaluating project implementation. But in critical differences with NEP, CNLM had only limited operational responsibility for PNC, and the Ministry of Health—a key player in nutrition—was left out of management. Management was AGETIP's responsibility, and AGETIP, with its limited nutritional knowledge but otherwise proven capacity for implementation, was largely able to implement the program by itself.

Beyond CNLM, the line ministries did not help much during the execution of the project, even though their representatives attended regular meetings. They had limited participation and so a limited sense of ownership of PNC. In one sense, their exclusion from implementation was intentional. But these ministries also acknowledged that their own limited capacities made it hard for them to participate more actively. Their lack of human and financial resources impeded their ability to effectively supervise activities and training. Given these limitations, the reliance on AGETIP to implement the program made sense, but it also prevented the various cooperating agencies from actually working together.

AGETIP's implementation of this program largely by itself at first might seem to offer a model of multisectoral action by means of directing or contracting others to do the work. Whereas the programs in both Senegal and Colombia (described in Chapter 6) did indeed contract out much of program implementation, suggesting such a model is viable, the AGETIP model did not actually integrate action across institutions, the focus of this study.

In addition, considering AGETIP as a success is highly questionable. It failed to integrate institutions, and it effectively created a body that duplicated existing interventions and coordinating mechanisms. In so doing, it simply emphasized the existing disconnects among institutions and sowed confusion. In these terms, it does not seem a likely model to emulate.

The experience also provides further evidence that an institutionally separate program is a weak basis for sustained action. Of course, this tactic is always an option, but because such a program exists independently and largely outside government agencies, it loses the integrative value of a multiagency program and the benefits that accompany interagency collaboration. It effectively has to build the entire structure for implementation, disregarding existing government programs and capabilities. Faced with likely institutional opposition, when the political or financial support is gone, the program will also disappear. This sequence of events is illustrated by AGETIP's experience. When stakeholders, including donors, NGOS, and public organizations, met to discuss technical and organizational aspects of a national nutrition program, AGETIP ardently defended its model of intervention but failed to carry the discussion.

Perhaps partially as a result of factors (both the locus of implementation being placed elsewhere and the participants' feeling they had little capacity to respond to the demands of implementation), CNLM meetings tended to be formal and did not stimulate discussion. Interest and impetus were lost. As a result, coordination among stakeholders in nutrition continued to be poor, even though it was a primary responsibility of CNLM.

The disconnect among potential partners is well illustrated by the fact that the National Food and Nutrition Service (Service National d'Alimentation et Nutrition), a division dedicated to nutrition in the Ministry of Health, initiated and implemented another national nutrition program alongside PNC, using separate funds raised by the Ministry and with no coordination with CNLM or PNC. The two interventions used different approaches and conveyed distinct messages. These programs thus not only duplicated work and failed to benefit from potential synergies, but they also actively contributed to disorganization and confusion among policy actors trying to reduce malnutrition, despite the existence of a supraministerial body intended to coordinate those efforts.

Not surprisingly, coordination between PNC and the Ministry of Health also failed on a programmatic level. As part of PNC, the severely malnourished were to be referred to health centers dependent on the Ministry of Health. Yet the World Bank's end-of-project assessment highlighted lack of expertise in nutrition case management, inadequate materials, and failure to provide needed special nutritional supplements among the many problems in making such coordination effective (World Bank 2001).

Opportunity for Change

Several factors coalesced to create a golden window of opportunity for change. First, the political context was highly favorable to a renewed engagement with nutrition. Although formally a multiparty democracy with more than 40 political parties and a history of entrenched civil liberties, Senegal was, in practice, a one-party state from independence until the March 2000 presidential election. The victory of Abdoulaye Wade in that election changed the political scene dramatically.

Wade's Parti Démocratique Sénégalais, which described itself as a liberal party, replaced the long-dominant Parti Socialiste, which espoused socialism and state control. The Parti Démocratique Sénégalais operated in a more pluralistic environment, and the new president was keen on embracing new ideas for development. In particular, Wade placed much greater emphasis on human development as a key element for getting Senegal out of poverty. Wade was more committed than his predecessor to promotion of the private sector, but he repeatedly emphasized the importance of addressing social concerns, such as healthcare, education, and unemployment. Wade himself advocated a decidedly Keynesian approach, assigning the state a major role in developing Senegal's infrastructure and in educating and training its workforce to compete in global markets. For Wade, improving nutrition was a critical component of creating a more productive workforce, essential to the future economic and social development of Senegal. This personal commitment may be key for creating higher political visibility for nutrition, as the presidency is the most powerful institution in Senegal's political system.

The First Lady, Viviane Wade, also became personally interested in the issue of nutrition. She asked Dr. Sall (at the time director of the Nutrition Unit in the Ministry of Health and known for his work on nutrition in the country) to enlighten her on the issue of nutrition. She was particularly interested in learning about a product named "spirulina," a highly nutritious local product. Dr. Sall used the opportunity to advocate for a preventive approach to nutrition, and the importance of having such a policy in the country. Since then the First Lady has remained a strong supporter of nutrition, making at least three presentations a year on the importance of nutrition as a public policy concern.

Deeper political commitment alone might not have led to a new approach to dealing with nutrition, if the current approaches had been effective. But as a second major factor, corruption in PNC provoked further calls for restructuring. Corruption within the organization weakened the position of those who would defend PNC. At least organizationally if not conceptually, this opened the door to substantial rethinking and replanning of future investments in nutrition.

In a way, just as earlier the devaluation of the CFA franc and its negative social effects had created a window of opportunity for the World Bank to introduce PNC and the notion of a multisectoral approach, the corruption scandal around PNC now favored a new discussion on the best way to reduce malnutrition, instead of a defense or simply a continuation of PNC. The end-of-project evaluation set out additional problems with PNC in addressing malnutrition—and significantly, gave some guidance on what a new approach should look like. For Claudia Rokx, the World Bank official in charge of the end-of-project assessment of the PNC, "the crisis situation in which PNC was involved . . . created the ideal scenario to start over" (CR).

And, indeed, Rokx used the situation to do exactly that. Rokx, an energetic nutritionist trained in Holland with a holistic view of nutrition, had replaced the previous World Bank staff who had designed, supervised, and promoted PNC. Assigned to review PNC as part of the end-of-project assessment in 2000, Rokx found PNC flawed in many respects. Now, named as TTL for the negotiations, she had the opportunity to make changes and implement her own vision. Dr. Sall, who was in charge of the Nutrition Department at the time, said he "felt a big change in the World Bank's views in regard to nutrition. Before, they insisted on food distribution but then they changed to a more global view" (GS).

Thus it is important to note that criticism of PNC and subsequent changes were due not only to some implementation issues, which might rightly be attributed to the Senegalese government, but also because the World Bank staff in charge of the renegotiation had a different conceptualization of how to understand and respond to malnutrition than the strategy encapsulated in PNC.

Moving Change Forward: Starting NEP

For Rokx and a small coalition of people, the predominant approach in Senegal to attacking malnutrition, furthered by PNC, revolved excessively around the idea of food distribution. Based on their technical knowledge of more effective interventions in nutrition, they believed that this focus needed to change. They organized a series of workshops with participants from all relevant ministries, representatives from the Ministry of Finance, donors, and NGOs. This platform was ideal for creating a common view of the causes of and most appropriate solution for malnutrition.

In these workshops among a relatively small, well-informed group, the participants discussed their ideas about the most appropriate approach for fighting malnutrition. According to the participants, the most difficult part was not creating a common view about the multicausality of malnutrition. Rather, it was for the actors in this group to agree on how to operationalize the idea.

Even the nonnutrition actors were already convinced that a multisectoral approach was needed, a point illustrated by PNC. This view was shared by the professional association of nutritionists in Senegal, the Directorate of Nutrition in the Ministry of Health, and other key donors, such as UNICEF. To them, working across sectors was an obvious requirement for reducing malnutrition. But how to do that was much less clear. So the operational questions became: How would they design, organize, and implement such a program? What, particularly, would be its institutional setup?

Helped by a new World Bank TTL for nutrition programs in Senegal, and coupled with the opening of a new space for action by President Wade, this core group, including representatives from the World Bank, the Ministry of Health, and other donors (such as the United States Agency for International Development [USAID] and UNICEF) urged a move away from food distribution to a stronger focus on prevention, behavioral change, and education. They wanted to target rural areas, where malnutrition rates were higher; they wanted to draw more on the collaboration of community agents and the participation of NGOs; and they wanted to institute a better setup to improve interagency collaboration.

To obtain the support of the Ministry of Finance and the Prime Minister's Office, this informal coalition employed strategic communications to make their case. One advocacy tool they used was PROFILES.[2] PROFILES was an approach and a tool developed by the U.S-based Academy for Educational Development (AED) and funded by USAID. PROFILES was designed to help decisionmakers at the national level understand the benefits to the over-all economy of fighting malnutrition. Using PROFILES tools, an analyst can estimate economic and social benefits and also program costs, so that policymakers can see for themselves the return on investment in nutrition. According to participants in these sessions, these presentations were quite successful and helped to convince nonspecialists of the importance of giving nutrition highest priority. The audiences for these presentations were people in government who could make decisions on nutrition policies, such as the representatives of the Ministry of Finance and Ministry of Health.

In addition to the use of advocacy tools, the informal coalition also organized workshops to discuss ways forward. One important result was that government officials who participated in these workshops also joined in negotiations with the World Bank over the new loan, meeting in Washington, D.C., and Dakar. The workshop discussions had clearly targeted, educated, and conferred ownership on those who could ultimately influence the govern-ment's decisions about the program.

The Senegalese government and the World Bank drew on lessons from the PNC experience to design NEP. First, CNLM was revamped and became CLM. Under the new project, this former coordinating committee became much more. CLM was now to serve as the main anchor for collaboration, not just as an advisory or networking body. Under the new loan, CLM gained significant operational responsibilities. Its roles were more clearly delineated than were those of its predecessor. CLM now had direct responsibility for implementing NEP, creating greater integration of action across sectors.

Second, NEP worked to gain the confidence and strengthen the imple-menting capacities of operational partners. The government and the World Bank recognized that in the previous project, the Ministry of Health felt excluded. As a result, the Ministry had created its own parallel program. This time, the Ministry of Health was central to the preparation of NEP and CLM and therefore had a greater sense of ownership from the outset. As detailed later in this chapter, NEP also provided operational and financial support for collaborating partners, including ministries and local governments.

Third, the government decided to place CLM under the Prime Minister's Office, not that of the president, where PNC was located. On one hand, participants felt the program needed a fresh start, institutionally speaking.

---

[2] See http://www.aedprofiles.org/. Accessed February 12, 2011.

They wanted to remove the new program from the President's Office, where AGETIP was located. On the other hand, to promote intersectoral collaboration and avoid giving ownership to any one ministry, they hesitated to place CLM in a single ministry, for example, the Ministry of Health. After substantial discussions, they agreed to place the new program in the Prime Minister's Office, a more logical choice than the President's Office, because the Prime Minister's Office was responsible for coordinating among ministries and often functioned as the locus of interministerial collaborations.

Fourth, these organizational arrangements were supported by a legal framework and fiduciary obligations. Executive Decree 2001-770, passed in 2001, created CLM and gave legal effect to the arrangements noted above. The financial contract (the loan) between the Government of Senegal and the World Bank to finance NEP obligated the government to fulfill these agreements and ensure interagency cooperation.

Transforming the Approach to Nutrition

In discussing NEP, government staff consistently make the point that NEP represents a substantive and critical transformation in the Government of Senegal's fight against malnutrition. With NEP the government went from a project approach to a program approach. For politicians, policymakers, and civil servants, this is a significant reorientation in institutional thinking. A project operates in a relatively isolated fashion, usually within one sector, and most likely has a finite life. Until NEP, and even with PNC, nutrition was treated through projects. A program, however, connotes a broader initiative and is usually embedded in a larger policy framework. A program approach helps generate cooperation among actors and sectors dealing with nutrition. The creation of NEP and CLM, then, was not conceived of as simply another nutrition project, but as the beginning of a process of the institutionalization of nutrition as a cross-sectoral effort in Senegal.

In this context, the first task of CLM was to finish the work of CNLM and draft a national nutrition policy. CLM would then be responsible for its implementation. In this way, NEP would be one of the instruments to achieve the goals set out in the policy document. Furthermore, even if CLM later discontinued NEP, CLM would still be responsible in the long term for implementing policies to reduce malnutrition.

Before the initiation of NEP, Senegal did not have a national nutrition policy. Believing such a policy was important to the long-term institutionalization of nutrition policies, the World Bank made creation of a nutrition policy a prerequisite for its loan. NEP could only begin after the Government of Senegal had drafted a nutrition policy for the country.

As experience with CNLM had shown, a mandate alone is not sufficient to ensure that things work well, especially multisectorally. Even under NEP, smooth multisectoral functioning depended less on interagency cooperation at the national level than on good performance of NGOs and cooperation among partners at the local level, as detailed later in the chapter.

Unsurprisingly, these new proposals for rather dramatic institutional change generated significant opposition. AGETIP and the young professionals hired for MICs vigorously defended PNC, as they clearly had something to lose from restructuring. Their points of view on the organizational structure and placement of NEP were debated heatedly in the workshops. The young professionals who were part of PNC and who would soon be unemployed organized demonstrations and strikes that were publicized by the media. They demanded to be recruited by the new program. The new manager of NEP did not want to hire them, as NEP did not need them. To settle the dispute, NEP agreed to pay salaries to former employees of PNC for two years, even if they did not work. With the young professionals quieted, the new organizational structure favored by the Ministry of Health and the World Bank was put into place.

Strains of the debates surrounding the creation of NEP exist even today. For example, historically, nutrition policies in Senegal were associated with food distribution. Although the core group and close allies now fully recognized that attaining nutrition security meant going beyond food security, not all influential actors were aware of or shared this perspective. Most still associated nutrition policies with food policy: for them a food distribution program was a perfectly adequate nutrition program. In addition, from a politician's point of view, a food distribution program not only attacked the problem but also provided visible proof of government action, with the politicians reaping benefits. Beneficiaries also liked receiving food, which fit with the traditional and widely understood conceptualization of the socialist state as provider. Moving away from food distribution was therefore not only a matter of changing the understanding of a few people but also one of overcoming resistance from groups with political interests in maintaining the existing system and its complex of food programs. Replacing the focus on food distribution with the idea that prevention, education, and behavior change should be the main pillars of a program against malnutrition was the most difficult part.

According to Dr. Sall, implementing this "new idea" remains difficult today. Debate on this issue is still "part of their fight," particularly with regard to the wider public, as the politicians are now mostly convinced that food distribution is not the answer to malnutrition. Of course, politicians continue to reap benefits from food distribution, even if it is not part of a nutrition program. For example, food is still distributed as part of the religious celebrations of the Muslim brotherhoods. The World Food Programme also undertakes some limited food distribution.

Summing Up: Getting Started

The creation of NEP built significantly on a previous project (PNC), but various influences in the internal and external contexts, along with key decisions about institutional design, were crucial to the initiation of NEP as a genuine, sustainable, and successful multisectoral collaboration. The framework presented in Chapter 3 has already indicated that many of these factors might be harbingers of success.

Internal Context

- Although an external agent, the World Bank functioned as an internal player—taking leadership to maintain investment in nutrition even after the closing of PNC.
- Top leaders created a policy space. Other actors stepped in to fill the space with policy frameworks and programs and to forge collaborations, new approaches, and new structures.
- Advocates worked to create a common view about the causes of malnutrition and appropriate policy responses among a wide range of actors, with special inclusion of and support from the Ministry of Health.
- Although not perfectly designed for nutrition, a previous program (PNC) had helped create a shared conceptualization among donors and ministries about the causes of malnutrition and the need to work multisectorally. It also highlighted challenges for such work, giving the NEP designers some clues as to what obstacles they needed to address (such as implementation capacity, strength of coordinating mechanisms, and community involvement).

External Context

- Key actors, including the new president and the donor community, believed nutrition was central to development and prioritized action on improving nutrition.
- The project timelines imposed a sense of urgency for action. PNC was ending, and a new investment needed to take its place. A decision had to be made to continue, renegotiate, or terminate PNC.
- A corruption scandal in PNC weakened any potential initiative to preserve the PNC structure.

- The program framework (as opposed to a more limited project approach) favored intersectoral collaboration, elevated visibility, and supported the idea of a long-term commitment.
- Various other factors in the economic, political, and legal environments favored start-up of NEP:
  - A favorable political context developed, stemming from political change-over, interest of the First Lady in nutrition, and commitment to the MDGs, and the appearance of a new TTL for the World Bank.
  - Donors, especially the World Bank, pressured the government to adopt a multisectoral, long-term policy in nutrition.
  - Project preparation funds were available for activities to build vision and commitment among partners during the design phase.
  - Legal frameworks, such as the government's new nutrition policy and the decree to form CLM, supported efforts to install NEP. The financial commitment with the World Bank reinforced these frameworks through legal obligations.
  - A coalition for reform came together as donors and government officials advocated for a preventive multisectoral approach to nutrition.

Institutional Links

- Design activities were broadly inclusive, involving ministries, NGOs, and donors, and even government officials not usually associated with nutrition —thus providing a basis for dialogue and stakeholder ownership of the program.
- Placing NEP under the highest authority provided a sign to other actors of the priority to be given to nutrition and its multisectoral nature. This placement provided a known, common space for coordination and operation.
- The coordinating mechanism had operational capacity and not merely coordinating responsibility.
- NEP could provide funding and capacity building as incentives to partners.
- Actions were taken to neutralize opposition from MICs and AGETIP to the new institutional mechanism.

Structuring Multisectoral Collaboration

The Government of Senegal intended to use the World Bank loan to pursue two main objectives. One objective was to anchor the program and policies in an institutional framework that sought not only high political visibility (through its association with the Prime Minister's Office) but also coordinated actions with relevant ministries in the area of nutrition. This objective resulted in the creation of CLM. The second objective was to establish a long-term, nationwide, community-based program to combat malnutrition in the country and achieve the MDGs. Basically, this objective resulted in the establishment of NEP.

The government seems to have accomplished both objectives. The program has transitioned successfully from a project to a program approach within an established policy framework. And the government's poverty reduction strategy explicitly mentions NEP as part of its investment in human development.

The overall objective of NEP was to assist Senegal in reaching the MDGs by supporting its nutrition policy, which was mandated to improve the nutritional status of specific target groups (children under five years of age and pregnant and lactating women). Two subobjectives of NEP were (1) to improve the population's nutritional status, particularly that of children under two years of age and living in poor or rural areas; and (2) to build the country's institutional and organizational capacities in the area of nutrition so as to improve policy implementation and evaluation.

NEP was conceived of as a long-term program and is the foundation of the nutrition policy of Senegal. It was designed to operate in three phases: Phase One (2002–05), Phase Two (2007–11), and Phase Three (2011–16). During Phase One (already concluded), the program was set up, and implementation concentrated on targeted areas of the country. NEP conducted pilot activities during this phase, experimenting with alternative modalities of interventions and learning which approaches were most effective. During Phase Two (currently under way), NEP is scaling up to cover all 11 regions of the country. It nevertheless maintains a focus on rural areas and regions with the highest prevalence of malnutrition. Phase Three was envisioned as a consolidation stage to allow time for institutionalizing what had been accomplished in Phases One and Two. However, as explained in more detail later in the chapter, despite the operational and financial success of NEP, the realization of this phase will depend largely on the willingness of the World Bank to continue to provide financial support.

NEP works across sectors and across levels of government, from the national government down to community leaders. Institutionally, NEP has its own personnel, but for operation it relies on multilevel and cross-sectoral collaboration with several ministries, NGOs, the private sector, local governments, and the communities themselves. NEP is not part of any line ministry but falls under the purview of CLM.

NEP has four activity components with various subcomponents (Figure 5.2):
1. Nutrition interventions, including growth monitoring and promotion (GMP), Integrated Management of Childhood Illness (IMCI), micronutrient supplementation, and community initiatives

Figure 5.2   Components and subcomponents of NEP

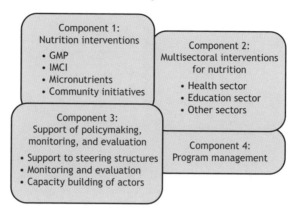

Source: Republic of Senegal, Nutrition Enhancement Program (n.d.).
Notes: GMP means growth monitoring and promotion; IMCI means Integrated Management of Childhood Illness; NEP means Programme de Renforcement Nutritionnel (Nutrition Enhancement Program).

2. Multisectoral interventions for nutrition, involving primarily the health and education sectors
3. Support of policymaking and monitoring and evaluation, including capacity building and support to steering committees involved in the program
4. Program management

Table 5.1 is more specific about the strategies that relate to these components and that NEP uses to reach its two major objectives. As Table 5.1 makes clear, although CLM exists to coordinate among national actors and strives to do so through coordination of strategic plans, much of the multisectoral nature of NEP occurs at the community level. This is in effect the ground level of implementation of a multisectoral program.

The organizational structure is slightly complicated, with intertwined and overlapping functions. Essentially CLM is the institutional mechanism that brings together the main actors in nutrition to coordinate nutrition policies and programs in a multisectoral way. It is supposed to plan, coordinate, and oversee nutrition policies in the country.

Specifically, the legal mandate of CLM is to assist the prime minister in defining national nutrition policies and strategies; ensure that the government's nutrition policy is implemented, including reviewing and approving project proposals and developing protocols with implementing agencies; facilitate cooperation among ministries, NGOs, and the private sector; approve the organizational structure of the National Executive Bureau (Bureau Exécutif

Table 5.1 Strategic orientation of the Nutrition Enhancement Program (Programme de Renforcement Nutritionnel, or NEP)

Objective	Strategy	
Improvement of the population's nutritional status	Growth monitoring and promotion (GMP of children zero to two years of age)	Promotion of key caring and feeding behaviors among mothers and child caretakers	Community-based distribution of products, such as bed nets and oral rehydration salts
	Vitamin A supplementation for children, iron and vitamin A supplementation for women	Food fortification	Promotion of foods rich in micronutrients
The country's capacity building in the area of nutrition	Support to sectors (health and education) through strategic plans	Development of multisectorality at the community level	Synergy building among programs

Source: Republic of Senegal Nutrition Enhancement Program (n.d.).

National, or BEN) and its annual plan and budget; provide technical advice on nutrition, design technical reference guides, and conduct studies and surveys as needed; manage national nutrition programs; and ensure the monitoring and coordination of funded projects in liaison with donors.[3]

The director of the Cabinet of the Prime Minister's Office chairs CLM. The members of CLM include key technical ministries involved in nutrition (such as Health and Education) and representatives of the mayors' association, rural communities' presidents association, and an umbrella association of NGOs associated with nutrition. CLM is thus similar in structure to the national nutrition coordinating committees in many other countries.

CLM oversees NEP, and from this perspective, NEP appears to be simply one more nutrition program in the panoply of nutrition interventions in Senegal. But NEP is not just one more program. Its size and operational and structural relations make it unique and have contributed to its success as a multisectoral organization. What are some of these structural characteristics?

First, NEP is a program under CLM, and therefore under the prime minister, rather than either simply a program of a separate ministry or a coordinating mechanism. It thus has a direct link to the prime minister, who has authority to coordinate among ministries and whose office is a logical locus of such efforts.

Second, CLM has BEN, which is composed of a subset of CLM members. BEN functions as a secretariat for CLM, providing administrative and technical support to the more inclusive policymaking body.

BEN's responsibilities are to assist CLM to (1) define the national nutrition policy, (2) design appropriate strategies for the implementation of national nutrition programs, and (3) manage nutrition programs. BEN develops an annual action plan and budget and submits it to CLM for approval. It also prepares a quarterly progress report for CLM and accompanies CLM during its visits to the field.

These activities and this structure are not so different from institutional arrangements in other countries. But BEN is not just a technical advisory council or administrative support for the supraministerial body. Rather, BEN has direct operational responsibilities for NEP.

The director of NEP, for example, is the chair of BEN. Thus BEN creates a very close connection between CLM and NEP. Importantly, BEN also functions

---

[3] It is clear that CLM and NEP gather multiple participants, but not all of them actually collaborate in the sense in which I use the term here. Even though the intention of CLM is to include many stakeholders in collaboration, some are actively involved (such as NGOs and the Ministry of Health), and others are less integrated into collaborative relationships (such as the Ministries of Education and of Industry).

as the Project Implementation Unit (PIU) of the loan from the World Bank. BEN is therefore also directly responsible for implementation of NEP. BEN is in fact essentially indistinguishable from the NEP implementation structure. This operational facet of BEN's responsibility, with its subsidiary but close connection to CLM, has been instrumental in its multisectoral work because BEN, in its role as implementer responsible to the prime minister and the World Bank, makes sure CLM fulfills its functions. Because it serves CLM and is also responsible for implementation of NEP, BEN can quickly access individuals and decisionmaking processes within the ministries when NEP needs support.

Those who designed NEP knew that multisectoral collaboration would not be easy. Consequently, they incorporated key lessons of development into the structure of the program, key lessons many donors have yet to learn. They understood partners would need time to develop capacities and learn how to work together. They knew developing capacities and effective institutional relationships would take time. They therefore thought of the development of collaboration among different technical ministries and other key actors in nutrition as a process. NEP was intentionally created as a program in three phases, with a 15-year horizon before it reached full strength.

This sort of approach, however, also must fit the standard operating procedures and philosophy of the donor agency. In fact, the World Bank has different loan products, and Bank staff chose a product known as an Adaptable Program Loan (APL). This product allows for a long-term commitment along with adaptations at the end of each phase (every five years). The intent was to allow for flexibility as needs changed and to learn and develop capacities as the program went along. And the 15-year time horizon demonstrated the commitment of the World Bank to the idea, which meant various political administrations could come and go, but the priority given to nutrition, as expressed by the loan, would remain.

But the World Bank team implementing the program later discovered that the loan did not function exactly as they thought. Instead of a continuous but adaptable loan, every five years the loan was actually renewed, not simply extended. New discussions about whether to extend the loan would take place at each juncture, with the possibility that the loan might not be extended beyond the current phase. In fact, that is what happened during the negotiation between Phase One and Phase Two. World Bank managers at the time did not want to continue financing a stand-alone nutrition project that looked small in the Bank's portfolio, despite the government's continued interest. The managers ultimately conceded to financing Phase Two, but with only a US$10 million investment, a considerable reduction from Phase One. In return, TTL and the government agreed that the Bank would not fund Phase

Three as a stand-alone project. As a result, efforts are being made to have the government take on more permanent ownership of the program (MMS29).

Figure 5.3A shows this organizational structure in some detail. The figure shows the two arms of NEP. Dialogue among national actors about coordination of their programs takes place as part of the ministerial arm. Theoretically the members of CLM, which essentially include all major players in nutrition in the country, can coordinate their actions, be it through the government, the private sector, or civil society. They reach the community through their own institutional arrangements, such as market structures (private sector), public–private partnerships, or decentralized services (such as local health clinics).

For implementation of the integrated program of NEP, the program works largely through the local government arm, and it is here that the multisectoral nature of NEP comes into full play. Here the integrated multisectoral package of components is implemented through BEN and more specifically the Regional Executive Bureaus (Bureau Exécutif Régional, or BER), local government structures, and NGOs. BERs are the regional-level implementation subunits of BEN. BERs work with local governments to determine implementation plans, which are then implemented by community implementation organizations (that is, NGOs).

Figure 5.3B gives more detail on the contractual and implementation arrangements for this local government arm. It shows the large responsibility assumed by the local governments and NGOs in implementing NEP and also how NEP coordinates and works through the ministries even for the local government arm. Working with BEN and BER, local governments contract local community-based organizations (which are also NGOs), who serve as implementing partners. CLM (BEN) pays the NGOs and also has financial understandings with the local government and the Ministry of Health, for example, on budget and how the program will be implemented. The Ministry of Health may work vertically and implement some of its decentralized services through providers at the district level. Using technical support and letters of understanding, these district-level providers coordinate with the local government and NGOs. The long-term goal is to have BEN turn over full responsibility for finances and administration (including selection, approval, supervision, and payment of the NGOs) to the local governments (MMS29).

Working Together: The Dynamics of Multisectoral Connections

Institutional Coordination and Operation

CLM is the central mechanism of institutional collaboration. It links and integrates nutrition actions both horizontally and vertically. An important charac-

Figure 5.3   Implementation structure of NEP

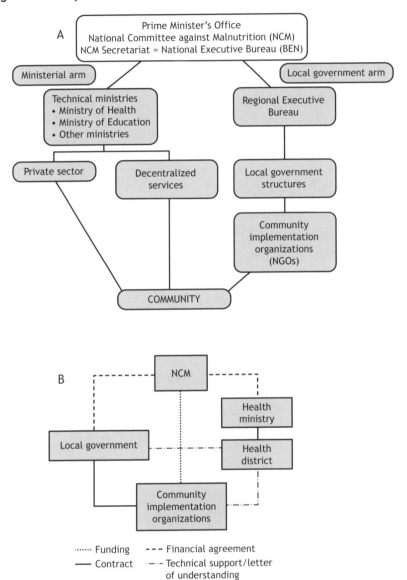

Source: Republic of Senegal, Nutrition Enhancement Program (n.d.).
Note: BEN means Bureau Exécutif National (National Executive Bureau); NEP means
          Programme de Renforcement Nutritionnel (Nutrition Enhancement Program); NGO means
          nongovernmental organization.

teristic of CLM—and one that many other multisectoral coordinating bodies do not have—is that CLM also manages the implementation of NEP. Thus CLM not only coordinates but also directly allocates and manages resources to develop and strengthen collaboration around nutrition. NEP and its structure gain further credibility because its national coverage and information monitoring system have allowed it to have a demonstrated impact on reducing malnutrition in the country. Thus it can show results on investment to government, civil society, and donors. Because CLM manages the implementation of NEP, it can bring together partners around concrete actions and can garner enough resources to develop activities that enhance the collaboration.

Through their participation in CLM at the national level, the ministries can become involved in the planning, design, and supervision of nutrition projects and programs. The perspective of Menno Mulder-Sibanda, the World Bank's TTL for NEP and Senior Nutrition Specialist for Africa, is crucial. He argues that even without specific instances of programmatic integration, cooperating in this way can lead to integration of nutrition considerations in their other work.

Multisectorality at the national level requires involving many stakeholders in the process. The aim is to involve all stakeholders, so that their perception of nutrition is positive and they take responsibility for their allotted tasks. Multisectorality at the national level requires involving all sectors, so that they recognize their role in nutrition and see it as part of overall development (MMS29).

Of course, such consciousness raising and mainstreaming are important but are not the same thing as integrated collaboration. As noted in Chapters 2 and 3, such cross-sectoral participation does not happen easily. Consequently, even though the conceptualization of NEP assumed different ministries would participate in order to influence nutrition policy in the country and that ministries would align their own policies with NEP, the program still had to actively pursue this participation. Fortunately, NEP had a budget specifically assigned to promote the participation of ministries and local governments and to strengthen their institutional capacities to carry out nutrition programs.

Collaboration of the ministries at the national level is still difficult. Although six years into NEP the local level understands the process, understanding at the ministerial level still lags. The local level has developed so much that as a general rule NGOs do not have to impose themselves on communities to lead or integrate efforts—the local government leads implementation (MMS29).

However, the line ministries have hesitated, perhaps because they are more capable and can function independently in their institutional routines. The Ministry of Health, for instance, still sees NEP to some extent as a competitor (MMS29). Yet even though the Ministry of Health "doesn't care," the

Ministry of Economy and Finance "gets it" and is "keen to see things work" (MMS29). From the perspective of institutional missions, this state of affairs is not surprising, as Ministry of Economy and Finance would favor a program that achieves social results at lower cost and has no stake in maintaining sectoral silos. But the Ministry of Health does.

In sum, the ministerial arm is working, though perhaps not optimally. At this stage, this ministerial harmonization "is important but least essential. The community is more important" (MMS29).

Still, with time the ministries seem to have developed more interest in collaboration through NEP, partly because it has shown results and so has become relevant to their own institutional missions. A recent example of a national-level coordination is the creation of the Committee for Food Fortifi- cation. The Committee includes public and private partners as well as donors and has been able to make good progress in a short time. NEP's structures have also allowed the Ministry of Education and the Ministry of Health to increase participation in implementation at the community level. Salt iodiza- tion under the Committee, for example, is working better than previous initiatives with UNICEF because through NEP, it can work directly at the local level to obtain cooperation from the salt cooperatives. And although the nutrition mandate of the Ministry of Education seems less obvious than that of the Ministry of Health, the Ministry of Education has arguably proceeded further. Starting with a pilot for health-nutrition education in schools, the Ministry has now scaled up and integrated the program into its own budget (MMS29). Simultaneously, NEP is aware of what is happening at the regional and community levels and so can work with the ministries at the national level to seek ways to complement their actions.

Effective Leadership

The institutional design and control of resources are undoubtedly crucial, but it is highly unlikely that CLM would have been as effective as it has been with- out strong, innovative leadership. A key factor in developing and strengthen- ing cooperation over time was the emergence of effective and clear leader- ship from Biram Ndiaye, director of NEP and head of BEN.

BEN has served as the engine of CLM, taking the lead in all of CLM's activities and in the relationships with key ministries, such as the Ministry of Finance. As secretariat of the CLM, BEN has been responsible for disbursing the budget, keeping CLM abreast of the accomplishments of the program, and reminding ministers of their budget commitments to nutrition.

Thanks to this leadership CLM has emerged as a clear reference point for nutrition policy for the government. Donors now turn first to CLM when they wish to fund a nutrition program. They look to CLM to make sure their activities coordinate with national policies and with NEP. Formerly they might have negotiated a one-to-one relationship with specific ministries, a common problem that conspires against having a consistent and effective nutrition policy in many countries. The judgment of the representative of the World Food Programme (WFP) is typical:

> CLM and its coordinator (Biram Ndiaye) are very active, serious, and it is a pleasure to work with them. Before the CLM, [WFP] had a program that was halted for five years because the government did not know what to do with it. Now the government sends them to the CLM to discuss their programs and coordinate their actions around the NEP. (JNG)

Leading Values: Technical Competence, Transparency, Team Building
One important element in creating this effective leadership was the transparent process used to hire the director of NEP. As a result, NEP not only acquired a qualified manager in Ndiaye but also one who was not seen as a political appointee. Ndiaye was technically solid, with a Ph.D. in nutrition from a prestigious university and international experience in nutrition programs. He had worked in Senegal on a previous nutrition project (PNC), so he knew the structures and the players. In addition, he emphasized developing managerial skills for himself and his team and spent time and resources in team building. Ndiaye believed in creating a sense of common purpose and a system of rewards based on performance. He took this job as a personal challenge. He wanted to show that "we can do a good and serious job in Senegal" (BN).

Ndiaye took responsibility not only for making sure that the NEP delivered results, but also for making CLM visible and functional. He oversaw all aspects of administration of CLM and NEP, organized the meetings, submitted progress reports, organized field trips to monitor the program, and made sure that all partners participated in it. Through his hands-on but respectful and transparent leadership style, he gained the respect of the different ministries with whom he worked.

Orientation and Organizational Flexibility
That leadership of interagency cooperation was not a formal part of government bureaucracy gave CLM greater discretion to act in a results-oriented manner and circumvent bureaucratic procedures and protocol. Personally, too, Ndiaye seems not to have harbored career political ambitions—and remained much more focused on achievement as measured by results rather than on political gain. This orientation reduced his need to respond to politi-

cal pressures. These are the types of managerial skills that have been identified as producing successful results in coordination in developed countries as well (Bardach 1998).

Such discretion is in part because CLM is accountable to the prime minister directly, so there is room for flexibility if the prime minister allows it. It also comes about because NEP is a World Bank-funded project with a separate management unit (the Project Implementation Unit). Thus specific targets are monitored not only by the government but also by the World Bank, and the NEP is responsible to both.

Operational flexibility is most apparent in the contractual arrangements used with local community-based organizations to implement the program. However, it is also reflected in the use of a performance-based system for evaluation of staff, a system outside the norm of government bureaucracy. Under this system, theoretically the director can fire an employee who is consistently underperforming.

Clearly Ndiaye was concerned about the capacity of his own staff, and he pushed them for results. At the same time, he believed in building their capacities to work as a team. This practice was not typical of the government, but it was an element of leadership that helped NEP staff deliver better results. One factor in NEP's favor is that CLM did not seem to suffer as much as other agencies from turnover among staff. Staff at BEN during Ndiaye's tenure, for example, did not change.

Working with the Community: Creating the Capacity for Flexibility

Genuine multisectoral collaboration under NEP has so far occurred largely at the community level, as NGOs, communities, and workers from the Ministries of Health and Education cooperate to implement NEP's components. It is worth noting, too, that different NGOs work in different geographic areas where the program was established, potentially allowing for variation in implementation.

Empowering the local level to implement the program (within the bounds of their capacities, the components, and the strategy of the program) has contributed to the organizational flexibility needed for success in working multisectorally. As has been observed elsewhere, collaboration among sectors tends to be more successful at the more decentralized levels (where workers on the ground interact on implementation) than at higher levels (where policy discussion and planning occurs).

These local workers appear to be closer to their clients and their needs and have a greater, perhaps personal, incentive to collaborate with one another to make their actions more effective. Because they are directly in charge of delivering the services, they can see problems more quickly.

Staff from the various cooperating agencies (local government, NGOs, and the clinics or educational institutions) often know one another. They can readily size up the local situation and suggest ways for partners to do their jobs better—independently or in collaboration—adapting solutions to local conditions and capacities. The results can be synergistic and extend beyond the performance of one organization. By improving the efficiency of health posts, for example, these posts may, in turn, extend the services provided by the community workers, increasing accomplishment and job satisfaction. Of course, this train of events assumes that higher authorities have given local workers the necessary flexibility and discretion to make judgments, and also assumes that local workers have sufficient capacity to do so.

For NEP, the presence of capable NGOs at the community level thus helped to enable this flexibility and build up local community capacities. NEP purposefully built this discretion and flexibility into the program. Those who designed NEP wanted to allow NGOs to develop their own ways of working with their communities, because community characteristics and capacities varied by region. However, NEP monitored the work to make sure actions led to good results and chose NGOs on a competitive basis, so the ones selected had a proven record of results at the community level.

The expectation is that local governments may take over many NEP functions in the future. Decentralization is progressing in Senegal, and it is planned for local governments to take more responsibilities in the implementation of public policies and programs, including nutrition. Before this handoff can happen, however, local capacities still need to be strengthened, and the role of CLM will have to be stronger than it is now.

Results Orientation, Monitoring, and Learning

A results orientation was also purposely built into the design of NEP. The design paid particular attention to the elaboration of monitoring and evaluation tools that the World Bank had found sound and comprehensive (World Bank 2007). Management used these tools to track results against expectations, helping them to improve performance and introduce modifications when needed. "Much emphasis was put on learning by doing which implied that the central level provided the bare minimum of instructions but maximum support, thereby allowing each implementing partner to develop its own strategies and solutions" (World Bank 2007, 9).

BEN's decentralized structure with six regional executive bureaus also helped. Closer to the action, BERs focused on strengthening the ability of implementing agencies and other stakeholders to contribute to outputs and outcomes. NEP's monitoring and learning system involved every partner and stakeholder in measuring and discussing results. Each partner was allowed to make their own contributions and take credit for results, thus enhancing ownership and incentives for participation (and, as part of a joint effort, providing a framework to pressure others to do a good job).

Monitoring takes place at three levels: (1) monthly monitoring of data collected at the community level, communicated to the regional and national levels and used for conducting regular supervision missions to project sites; (2) performance evaluation of each community subproject by before-and-after population-based representative surveys, which formed the basis of the performance evaluation of the implementing partners when preparing Phase Two; and (3) an independent impact evaluation.

Program feedback, for learning and sharing in success, was also important in keeping the partners interested in cooperation. As a result of the strong commitment of Ndiaye and NEP partners to having a successful program and their administrative and political savvy to make it work on the ground, NEP was able to reduce malnutrition significantly while costing less than PNC. In PNC, the cost per beneficiary for six months was US$40; it was US$67.70 if the child received food supplements. For Phase One NEP, the costs were much lower: a median cost per child of US$3.70 in rural areas and US$5.00 in urban areas. Routine monitoring data showed a clear decline in malnutrition rates from 18 percent in December 2004 to 10 percent in December 2005 in the geographic areas of intervention (World Bank 2007).

Success Leads to Success

The program is considered the best performing program in the World Bank portfolio in Senegal and an example of good implementation elsewhere. Through CLM, BEN shared this accomplishment with all participating ministries, making them feel integral to the effort. Partners were thus able to benefit from the good image of the program. This sharing in success also applied to the Government of Senegal in general and to the Office of the Prime Minister, to which CLM and NEP were directly attached. The good results of the program gave a sense of pride to the government, which committed publicly in international forums to the achievement of the MDGs and in particular to the reduction of malnutrition. It was also a good negotiating point with donors, as the government could show them impact and return on their investments. The ability to bring in more resources, in turn, reinforced the government's commitment to reducing malnutrition and to NEP in particular.

One specific example is how participation in the program helped the Ministry of Health improve its own performance, creating a strong incentive to remain in the partnership. Based on proven success, and using links with the Ministry of Health, NEP became a major mechanism to roll out programs in infant and young child feeding, IMCI, and mass and routine distribution of vitamin A supplements. Using the NEP structure, the public service delivery of vitamin A supplements and insecticide-treated bed nets greatly improved. NEP also improved the delivery of health services to poor areas.

The collaborative structure of NEP allowed for program integration that had not been possible before. According to the World Bank's (2007) end-of-project assessment for Phase One, NEP integrated GMP with community-level IMCI. NEP also integrated promotion of feeding practices, delivery of essential health services (such as immunization, vitamin A supplementation, and deworming), and the prevention and treatment of malaria. "This approach was a strategic way to work more closely with the health service delivery system and to promote measures that help prevent malnutrition" (World Bank 2007, 7). This integration further promotes collaboration with the Ministry of Health by demonstrating the value of NEP. In the estimation of at least one World Bank staff member (MMS29), such demonstrations of success have prompted interministerial coordination, rather than first having institutional coordination that then led to success. In this view, coordination and success are synergistic over time. Working together for a specific objective of mutual interest forges ways of working. Achieving success solidifies and incentivizes the collaboration.

Paying Attention to Partners: Incentivizing Collaboration

Partners involved in a collaboration need to remain satisfied with their involvement in it, and NEP provided financial and personal incentives for staying involved. Ndiaye remained personally attentive to the needs of partners, and NEP funded training, equipment, and technical support for participating ministries. These activities helped NEP achieve its objectives by strengthening ministerial capacities, so they could fulfill their roles and responsibilities. But funding also helped to maintain ministerial interest in the collaboration. As noted in Chapter 3, money may be an important lubricant for intersectoral collaboration. That seems to be the case in Senegal, where organizational and personal incentives can be weak and where actors, such as the ministries, are only now seeing how they can use NEP's structures to accomplish their goals.

NEP worked to strengthen capacities across the board, however, and not just with ministries. NEP has systematically strengthened implementing capacities for NGOs, for example. Participating NGOs, which played a key role in the implementation of NEP at the community level, benefited from extensive training and received technical assistance when monitoring detected problems. They also benefited from their involvement in a national program, which gave them more visibility.

Thus part of the maintenance management of the collaboration was allowing partners to share in the prestige that NEP acquired. Even though the creation of CLM was key for coordination, it was the successful management for results and an intelligent use of strategic communication to make those results known that brought more players on board. NEP could also personalize these results by encouraging partners to visit the field. Partners could then monitor and understand what was going on and could show success to donors and other possible supporters. The NGOs, in fact, have become a strong constituency for NEP.

Government Commitment

The overall political environment is also favorable to NEP. The Government of Senegal, through the Prime Minister's Office, has shown a high level of commitment to the country's nutrition policy and programs in different ways: (1) strong commitment to the MDGs related to nutrition, (2) incorporation of nutrition as a development priority in the national Poverty Reduction Strategy Credit (PRSC), (3) design and approval of the national nutrition policy with defined objectives to reduce malnutrition, (4) creation of CLM, and (5) financial resources through the budget, which should cover one-third of the expenses of NEP in Phase Two. The rest of the funding comes from the World Bank loan, which, of course, is government money as well. However, given the history of many of these programs and the difficulty of sustaining them once external funding ceases, incorporation of part of the funding into the government budget may be important to sustain expenditures over time. Traditionally, items that get incorporated in the budget are not easily taken out of it. That is what makes visibility of success and initial steps by ministries to take on nutrition in their own budgets so important.

Sustainability: Potential and Challenges

Several factors, some of which have contributed to the functioning of this collaboration, are also responsible for its sustainability so far. First, the Government of Senegal has a strong commitment to the MDGs, particularly the reduction of malnutrition. NEP's demonstrated success has contributed to strengthening this commitment. Success has made partners in the collaboration interested in seeing NEP continued. It has made the program credible to donors and the government, which improves the chances for continued support. The continued flow of financial resources for funding of CLM and NEP has undoubtedly contributed to sustaining collaboration, especially because financial resources are part of the incentives that help promote the collaboration.

Based on this success, the government publicizes this commitment, thus creating an environment that favors keeping nutrition on the policy agenda. It also creates support for continuation of the current institutional arrangements. A Senegalese delegation headed by the Minister of Planning and Sustainable Development, for example, proudly presented the NEP achievements at the "Countdown to 2015: Tracking Progress in Child Survival" Conference in London in December 2005. The international recognition that followed led Senegal to offer to host the next countdown conference in Dakar. At the same time, the prime ministers of Madagascar and Senegal published a letter to the editor in *The Lancet,* one of the top international journals for health, describing their activities and asking their peers on the continent to follow in their footsteps. A national seminar on maternal-child health was organized in December 2006 with support from all parties involved.

As discussed, the interest of national-level partners (the ministries) also seems to be growing. The small-money funding of specific activities in the ministries was intended to support their involvement with NEP. But it also means that nutrition activities have been present in their work and minds for many years. They have examples of how to integrate activities to support nutrition in their own actions and in collaboration with others. The experience, success, and consistent presence of NEP are slowly accomplishing what the short experience of the nutrition cells in past years could not. And now the ministries are beginning to lobby for their own budgets to support their own nutrition activities (MMS29).

Second, because this collaboration depends on the availability of financial resources to sustain the activities—both the nutrition activities at the community level and the ones related to incentives, institutional strengthening, and collaboration—a long-term commitment of external funds is very important. The initial commitment of external funds over an extended period (in this case 15 years) has been key. The long-term commitment allowed partners to believe that they had time to develop a program, learn from mistakes, and institutionalize NEP in the government structure. The long time frame also gave participants a different reference point: instead of creating and defending a project, they could work across sectoral and organizational boundaries to create a program, one that government officials knew would extend beyond their elected or appointed mandates, but also one that, through the external partners, they could continue to participate in even after they left government.

This long-term approach is not often taken, but it seems essential to sustainability of investment. Low-income developing countries like Senegal have very limited budgets and limited capacities. It takes time for them to build capacities for decisionmaking, management, and implementation, even if the political commitment is there. The World Bank had promised a loan with a long-term horizon of 15 years, which was expected to be enough for the government to find resources to fully fund the program in the future. In Phase Two, although the World Bank's commitment is uncertain, the government has already committed to funding one-third of the program's total budget, and the NEP is seeking to raise other external funds.

Third, the continued support of the World Bank and other international organizations (such as UNICEF) for Senegal's efforts has helped keep the government's attention on nutrition. These organizations have provided an enabling environment for collaboration among agencies on nutrition. Together with domestic stakeholders, they have created an informal coalition for nutrition. Through informal coordination and advocacy, they have kept nutrition high on the development and investment agenda and have defended NEP when needed.

These interested parties have not only put nutrition on their action agendas, but they have also reached a common understanding that reducing malnutrition requires a multisectoral approach. This convergence creates a uniform discourse coming from the agencies, donors, and other stakeholders with the government and pushes them toward finding ways to implement the concept in practice. In some cases, agencies, such as WFP, cannot easily integrate into the nutrition paradigm, but neither do they oppose the approach. In fact, WFP has been willing to cooperate with CLM and provide food to communities during periods of shortage, but they have agreed not to otherwise intervene.

At the same time, CLM has several weaknesses that work against sustainability. One of the fragilities is the possible dependence on external funds to sustain nutrition programs. In this case, the commitment of the World Bank in financing NEP is important, as it is currently the only donor that can provide the amount of money required to sustain action at a national scale. The World Bank's commitment to nutrition cannot be taken for granted, as the number of nutritionists on the staff is quite small and there are different views in the Bank on the importance of nutrition vis-à-vis other issues.

A second weakness is that the Ministries of Health and Education are still not fully integrated in implementing NEP. Lack of involvement of other ministries (such as Agriculture and Water and Sanitation) in nutrition makes the continuation of multisectoral collaboration at the ministerial level for nutrition more vulnerable if World Bank funding ceases. The lack of ministerial ownership also makes an exit strategy for the World Bank more difficult.

Third, what appeared as a strong point for collaboration among agencies could have turned into a drawback if NEP had grown to depend too much on strong leadership, such as that of Ndiaye. In 2008, Ndiaye left the program and was succeeded by his deputy. But Ndiaye had prepared her to continue his management style. The training and mentoring effort worked, and the NEP and BEN are still strong.

Fourth, in Senegal, the turnover of public officials is high. The president exercises a great deal of discretion in appointments and other administrative decisions, which means public administration is unpredictable. Although NEP has experienced some stability because the party in power has not changed since its initiation, prime ministers still change often. Each one has had a different style and policy preference, and many of the bureaucrats with which NEP interacts have also been replaced. New decisionmakers are constantly arriving, each with different levels of technical ability and understanding of nutrition. Cooperative arrangements in such organizations as BEN and CLM tend to be the informal creation of a particular political moment. This political turbulence makes the management of a largely voluntary collaboration more challenging.

A savvy manager who can handle this changing environment is very important for the survival of these types of interagency collaborations. Ndiaye, for instance, noted that he had to invest substantial time in educating every new public official who arrived at CLM. The advocacy work had to be done again and again: explaining the importance of nutrition, showing the value and success of NEP, and gaining their understanding and commitment. It also helped that Ndiaye was more a technician than a politician. He was not afraid of losing his post. As a result, he could be bold and assertive and was more able to resist some of the pressures to politicize the program.

An example of this pressure, which also illustrates the importance of having a strong coalition of support, was an attempt to move CLM from the Prime Minister's Office to the Ministry of Solidarity. NEP and World Bank staff both judged this change to be detrimental to keeping nutrition as a high priority on the agenda, given that it would take NEP out of the Prime Minister's Office. This move would undermine the priority given to nutrition and weaken its multisectoral nature—and place it in a relatively weak ministry. Members of the donor coalition, NEP staff, World Bank officials, NGOs, and the media mobilized against the change, and so the government relented. NEP remains in the Prime Minister's Office.

A fifth fragility of the sustainability of the collaboration is maintaining the incorporation of nutritionists in the collaboration, as they are the professionals with the best understanding of the problem. Ideally, each ministry should have a nutritionist on staff as a way of establishing a better dialogue among different disciplines. Senegal has a university that trains nutritionists, but the number of graduates is not yet enough to cover the country's needs.

Summing Up: Working Together

Internal Context

- Strong leadership and interest continued after start-up, from internal management, the World Bank, and the donor community.

- The first director of NEP was a highly effective leader, with strong skills in negotiation, maintenance management, and building internal capacity. Further, he ensured continuity in leadership by mentoring and training his successor in these same skills. She was able to take over and keep NEP running strong.
- The director was effective at maintenance management and was always attentive to partner demands. He educated newcomers as needed and created incentives for continued participation, such as complementary funding, training, and public acknowledgment of their contributions to success.
- A focus on results and the use of a monitoring system to measure and learn from them helped manage and incentivize the collaboration. Learning by doing was a key principle as the program modified implementation over time. It is unclear whether this focus helped to reduce sectoral divisions.
- The program had sufficient financial resources to carry out activities and to encourage participation from partners.
- Local capacity was a known weakness, but reliance on qualified NGOs and emphasis on training allowed the program to work well at the local level.
- Flexibility was a hallmark of the program. The government gave NEP substantial administrative flexibility, outside normal rules, and NEP allowed significant flexibility in implementation, adapting to the local level and implicitly empowering operating partners (NGOs and local government).

External Context
- Shifts in the political landscape (especially changes in bureaucracy and decisionmakers) posed challenges to program stability, but the group of advocates provided pushback to threats. This experience may provide some indication of how to weave nutrition as a priority into the social fabric and preserve focus and institutions in the face of change.
- Lack of World Bank support for NEP as a stand-alone program has challenged its financial sustainability. But the success of the program may support continued prioritization in the government budget and make financing more attractive to other donors.
- Urgency was instilled by the program and project timelines. Nevertheless, obligations to the World Bank are important for maintaining focus on achieving planned outputs and outcomes.

Institutional Links
- As a program that could provide operating funds and that shared success with partners, NEP operationalized the links among CLM, BEN, and itself in a way that simply trying to coordinate or align efforts would not.

- Quarterly meetings kept nutrition on the minds of the core group in BEN and CLM.
- Ministries had initially little interest in the program, except as perhaps interested but supervisory parties. The success of NEP has now prompted them to establish more integrated cooperative links, as NEP now provides a structure for addressing malnutrition that is of interest to donors and provides a way to improve delivery of their own programs.
- There is still less integration among sectors at the national level—and perhaps more skepticism and resistance—than at the local level. Vertical implementation of a multisectoral package, with some local representation of national ministries, still seems easier than trying to coordinate across ministries. However, the success of the local government arm and of BEN now gives ministries ideas and opportunities for collaboration.
- Insisting on a long-term perspective and emphasizing the concept of process when instigating institutional development and collaboration represent good development practice.
- The linking mechanism is complicated and has overlapping structures and a division between a ministerial arm and a local government arm. But the stronger local arm has led to increased integration of national actors. The inclusion of national actors in program development, attentiveness from BEN, and mechanisms for coordination (CLM) that have actual supervisory responsibilities are among the factors that have prevented these high-level actors from establishing parallel structures.

The case of Senegal demonstrates how a nutrition program can work across sectors and levels even under difficult constraints, including limited capacities and a resource-scarce environment. The experience of NEP reflects many of the elements that the framework discussed in Chapter 3 suggested should be present for success—particularly the importance of creating a common vision, promoting joint ownership, paying attention to capacity, and having the mandate to operationalize the collaboration. Having a strong manager of the collaboration mechanism who incorporates these values also seems critical, as does pushing integration down to the local government level.

Of course, several challenges exist to the sustainability and effective operation of NEP. Despite these challenges, NEP continues, with reasonably bright perspectives that financing will be found for Phase Three and scaling up. But it is a shining certainty that Senegal has demonstrated a way to work effectively and multisectorally to make a real impact on malnutrition.

CHAPTER 6

MANA: Improving Food and Nutrition Security in Antioquia, Colombia

JAMES GARRETT

T he Food and Nutrition Improvement Plan of Antioquia (Plan de Mejoramiento Alimentario y Nutricional de Antioquia, or MANA) began in
2001 as an outgrowth of one Colombian politician's passion to reduce
child mortality from malnutrition. Probably very few people in Colombia's
mountainous department of Antioquia know what the letters of MANA stand
for. But thanks to successful, energetic promotional campaigns among politicians, communities, and other stakeholders and an effective synthesizing
of new and existing programs across multiple sectors, quite a few people
know MANA. This chapter explores the research questions and hypotheses
described in Chapter 4 in the context of this program.

The Department of Antioquia

Antioquia is one of the departments of Colombia (Figure 6.1). It is located
in the central northwestern part of the country but has a narrow strip that
reaches to the Caribbean. Most of its territory consists of high mountains and
steep valleys. The department covers 62,840 square kilometers and has an estimated population of about 5.7 million, according to a 2005 census. The department is probably better known for its capital, Medellín. Medellín is the second
largest city in Colombia, with about 2.2 million people in the municipality and
3.7 million in the metropolitan area. Although known for its mountains, Antioquia's geography represents a broad range of climate and landscapes, including
seashore, plains, lakes, rivers, swamps, forests, and jungles (Colombia 2005;
Gobernación de Antioquia 2006; Alcaldía de Medellín 2006).

The mountainous terrain has resulted in a degree of developmental isolation for Antioquia. It was affected less than other parts of the country by the
armed conflict that wracked Colombia during the nineteenth century, and
instead of the estates found in much of the rest of the country, smaller farms

Figure 6.1   Political and topographical maps of Antioquia, Colombia

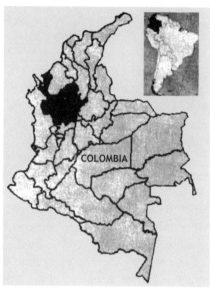

- 62,840 square kilometers
- Varied terrain, largely mountainous
- 5.7 million population
- 3.7 million in metropolitan Medellín

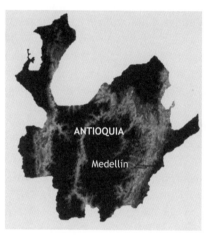

Sources: GADM (2010); Jarvis et al. (2008).

with relatively fewer financial and natural resources predominated. These circumstances gave rise to an entrepreneurial, industrial spirit, and in time significant intraregional trade and commerce developed (Wikipedia 2009).

Mining, agriculture, and manufacturing were the mainstays of the Antioquian economy during the nineteenth century and most of the twentieth (Wikipedia 2009). Agriculture, mining, and manufacturing are still important, but services now account for at least 60 percent of the economy. Information technology and medical services are well developed. Antioquia now provides 25 percent of Colombia's nontraditional exports and 15 percent of its gross domestic product (GDP) (Colombia 2004; Gobernación de Antioquia 2006).

Current political institutions arise, for the most part, from the 1991 Constitution. Although not a federal government, Colombia is decentralized in many respects. For instance, more than 40 percent of spending is allocated by subnational governments (Alesin 2005). Colombia's departments and municipalities have less autonomy than Brazilian states or Argentine provinces, but the constitution and the electoral process confer on them substantial political legitimacy. In addition, decades of guerrilla warfare have led to de facto, if not constitutional, autonomy in large sections of Colombia, including parts of Antioquia (Dillinger and Webb 2001).

Colombia weathered severe economic and political crises from the late 1970s to the mid-1990s. Severe economic recession; the rise of guerrilla groups, particularly the Revolutionary Armed Forces of Colombia (Fuerzas Armadas Revolucionarias de Colombia, or FARC); and the emergence of the cocaine trade in the 1980s turned the cities, suburbs, and countryside in Antioquia into battlefields for narcotraffickers, the military, police, and paramilitary and guerrilla groups (Hylton 2006; Wikipedia 2009). During the next two decades, Antioquia experienced intense violence, and an estimated 40,000 of Medellín's population between the ages of 14 and 25 died violently (Hylton 2002). The assassination of prominent narcotrafficker Pablo Escobar in 1993 marked the beginning of the decline of the Medellín Cartel and of violence in Antioquia (Kurtz-Phelan 2007; Colombia 2009).

The situation has improved, but the FARC and other armed groups still operate in the department, and social and economic development still lags (Colombia 2009; U.S. Department of State 2009). Compared to other departments in Colombia, Antioquia is poor. According to the 2005 census, Antioquia's overall poverty rate, as measured by Unsatisfied Basic Needs, is 22.6 percent, compared to only 9.2 percent in the Department of Bogotá. The poverty burden is even higher in rural areas, at 47.1 percent as opposed to 15.4 percent in urban areas (Colombia 2005).

Methods and Data for the Case Study

For two weeks in June 2006, I met in Antioquia with a variety of stakeholders. I interviewed more than 60 people affiliated with MANA. These individuals had worked with MANA at different points in its history (from conception to the present) and had played various roles in the program (including conceptualizing, managing, implementing, and observing it). I conducted focus-group interviews with the implementing partners of each of the six programmatic components of MANA. These discussions usually lasted between one and two hours.

These groups included universities, regional development associations, professional associations, and private-sector firms. I also conducted two focus-group interviews in the field with the counterpart municipal staff who were responsible for implementing the program at the municipal level, one in a rural area and another in an urban community. In addition, I held meetings with a regional implementing team. This group was composed of the different operational partners at the regional level, each of whom is responsible for implementing a different component. This coordinating group is responsible for working together among themselves as well as with the municipalities to make sure that MANA is implemented in a coordinated way. I also met with the consulting firm responsible for, on the demand side, strengthening the municipalities' abilities to fulfill their obligations to the program (particularly planning and management responsibilities) and with representatives from national programs with whom MANA coordinates on some activities.

MANA staff set up the focus groups but invited representatives of all implementing organizations affiliated with the component. MANA staff did not participate in the meetings. I separately held formal meetings with the program director and the senior managers of MANA and had informal conversations with staff responsible for overseeing specific components.

In addition, I conducted extensive key informant interviews with the principal actors, that is, those individuals who had started MANA, those who managed it, and those policymakers who played a role in its initiation and implementation. These individuals provided in-depth histories of the initiation and development of MANA. Key informants included the director of MANA; principal staff from the Ministry of Health who were responsible for initiating MANA; partner staff at the Ministry of Agriculture and Ministry of Education at the time MANA was being developed; the minister of planning and the governor's special adviser at the time of the creation of MANA; the current governor of Antioquia and relevant ministers (Health, Education, Agriculture, and Planning); and a legislator whose committee provided oversight of the program.

The interviews used open-ended questions, largely following the guide shown in Table 4.1, although these were adapted to the appropriate time period for each group or individual. I took extensive notes, distinguishing between summaries of the conversations and verbatim records. In almost all cases, the conversations were also tape recorded. Given the written record, the interviews were not transcribed, but the tapes could be referred to as needed during analysis.

I then consolidated the written responses to the interviews. This effort was fairly straightforward as I had followed the outline provided in Table 4.1 and had asked each focus group similar questions. With those who had been with MANA from the start, I pursued the entire chronology. No quantitative software was used. I consolidated and analyzed all interview notes, paying attention to the highlights and explanations proffered by informants but also relating responses to the components of the conceptual model and hypotheses.

PowerPoint presentations, government documents, communications materials, and other studies and documentation on MANA complemented these interviews. Although there was no specific search for noncorroborative evidence, I tried to interview all sides of the partnership from different perspectives over time. As part of MANA's learning process, implementing organizations and community partners had prepared presentations and documents on lessons learned that proved especially useful.

Getting Started

In 2000, Guillermo Gaviria of the Partido Liberal political party was elected governor of Antioquia. He was soon recognized as one of the outstanding governors in the country and began to rise on the national stage. In an area convulsed by drug lords and armed rebels, he preached nonviolence. Inspired by the example of Gandhi, Gaviria saw the root of violence in deprivation and focused his administration on achieving greater equity and social justice (Wikipedia 2008). As part of his political campaign, Gaviria set out on a series of walks throughout the countryside to better understand the conditions and concerns of those living there. Nutrition, and more specifically, child mortality from malnutrition emerged as one of the major concerns in these communities.

Although the mortality rate among children under five years of age due to malnutrition had actually declined dramatically in Antioquia during the 1980s, the rate began to rise again in the mid-1990s. The certified mortality rate had declined from 94.0 per 1,000 live births in 1980 to 17.5 in 1990, and then to 9.3 in 1994. The rate then began to rise rapidly, to 17.2 in 1999. In 2000 and 2001, the period of the gubernatorial campaign, the rates jumped again, to 32.9 in 2000 and 31.6 in 2001 (Figure 6.2). Although the reasons for this spike are unclear, violence from guerrilla and paramilitary groups continued during this period, and may be related to the increase. Table 6.1 shows the rates of chronic and acute malnutrition during this period.

Relative to many developing countries, the prevalence of malnutrition and the child mortality rates were actually fairly low, but the image of a child dying from malnutrition was a powerful one. It becomes more powerful when one can argue that such deaths are preventable. Gaviria took up child deaths from malnutrition as a signal indicator for success of social policy in his administration. Deaths from malnutrition represented a concrete indicator in which progress could be measured, yet one for which his administration could conceivably make gains. Gaviria's adoption of the issue raised the political visibility of malnutrition and gave his administration a strong political point around which to rally social action—specifically, action on hunger and malnutrition. Other results of this prioritization were a shared focus on results among ministries and a transformation of nutrition from being simply a project to being a social issue that required a programmatic response.

Figure 6.2   Mortality rates due to malnutrition for children under five years of age, Antioquia, 1980–2005

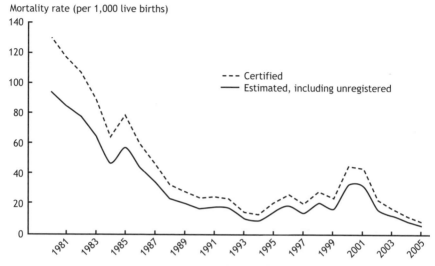

Source: Gobernación de Antioquia, Plan de Mejoramiento Alimentario y Nutricional de Antioquia (2006c).

Table 6.1   Rates of malnutrition in children under five years of age in Antioquia, 2002 (percent)

	Malnutrition	
Region	Chronic	Acute
Valle de Aburrá	39.7	18.0
Oriente	42.8	15.9
Suroeste	43.0	11.6
Occidente	42.2	16.5
Norte	49.0	21.2
Nordeste	47.9	20.1
Magdalena Medio	45.6	17.1
Urabá	51.4	16.1
Baio Cauca	55.0	21.4
Medellín	33.6	16.7
Overall	46.0	18.0

Source: Álvarez et al. (2004).
Notes: Malnutrition is defined as below –1 standard deviation from the U.S. National Center for Health Statistics (NCHS) mean z-score. Chronic malnutrition is defined in terms of height-for-age and acute malnutrition in terms of weight-for-height.

Once in office, Gaviria continued to press for action to reduce malnutrition in Antioquia. He turned to the minister of health to devise a plan of action. This Ministry was one of the stronger ones in the departmental government in terms of financial and human resources. Gaviria decried the fact that Antioquia did not collect indicators of malnutrition at the time and argued that "*el gobierno que no mide, no sirve* [the government that doesn't measure anything, isn't worth anything]" (DCHA).

Staff initially suggested building a program to reduce malnutrition around the eight lines of action in the national food and nutrition strategy, a strategy that existed on paper but had never been implemented. He rejected that option. Influenced by experience elsewhere, Gaviria suggested replicating the Peruvian Vaso de Leche (Glass of Milk) program in every municipality.

Although the implementation of a glass of milk program may have promoted community development and empowered community leadership, from the point of view of many technical experts, this sort of program has limited impact on the nutritional status of children in the age range of zero to two years of age, generally considered the most vulnerable period. Even if the program functions efficiently, it does not primarily target and so does not usually reach this group, nor will a "glass of milk" meet the most pressing nutritional needs of these small children. The most important factors for improving nutritional status of these children are exclusive breastfeeding up to six months of age and provision of appropriate weaning and complementary foods (meaning energy- and micronutrient-dense foods) beyond that age.

The senior technical staff in the Ministry of Health were consequently reluctant to implement the idea. "He thought nutrition was a problem of the stomach," they said. They urged the governor to support a more inclusive approach to nutrition. Gaviria was willing to listen to his advisers but continued to press for action: "*Tenemos que hacer algo* [We have to do something]," he said (MM17).

Initially, however, even the senior civil servants in the Ministry of Health who had been given the responsibility to "do something" were not sure what to do. Patricia Monsalve was the health services administrator. Angela Molina was an epidemiologist. Both were highly competent and experienced. They also knew how to maneuver within the government bureaucracy. Another member of the initial team, Alberto Gómez, had years of practical field experience.

In interviews, all acknowledged that at the beginning, being based in the Ministry of Health, they knew little about broader conceptualizations of nutrition or food security. National government agencies also provided little guidance. The national government had various plans and programs, but there was no overarching strategy, prioritization, integration, or, indeed, political commitment for food and nutrition security.

Monsalve and Molina turned ignorance to their advantage. Perhaps partly because of their own background in the sciences, they had a keen interest in learning and gathering evidence for understanding and devising practical solutions to problems. They did not appear to fear their initial lack of expertise in the area and instead responded energetically to the governor's mandate. "Initially we didn't know anything about the topic, and we thought it was a health problem. But we concluded it shouldn't be a health problem. [The questions became:] How do we fight hunger? How do we change minds?" (MM17).[1]

Instead of floundering and not doing anything, forging ahead with a health-centric program, or simply replicating what existed elsewhere, the two began a process of reflection and self-education. Their initiative was two-pronged. First, they began to find out what exactly was meant by "food and nutrition security" and to understand its determinants. Second, they began to engage others, particularly those in other ministries, to determine how others understood the issue and what the other ministries were doing.

Monsalve and Molina uncovered helpful resources (such as the website of the Food and Agriculture Organization of the United Nations [FAO]), which provided a conceptual framework for understanding food and nutrition security, and documents from other organizations and researchers. Within this framework, they identified existing policies and programs across the departmental government that were ostensibly aimed at reducing hunger and malnutrition. Importantly, they then worked with counterparts from other sectors, such as the Ministries of Education and Agriculture, to develop a definition of the problem they understood and shared. In these initial discussions, they focused on understanding and solving the problem, not on the activities of the sectors themselves.

They quickly found that despite concern with high levels of malnutrition and the existence of various indicators (such as low birth weight), they did not have any information on the levels or spatial distribution of malnutrition in Antioquia. The national Demographic and Health Survey (DHS) had only recently been undertaken. Monsalve and Molina did some initial analysis of food insecurity and malnutrition in Antioquia with available data that sparked intense high-level discussions. In 2000 and 2001, they were given a separate budget, with a timeline of one year, to define and develop a plan. This was the origin of MANA.

A director was appointed for MANA, bringing a more sectoral, agriculturally based perspective. Following the governor's lead and not those of her techni-

---

[1] The codes for the interviews are listed in the references.

cal advisers in the civil service, this director believed that the "glass of milk" program should be the flagship component of the plan. The glass of milk program fit traditional concepts of a food and nutrition program, and she was able to get funding for such a program from the departmental government very quickly. Her own political interest in supporting and carrying out the governor's wishes overrode more thoughtful technical advice on how to address the problem and actually achieve the goal set out by the governor. The work by Monsalve and Molina had helped to identify the problem, but the solution chosen was at odds with what their evidence suggested. Between January and July 2002, negotiations over milk production and distribution continued with the private sector.

A few events in the first half of 2002 then changed the course of MANA and gave technical advice more prominence in MANA's development. For various reasons, including the impetus she was giving to the "glass of milk" program, which seemed at odds with a more health-centric approach to malnutrition, the director was having continuing disagreements with the minister of health. And in April 2002, the FARC kidnapped Gaviria.

As part of his approach to governance, Gaviria had continued to undertake various walks, or marches, through the countryside for the sake of peace and social justice. On April 21, 2002, while he was leading a March for Nonviolence, he was kidnapped by the FARC, along with an ex-minister of defense and his peace adviser, Gilberto Echeverri. For more than a year, national and international governments and groups pressured the FARC to release the hostages. In May 2003, as army troops closed in on a rebel encampment as part of a rescue mission, the FARC murdered Gaviria, Echeverri, and eight soldiers, who were also fellow hostages (PBS Online News Hour 2003).

Eugenio Prieto replaced Gaviria as interim governor (April 2002 to December 2003). MANA's director was not so close to Prieto as she had been to Gaviria. At the same time, Prieto was prone to listen to technical arguments, and he wanted results. On both counts, the director was struggling.

During the rest of 2002, the program, such as it was, continued to try to develop an operational plan. Ultimately the director was replaced. A new director, Dora Cecilia Gutiérrez Hernández, arrived in June 2003. With so much attention on the "glass of milk," little progress had been made in defining, finalizing, or implementing other aspects of the program. In the meantime, the earlier director had managed to upset many of the partner ministries by essentially attempting to take over programs and responsibilities that they viewed as their own (MC27). Proceeding in this way had aroused institutional (some might say political) sensibilities over operational territory, making cooperation across agency lines even more difficult.

The new director's priority problem, then, was to win back the confidence of MANA's presumptive operational partners. Gutiérrez quickly emphasized principles of respect and transparency and of working in partnership with other agencies, not imposing outside ideas on their way of working. "In negotiations," she said, "your word is important. We respect their ways of working, and they respect ours. And where we might work together, we ask how" (GHFV).

This attitude partly reflected Gutiérrez's own background of working in the nongovernmental organization (NGO) sector. Limited resources there required fundraising skills and the ability to collaborate with others (not simply ordering them around or defending one's own agency's point of view) and with communities. She excelled at forming teams and appreciating the strengths of her staff and potential partners.

She also knew how to build an organization and believed that an essential element of being successful was, in short, being successful—actively demonstrating to your partners and clients that you were achieving results. Taken together, these ideas transform management mentality to one that prioritizes shared results and allies, as opposed to individual ownership of accomplishments and competition with other institutions. It also elevates the role of evidence and the monitoring of management and impact to establish a shared and neutral basis for discussion of the effectiveness of collaboration.

Such an approach may seem apolitical, but in fact it is not. Gutiérrez was keenly aware of the need for political support if a program was to be successful and sustained, although she marshaled that support on her own terms. "When we have intelligent politicians," she said half jokingly, "We have to take advantage of them" (GH01). At this moment, she seemed to suggest, the political leaders in Antioquia were willing to listen to the evidence and work together to achieve a common goal of reducing hunger and malnutrition in the department, and they seemed less interested in promoting their own personal or institutional agendas around the issue. She seemed willing to press that political advantage and get them on her side, or at least on the side of the program.

Although she clearly thought about the upper levels of politics, she also felt programs could lose support if they failed to reach down to the community. "The problem with Zero Hunger [in Brazil], for instance, is that it did not get down to the level of the community. MANA should be a community-level program, so that the community is aware of it, the community monitors it, and they know what they're due" (GH01).

So Gutiérrez's approach responded to the political imperatives felt by politicians across multiple levels: MANA would not hesitate to publicize the role of partner ministries, allowing them to share in success, and it would provide local leaders with additional resources and a visible program that reached deeply into their communities. In this way, Gutiérrez built the political support—the ownership—the program needed.

Through consultation and negotiation, through securing mutual agreement on goals and action, she fairly well neutralized the institutional fight response that the previous director had engendered. MANA and the Ministry of Health no longer threatened the other ministries; instead they were seen as partners that could produce political benefits for the others. Specifically, even as MANA incorporated actions of other ministries into its operations and granted them the recognition they wanted for themselves or their agencies, MANA's new approach largely allowed them to continue to operate their own programs. It thus left them control over action in their own spheres. This approach shifts the potential impact of politics, which usually means defending or promoting personal or institutional goals over societal ones, from a negative to a positive force.

When Gutiérrez arrived, the program was still on paper, but thanks to the continuing efforts of Monsalve and Molina, it was well designed and still engaged the interest of operational partners. Throughout this period, Monsalve and Molina had continued to bring stakeholders together, initially from the Ministries of Agriculture, Education, and Health. Significantly, these meetings were not one-offs but took place fairly frequently over a period of time. No large workshops or conferences were held, just meetings among colleagues in other ministries also working on food and nutrition issues. Colleagues in the various partner organizations thus had multiple opportunities to meet with one another privately and on a small scale to determine follow-up actions and obligations. Almost 45 formal and informal meetings were held during this initial period.

In these meetings, the institutions began to discover that they were working on the same issues, but their efforts were disjointed. There was no information system to discover what each one was doing. Such disorganization was partially a result of the lack of prioritization that had been given to food and nutrition. These meetings encouraged understanding and ownership. "If [you are] not present in the process of analysis, and of creating a vision, of understanding and of capacity, it doesn't belong to you. You aren't committed to do anything" (MM17).

In this sense, the creation of MANA was a true initiative: it was not just a statement made at a single conference or high-level meeting. Rather, the core members from the Ministries of Health, Agriculture, and Education, in particular, met multiple times to discuss issues both big and small. These meetings provided genuine opportunities for personal exchanges of ideas, perspectives, and ways to proceed.

Many times the conversations were not easy, as staff from different ministries had different ideas about what food and nutrition security meant. Through multiple individual meetings, the different organizations hammered out a shared vision, what each could do, and how they could work together. This initial group was composed of people who were already interested in and working on nutrition, with their passion perhaps making development of a sense of common purpose easier.

Two of the key individuals outside the Ministry of Health, Alírio García of the Ministry of Agriculture and Marta Celis of the Ministry of Education, recalled:

> We had difficulties in the institutional part, with the ideas of each profession. Agriculture thought agricultural development was more important than anything else. But in food security there is also health and education. We had mistaken ideas. We didn't yet have an idea of what "food security" was. We lacked a deeper conceptualization. We built the project together, based on . . . the mission of each [ministry]—agriculture, health, education. And so we dissolved the barriers, and problems became strengths, as we learned from one another. For this to work, you have to get people together so they live in the same house. (AGMC)

Notably, this initial process of consultation and conversation occurred at the level of other technicians, not upper-level policymakers, such as ministers or the governor. In part this reflects the structure and capabilities of the government in Colombia and in Antioquia in particular. The civil service is composed of experienced professionals who are well respected, knowledgeable, and competent. Although policymakers may change, depending on the administration in power, the civil service carries on regardless of party. This continuity gives civil servants an understanding of policies, programs, institutions, and decisionmaking structures (of their own agency as well as others). In many cases, civil servants know one another, even if they work in different ministries. These characteristics—stability, competence, and institutional knowledge—mean that ministers can confidently turn to these technicians for advice. It also means that senior civil servants in each ministry are accustomed to making arguments based on technical rather than political grounds.

Interestingly, outsiders might interpret disagreements among the actors as expressions of bureaucratic politics, as each organization struggled to defend its programs and put boundaries around institutional turf. Yet in the separate key informant interviews of the four main staff members involved in these initial discussions (from the Ministries of Health, Education, and Agriculture), all said that it was the different paradigms of understanding each brought to the table that provoked the heated debates. They each were aware of maintaining the prerogatives of their home ministries, but not one mentioned politics or defense of turf as a cause of the disputes. Bringing conceptual models and evidence to the discussion helped them to stay focused on the goal they shared and were working toward and the role each ministry could play. Thus MANA's evolution as a joint integrated program tended to minimize the potential for boundary wars.

This process incorporated many elements known to promote successful collaboration and organizational change. Monsalve and Molina based their arguments on solid evidence. By approaching other key actors with some humility and being open to the perspectives or needs of others, they were able to encourage a common vision of the problem and potential solutions. Through the process, participants deepened their own understanding of the issue and of how their organization and programs could help while maintaining the integrity of their institutions. The process also resulted in genuine institutional ownership of the issue and solutions.

> We formalized a process of consultation, of creating a space to continue the conversation, perhaps a committee, so as not to lose coordination of the project. Through working groups, we gained space and took action little by little, with knowledge and commitment. It was a slow process of change. Each person was protecting their own institution, but they all did work together. The process was to understand the issue through learning by doing. (MM17)

The conversation among ministries soon expanded to include actors outside government. Invitations to participate went to a broad range of actors who had an interest in the issue and not just those with an operational role. Monsalve and Molina included not only other departmental government agencies with which they might coordinate operationally but also other actors who could contribute to the program or who might have an interest in the issue. In the end, 17 governmental and nongovernmental entities formed part of a *mesa de trabajo,* or working group, including universities, NGOs, and the private-sector groups (such as regional development authorities or producer associations). Government organizations included the departmental Ministries of Health, Agriculture, and Education; national agencies, such as the Colombian Institute for Family Welfare (Instituto Colombiano de Bienestar Familiar, or ICBF); and the public university, the University of Antioquia. The group received some financial support from the Swiss government and the World Food Programme (WFP). Table 6.2 lists the partner organizations to July 2006.

These other actors provided technical and financial support, insight, and expertise. At later stages these organizations and individuals often became operational partners as well. The leadership style of Monsalve and Molina, later supported by Gutiérrez, was also important: in addition to including many sectors, they appear to have genuinely listened to the views of others and ultimately devised ways to incorporate responses to the institutional needs of those potential partners.

Table 6.2 MANA's partner organizations, 2001–July 2006

Organization name	Organization type
Instituto Colombiano de Bienestar Familiar (Colombian Institute for Family Welfare)	National government social welfare agency
Fundación Banco Arquidiocesano de Alimentos de Medellín (Food Bank of the Archdiocese of Medellín)	Nonprofit religious-affiliated nongovernmental organization
Ecopetrol	State-owned enterprise
Cornare (Corporación Autónoma Regional del Río Nare) (Río Nare Regional Corporation)	Regional development association
Corantioquia (Corporación Autónoma Regional de Antioquia) (Regional Corporation of Antioquia)	Regional development association
Comité Departamental de Cafeteros (Departmental Coffee Growers Committee)	Private-sector association
ReSA (Red de Seguridad Alimentaria) (Food Security Network)	National social protection program
Cormagdalena (Corporación Autónoma Regional del Río Grande de la Magdalena) (Regional Corporation of the Río Grande de la Magadalena)	Regional development association
CISP (Comité Internacional para el Desarrollo de los Pueblos) (International Committee for the Development of Peoples)	Italian nongovernmental organization
Ocensa (Fundación Oleoductos de Colombia) (Colombian Oil Producers Foundation)	Private-sector foundation
Central Mayorista (Wholesalers Union)	Private-sector association
Clínica Santa Ana (Santa Ana Clinic)	Private health service
FEDEPANELA (Federación Nacional de Productores de Panela) (National Federation of Brown Sugar Producers)	Private producer association
Noel	Private-sector firm
Nestlé	Private-sector firm
Fundacion Educativa El Café (El Café Educational Foundation)	Private-sector funded foundation
Universidad de Antioquia (University of Antioquia)	Public university
Universidad Pontificia Bolivariana (Pontifical Bolivarian University)	Private university

(continued)

Table 6.2 Continued

Organization name	Organization type
Universidad La Salle (La Salle University)	Private university
Tecnológico de Antioquia (Technological Institute of Antioquia)	Public technical institute
Universidad Catolica de Oriente (Catholic University of the East)	Private university
Corporación Educativa COREDI (COREDI Educational Corporation)	Private educational institute
Politécnico Jaime Isaza Cadavid (Jaime Isaza Cadavid Polytechnical Institute)	Private technical institute
Fundaunibán (Fundación Social de Uniban) (Uniban Social Foundation)	Private-sector foundation
Augura (Asociación de Bananeros de Colombia) (Banana Producers' Association of Colombia)	Private-sector association
IKALA	Private-sector consulting firm
Sofasa (Sociedad de Fabricación de Automotores) (Automotive Makers Society)	Private-sector corporation
Programa Mundial de Alimentos (World Food Programme [WFP])	International multilateral organization
Organización de Las Naciones Unidas para la Alimentación y la Agricultura (Food and Agriculture Organization of the United Nations [FAO])	International multilateral organization
OPS (Organización Panamericana de la Salud) (Panamerican Health Organization [PAHO])	International multilateral organization
INCAP (Instituto de Nutrición de Centro América y Panamá) (Institute of Nutrition for Central America and Panama)	International multilateral organization
Federación Nacional de Cafeteros (National Federation of Coffee Growers)	Private producer association
Colanta (Cooperativa Lechera de Antioquia) (Dairy Cooperative of Antioquia)	Private-sector cooperative
Land O'Lakes	Private-sector firm
ISAGEN	State-owned enterprise

Source: MM17.
Note: MANA means Plan de Mejoramiento Alimentario y Nutricional de Antioquia (Food and Nutrition Improvement Plan of Antioquia).

Interestingly, Monsalve and Molina, along with Mauricio Hernández, an adviser close to the governor, also initiated a more formal process, Situational Strategic Planning (Planificación Estratégica Situacional, or PES). PES was an approach to planning and management developed by Carlos Matus, a prominent Chilean economist and professor of management. Using PES, participants from various institutions learned how to analyze and address a given situation.

The PES approach stressed the importance of specifying initial conditions, available resources, and intended results and objectives. The course trained managers to analyze the strengths and weaknesses of different actors (and potential partners). It helped managers to determine what actions were necessary to overcome bottlenecks or take advantage of opportunities and what factors would determine the success or failure of those actions. Using PES, the participants analyzed the problem together, constructed problem trees, and determined how to respond. They also came to understand nutrition as a human right.

These efforts resulted in several products, some of which were important in guiding overall actions. By April 2001, the group had developed a brief analysis that named the problem (high levels of malnutrition in children 14 years of age and younger in the Department of Antioquia) and the program (Departmental Food and Nutrition Security Plan). The analysis noted various symptoms of the problem, including high levels of poverty, infant mortality, and chronic and global malnutrition; lack of detailed information on the problem and its causes; and lack of effective programs and of coordination and strategies among pertinent institutions. The analysis contained many of the initial ideas that would form the axes of action for MANA. Just creating a platform—for contemplation, planning, and action—energized the participants because, despite their interest, the government had never previously talked about nutrition (MM17).

The group decided to implement PES in each partner organization. The participants would identify bottlenecks on an action map and try to understand the cause of the bottleneck: things they could not do because they did not have money, it was beyond their authority (it required national- or municipal-level attention), or it was an issue far beyond their ability to tackle (unemployment, for example). Said Monsalve and Molina (MM17): "They built the map with their visions and their knowledge, so that they could see how their ideas were reflected. They believed in it, but everything was mixed together—[the contributions from] agricultural technicians with [those from] people from health, for instance." These analyses often helped identify bottlenecks to action in each organization. For example, the universities discovered that their current curricula did not really prepare their students to work in nutrition at the level of programs or the community.

Monsalve and Molina operated within a reasonably supportive political environment. Although Hernández was a continuous link to the governor, Monsalve and Molina also had access to the governor when they needed it. The governor was, they said, a "good ally." He had a personal interest in the program and helped to raise funds nationally and internationally (MM17). Thus they were able to obtain the governor's support at critical moments. That was important for gaining the support of other partners in the government, even if the other actors were not initially sure of the way forward or their particular role, because "when the leader understands, that knowledge radiates to everyone" (MM17). It was also important that MANA had, even from the beginning, enough funds to get planning and then operations started. This stability created further confidence among partners from the beginning.

These observations suggest that it is not critical to involve the highest level decisionmaker on a daily basis or even actually have him or her lead the initiative, but it is important that the top level take ownership and make clear that the issue is a priority for the administration. Making sure at least initial efforts have funding, even if permanent sources must be found later, can be an important demonstration of commitment. In addition, it does not hurt that others also know you have a direct line to the decisionmaker when needed!

Gaviria's management style also helped to establish networks and to get various agencies to work together. He listened to people and gathered broad support for action. Key informants suggested that despite the first director's insistence on a milk program, Gaviria himself focused on achieving results rather than implementing any particular program, and he was open to reason. He emphasized the importance of measurement and of holding staff accountable. MANA moved forward under Prieto, who continued this orientation.

At the same time, either through luck or astuteness, well-trained, well-placed, and committed civil servants were assigned to this task. In some sense, having an organizationally blank slate and not knowing much about nutrition or nutrition interventions helped. Monsalve and Molina worked to create a program that simply made sense conceptually and technically, without needing to defend specific programmatic or institutional prerogatives. Monsalve and Molina's use of proven consensus-building tools was also key, as was their openness to new ideas and the contributions of others.

This experience highlights the importance of personalities and leadership at all levels in making collaborations work. The importance of respect and collegiality that these individuals demonstrated—two human rather than technical elements—is often ignored in analyses of organizational collaboration. Said Monsalve and Molina, "A lot of times the plans think about the institutions and not the people" (MM17). By thinking about people and their personal and organizational perspectives, they were able to bring others together and achieve their own goals.

This sort of lateral leadership appears to be critical to multisectoral collaboration, where the leader has no direct authority over actions of other partners (Fisher and Sharp 2004). Monsalve and Molina did exhibit leadership, but it came gently (although emphatically) from the side, in ways that even Fisher and Sharp (2004) do not exactly capture (their focus still seems to be on the traditional leader of a collaborative project rather than on an initiative or program).

Summing Up: Getting Started

Table 6.3 provides a brief timeline of this start-up phase. A close reading and interpretation of MANA's experience with starting up the program highlights the following issues, corresponding to the main elements of the conceptual model.

Internal Context

- Leaders and managers appeared to share a similar style, with an approach of inclusion and co-ownership, a learning mentality, a focus on results and use of evidence, and respect for others and their institutions.
- Leadership emerged at various levels and at different times to accomplish different things, from high-level authorities and political appointees (governor and director) to civil servants (in the Ministry of Health and other partner ministries).
- Those responsible for designing the program set out processes to create similar understandings of the problem across sectors, a consensus on solutions (including how each agency could contribute), and a vision for how to get there.
- The designers were senior officials with strong technical capacities and the authority to lead the design process, including the ability to call meetings and make initial decisions about program objectives and design.
- The lead organization provided partners with incentives to collaborate— personal (own interest), organizational (mandated to make a collaboration work), and financial.

External Context

- The highest political authority in the department made reducing hunger and malnutrition a public priority.
- Public commitment created a sense of urgency and an incentive for officials across government sectors to act (rather than defending their own programs).
- Higher authorities held participants accountable for achieving results.
- A series of meetings and monitoring from the top maintained the sense of urgency; outcomes were defined for subsequent meetings and a timeline was set up.
- Participants assigned to develop the program had a budget to undertake initial planning and design activities.
- The influence of politics on the collaboration was diminished through inclusiveness, use of evidence, respect for institutional missions and procedures, and incorporation of those ways into the program, instead of competing with them or trying to eliminate them.

Table 6.3   Timeline for start up of MANA

2000
March
Governor calls on Ministry of Health staff to develop a plan.
June
PES is initiated at the departmental and partner levels.
November
Working group's problem analysis is consolidated.
After the elections, the Health Section drafted the initial analysis, "Bottlenecks, Operations, Demand for Operation and Action: The Macroproblem of Health." The primary problem was defined as deterioration in the health of the population of Antioquia, especially through inefficient and ineffective management of health promotion and prevention.
Reducing malnutrition is first stated as a public policy goal.
Analysis includes goals of reducing overall malnutrition, improving micronutrient fortification, promoting breastfeeding, and integrating care for children under five years of age (including deworming, micronutrient supplementation, good feeding practices, food fortification, complementary feeding, and nutritional rehabilitation).
Implementing partners are targeted. They include the following:
- Ministry of Agriculture, municipalities, and the Colombian Agricultural Institute for improving agricultural production
- ICBF and NGOs for complementary feeding and nutritional rehabilitation
- ICBF, food industries, and the National Institute of Food and Medicine Surveillance for increasing production of nutritious food products and improving micronutrient fortification
- Secretary of Education for providing rural schools with productive, environmentally sustainable projects
- Local organizations for empowering communities

2001
April
Lines of action are developed through further PES analysis, with production of a situation analysis for the department.
The working group designs strategies to address the problem. The Departmental Subcommittee on Food Security, a subcommittee of the Departmental Committee on Social Policy, is officially established.
Requirements for participation are developed, including municipal agreements that require the formation of coordinating committees.
Work to create support structures for the program is begun: this involves developing budgets, obtaining materials, creating beneficiary lists, and identifying community workers.

2002
January–July
Complementary feeding component includes milk, and negotiations continue with suppliers.
April–September
Contracts begin to be set up for financing and operations.
December
First press release is made announcing the Departmental Plan for Food Security and its six programmatic components.

Source: MM17.
Note: ICBF means Instituto Colombiano de Bienestar Familiar (Colombian Institute for Family Welfare); MANA means Plan de Mejoramiento Alimentario y Nutricional de Antioquia (Food and Nutrition Improvement Plan of Antioquia); NGO means nongovernmental organization; PES means Planificación Estratégica Situacional (Situational Strategic Planning).

- Elements of serendipity came into play: The initial director, who had a more traditional, sectorally focused management style, was replaced. The lead staff in the Ministry of Health were technically competent and interested in pursuing a multisectoral approach, and they were ready with a plan when the opportunity came.

Institutional Links
- Organic linking mechanisms emerged from common understanding, sharing, and discussion of evidence.
- The process of emergence took time—time to reach agreement on the problem, solutions, and vision among a core group; to reach out and gain support of others; and to deal with and respond to changes in management and the political environment.
- The program moved forward with other agencies when management became more transparent and inclusive, paying attention to partner needs and operational routines.
- Broadly inclusive partnering in initial stages, including in-depth discussions about vision and how each partner could contribute, strengthened the commitment by partners to the institutional links.
- Systematic processes were used to gather and guide the contributions of others, helping to maintain the focus of the program as it was developed.

Some other factors not readily identified in the framework established in Chapter 3 also appeared to have influenced the initiation of MANA. The strong focus on results, and not just on a routine implementation of some monitoring mechanism, stands out. The pressure from the governor's office, as part of a campaign pledge, was constant throughout, so that staff were continuously held accountable. Both Gaviria and Prieto appear to have held ministers accountable for action.

The beginnings of MANA appear to emphasize the importance of a people-oriented perspective, not just a focus on institutions. This description of start-up also suggests that Monsalve and Molina had a particular approach to getting started, and that Gutiérrez had a particular management style. These observations suggest that a strategy (a complete bundle of elements working together) was critical to success, rather than the specific presence or absence of key factors (as the description of hypotheses in Chapter 4 or summary comments on factors above might suggest). The approach seems to involve an inclusive process of building consensus about the problem and its solutions; of respecting the institutional mission and procedures of others and helping them see how their agency could contribute to achieving a common goal and vision; and using evidence and reason to support the discussion. These sorts of elements are largely present in lateral leadership, a style that seems particularly well suited to managing complex systems (such as multisectoral programs), where the leader has little direct line authority and so must rely on persuasion and incentives to create alliances for working collaboratively.

The implementation of a particular approach designed for analysis with multiple stakeholders (PES) was also uncommon. PES allowed partners to conduct a systematic problem analysis in a fairly institutionally neutral fashion to identify solutions and managerial or institutional obstacles. They contextualized the approach by incorporating personal contributions and available data. The replication of this type of analysis in other agencies led to a shared conception of the problem and appropriate action. Holding multiple small meetings with defined outcomes and follow-on steps, rather than large high-level workshops, kept momentum going. This process also allowed for a rather organic emergence of ways of working and of the programmatic structure of MANA. Technical and financial capacity seems more important at this stage than operational capacity.

The large role played by information has not been noted in previous analyses. Monsalve and Molina used the internet to find conceptual frameworks they could use. They brought in recent data on nutrition conditions to understand the problem and raise awareness. Their direct line to the governor may have created friction, because it allowed them to circumvent the director if necessary. And it also demonstrated the governor's interest in hearing a technician's point of view and getting a grasp on the extent of the problem and on goals he could use to monitor progress.

The significance of senior civil servants in pushing the program forward may be telling. When a new director proved receptive to creating partnerships with other ministries, the groundwork done by Monsalve and Molina quickly paid off. The problem analysis progressed, as did the writing of an initial strategy paper that identified policy objectives and institutional structure. Thus high-level authorities may need to establish the issue's priority and create initial political space, but mid-level technicians can then fill in this space with interventions and collaborative mechanisms to move the initiative forward.

Leadership, management styles, and certain approaches to collaboration thus emerge as highly influential elements here, more strongly than most of the literature on collaboration, especially in nutrition, seems to suggest. Specific personalities appear to play key roles at critical times. The lack of emphasis on these factors in the literature may be because most studies tend to focus more on the causes of failure, citing mostly institutional issues or bureaucratic infighting over turf. The MANA experience seems to suggest that inclusive leadership, expressed in a variety of ways at different times by different individuals, may be a key factor in success that until now has been largely overlooked.

The richness of these differences in leadership is notable and perhaps even critical. As the top decisionmakers, Gaviria and Prieto led by setting overall priorities and goals and by focusing others on achieving results. Gaviria's leadership was important to creating the political space for nutrition. Monsalve, Molina, García, and Celis led at the technical level. They carried great weight within and among ministries as senior civil servants. They commanded respect for their technical knowledge but, within usual political limits, they also possessed influence. They had the authority to call meetings and negotiate across agency lines. They were the ones who took up the challenge to fill the space Gaviria had created and that Prieto continued to want filled.

And Gutiérrez, in her position as director, a political position, made many of the final operational decisions and infused MANA with an inclusive style of collaboration. She also thought and operated as a politician. Her role in managing politics was crucial to keeping the program functioning as both a program and a cross-sectoral endeavor. Gutiérrez had to manage that critical political space between the governor, ministers, and civil servants. She had to manage politics, as they might affect the program more than the policymakers (who were focused more on high-level strategy and policies) and civil servants (whose role was understood to be technical and therefore apolitical).

There seems to be, then, a variety of leaderships across levels and over time. The appearance of a particular kind of leader at specific junctures in the development of a program—namely at initiation, creation, and operation —seems critical. The content and source of leadership may thus vary by the need of the program at a particular moment in time. For this reason, multisectoral work requires a series of leaders who are able to initiate, create (design), and operate (implement and manage) a program.

Working Together: The Dynamics of Multisectoral Connections

This section considers what happens after a program gets started. How do the partners actually work together on a daily basis? What makes for a successful collaboration? And what are the challenges? Unsurprisingly, in a complex system, it is the interaction of a variety of factors and not one single factor that seems to lead to operational success. MANA's experience suggests key elements of such an approach, which this section describes in more detail.

MANA ultimately was composed of six components, or axes of action (Figure 6.3):

- Community Alternatives for Complementary Feeding (Alternativas Comunitarias de Complementación Alimentaria). The target population was children under 14 years of age, with a special focus on pregnant women and

Figure 6.3   MANA's six axes of action

Complementary feeding
Health services
Rights of the child
Nutrition surveillance
Agricultural production
School curricula

Source: Adapted from Gobernación de Antioquia, Plan de Mejoramiento Alimentario y
           Nutricional de Antioquia (n.d.).
Note: MANA means Plan de Mejoramiento Alimentario y Nutricional de Antioquia (Food and
           Nutrition Improvement Plan of Antioquia).

children under six years of age.[2] In addition to providing food assistance
for children between six months and six years of age (in the form of a
fortified snack), this component implemented a school curriculum on good
dietary habits and a healthy lifestyle. It also provided dietary counseling
to those responsible for school cafeterias. The Ministry of Education was
largely responsible for this component.

- Introduction to Health Services (Inducción a los Servicios de Salud). The
  main purpose of this component was to promote access to health services
  for children under 14 years of age and their families. Activities at the
  community level included promotion of breastfeeding, establishment of
  nutritional rehabilitation centers, integrated attention and complementary feeding for pregnant women experiencing low weight gain, and development of local plans to prevent child mortality from malnutrition. The
  component trained staff at health facilities in food security, the treatment
  of malnutrition, and the Food and Nutrition Security Plan. It also helped
  train local leaders to assist with nutritional surveillance activities.

[2] The inclusion of children up to 14 years of age shows that MANA was not solely a nutrition program, which might choose then to focus on the most highly vulnerable age range of zero to two
years of age. It was also a food security program. One of the major avenues to improving food
security is education. This component's educational curriculum targeted school-aged children to
teach them about food and nutrition, especially healthy diets.

- Treating Children Well (Nutrición con Buen Trato). Many parents seemed to see malnutrition or poor growth of infants or young children as a given. Until these children reached a certain age and seemed likely to survive, they did not consider these children as worthy of much attention or care. Parents paid little attention to their sick or malnourished children. This component emphasized the rights of the child and aimed to promote cultural change. MANA developed a short course that could be used to educate parents and community leaders (who would then train others) on the rights and value of children. The component also worked to strengthen the Social Policy Councils at the municipality level and other community organizations.
- Nutrition and Food Security Surveillance System (Sistema de Vigilancia Alimentaria y Nutricional). The information system was intended to provide data for measuring the food and nutrition problem in Antioquia and for improving program management at department and municipal levels, including interaction with sentinel sites and community leaders. The data could also be used for research.
- Productive Agriculture Projects (Desarrollo de Proyectos Productivos Agropecuarios). Although operated largely through the Ministry of Agriculture, this component also coordinated with the Ministry of Education to provide training materials for schools and the agricultural extension service. The objective of this component was to improve food and nutrition security of the most vulnerable rural families by helping them to increase and diversify household agricultural production in environmentally sustainable ways. Extension agents provided guidance about diets; food preparation, preservation, and hygiene; farm management; agricultural production techniques; and community organization. Participating families received access to credit and an initial stock of pigs and seeds to help them transition to more sustainable and more productive techniques.
- Educational Projects (Proyectos Pedagógicos). Working through rural educational institutions and centers (including formal schools and community centers), this component designed new materials for use in classrooms and adult training. Community organization and participation were priorities. The component provided a platform for learning and improving incomes and lifestyles at the local level. The approach emphasized holistic learning and pedagogical processes. This emphasis permeated other components of MANA as well. Topics taught included business management, agricultural production, food practices, healthy lifestyles, and rights and obligations regarding health. Through community organizations, the component organized and funded related Productive School Projects. Staff also advised on other educational projects that could tie in to MANA's objectives, such as the Institutional Education Project and the Municipal Education Project.

Given the consultative process and the focus on results (and thus on making sure that all needed actions were integrated into the program), the programmatic content of MANA is not surprising. The six components (or axes) cover the main determinants of food and nutrition security at the household level. Their activities were designed to increase incomes and access to appropriate foods, improve feeding and caring behaviors, and increase access to health services. At the same time, the program addressed some of the larger, more complex contextual determinants of food and nutrition insecurity. The program focused on education; the capacity of individuals, communities, and staff; awareness of rights, especially of the child; and the creation of a management information system.

In the spirit of collaboration and integration (which one might also interpret as a political calculation to minimize interministerial conflict), instead of trying to re-create what existed elsewhere, staff built on and integrated existing programs from partner ministries. This was particularly true of the agricultural, pedagogical, and complementary feeding components. The approach was likely due to various factors, such as the development across a diverse group of partners of a holistic vision of food and nutrition security, which included the importance of education and agricultural production and the inclusion of strong proponents of agriculture and education in the core team who argued for their programs' inclusion. Another significant factor was the apparent understanding by the Ministry of Health staff that their own institutional advantage lay in health-related actions and that the design and management of other components was best left to others. Through consultation, staff from the various ministries thought about how each could contribute. Ultimately MANA emerged as a coordinating body or umbrella organization that integrated these different components and oversaw implementation at the municipal level.

MANA had three organizational levels: the overall coordinator, the headquarters coordinators of each program component, and the regional teams (composed of the contracted operational partners, who were responsible for delivering and implementing the program components in the municipalities). Each partner on the regional team was responsible for one of the six components, or axes. The operating partners affiliated with each component (those implementing the education axis, for example) also met from time to time. In addition, a separate team was responsible for working with each municipality to build community capacity to demand and implement the program.

A close study of MANA sheds light on the relative importance of the various internal and external factors suggested by the literature and also uncovers other factors. In MANA, as in Programme de Renforcement Nutritionnel (Nutrition Enhancement Program, or NEP) in Senegal (see Chapter 5), collaborative and visionary leadership along with structural flexibility and the appreciation of the efforts of partners was key. Also, as in Senegal, involvement of local communities seemed to be an important element of success. Previous analyses have tended to overlook these factors in explaining success in working multisectorally. This section describes other factors that emerged as being important to operational success.

Leadership from Below? Involving Civil Servants

The participation and leadership of technical civil servants contributed to MANA's initial political and organizational success. As explained in the previous section, preliminary discussions about program content occurred largely at the technical, rather than the political, level. Thus the principal issues of coordination and technical disagreements were largely resolved by the time those questions reached ministers. The cadre of civil servants also provided some stability. Even if ministers changed, competent technical counsel and institutional memory remained. Even more important, the governor himself had set the policy goal—to reduce malnutrition—so that even if there were changes of ministers, the new ministers still would have to respond to him and work to achieve the continuing, overarching policy objective. This accountability provided an incentive for ministers to achieve results. At the same time, MANA provided the administration and ministers with a signature program through which they could increase visibility in communities and claim success without much additional administrative effort.

This approach differs from an organizational structure in which a higher political authority, such as the prime minister, might guide the process or manage an institution or coordinating body. Instead, coordination largely took place at a technical level. No additional high-level coordination seemed necessary, because the ministers knew that they would be held accountable for results. So rather than having the prime minister lead the program, it can be sufficient to know that nutrition is on the prime minister's (or governor's) agenda and ministers will be held accountable for results.

Creating Vision and Building Commitment through Communications

Strategic communications raised awareness of the problem among a wide range of stakeholders and built widespread commitment. When MANA began, government, families, communities, and professionals did not consider food or nutrition security a priority. A national food security strategy existed but was dormant.

As Gaviria raised the profile of hunger and malnutrition and MANA began to come together, many people—mayors, for example, and even doctors—did not believe that malnutrition was a priority problem. One of MANA's first steps was thus to gather data on the prevalence of malnutrition and malnutrition-related deaths. The Ministry of Health used a more inclusive cutoff to determine prevalence of malnutrition than that most often used internationally (children whose Z-scores were more than 1 standard deviation below the mean National Center for Health Statistics [NCHS] standard rather than 2 standard deviations below). This change had the effect of including not only those who were traditionally considered malnourished but also those at risk. Including the vulnerable is certainly technically defensible from a public health point of view, and it also served to highlight the extent of the problem and encourage urgent action.

MANA communications publicized the program through a variety of media, and staff made presentations wherever they could. Staff discussed their program and presented statistics on malnutrition in Antioquia to politicians, bureaucrats, and civil society organizations in conventions, professional meetings, and regional assemblies. They also contacted the mass media, the private sector, and universities. As a result, after only a few years of operation, community residents, students, municipal leaders, government ministers, parliamentarians, and other partners (such as those from universities or development associations) knew about MANA, its underlying analysis, and action plan.

The communication strategy had a few key elements. First, MANA targeted those directly concerned with interventions to combat hunger and malnutrition as well as those who could indirectly influence the success of those interventions, such as regional development associations. The idea was to get political society at large to view nutrition as a development priority.

Second, the logo designs were lively, easily accessible, and memorable. The MANA logo itself was a stylized family standing superimposed on an outline of a map of Antioquia (Figure 6.4). Third, MANA put the logos on almost all program materials, including vehicles, food, and publications. MANA became well known throughout the department, especially at the community level. Fourth, MANA communications supported each component individually across ministries. For example, MANA produced pedagogical materials, including curriculum guides and workbooks, for the educational component. Staff prepared and shared documents among partners, thereby encouraging a team mentality. And fifth, the design guidelines allowed the seal of the Government of Antioquia and the Health Directorate to appear, but not that of any particular ministry. At the same time documents could include the logo of the relevant operational partner. This practice reduced intragovernmental conflict over credit for the program and increased buy-in from nongovernmental partners.

MANA also produced compact discs with PowerPoint presentations to describe the program, its progress, and its achievements. Staff could use these

Figure 6.4   MANA: Program development and general logo

Objectives:
• Ensure food and
  nutrition security
• Prevent deaths
  from malnutrition
Concept developed:
  2000 to 2001
Piloted:
  2004
Expanded:
  2006

Source: Gobernación de Antioquia, Plan de Mejoramiento Alimentario y Nutricional de
           Antioquia (n.d.).
Note: MANA means Plan de Mejoramiento Alimentario y Nutricional de Antioquia (Food and
           Nutrition Improvement Plan of Antioquia).

presentations to explain the program to potential partners, municipalities, and community residents or for reporting to ministers and parliamentarians.

This communications strategy greatly increased the visibility of MANA throughout the department. MANA became known not only for its logo but also for its actions and its presence in the community. The materials that MANA produced also became integrated into the program operations in other ministries.

Experience with Collaboration

MANA was new but was able to build on existing programs. Some partners already had a history of collaboration. Importantly, since 1996, the Ministry of Agriculture and the Ministry of Education had worked together on school agriculture projects. As a result, they had already worked through many of the operational challenges posed by cross-sectoral collaborations. Specifically, they knew about the importance of creating a shared vision and ownership among partners rather than focusing only on the technical aspects of a project:

> [In our initial program] we had a problem with school gardens. We gave inputs [to the schools], but they were wasted. They planted the gardens with corn or beans, but then they abandoned them. The people didn't take ownership. And the gardens died when the school let out because [they thought] it belonged to [the agricultural exten-

sion service] or the Ministry. And so the agriculture sector saw they needed to involve Education, because it wasn't Agriculture's problem but one of community education. Then we co-financed a project. Agriculture put in money, and Education put in money. And together we trained teachers and agricultural professionals. The agricultural technicians learned to be teachers. And the teachers learned about agriculture. (AGMC)

The first years of this joint program, however, depended almost entirely on the vision and goodwill of two staff members, Alírio García in Agriculture and Marta Celis in Education. For them, MANA now presented an opportunity to get funding for their program and so institutionalize it:

To accomplish our vision, we had to find the resources somewhere. And there was money in Health. Well, we said, let's make an agreement. And so that's where we began. [The Ministry of Health] invited us because they had a food security program. And they came to Agriculture, because Agriculture had something to do with production. And Agriculture included the agriculture-education project. We started up a unit to work together. (AGMC)

In perhaps an amusing extreme of participatory ownership, they named the new initiative the "healthy productive education project," basically using the title to cover the bases with all three ministerial "owners" of the program.

Organizational Placement of MANA

In the beginning it was uncertain where to house the coordinating unit for MANA, as it included programs and staff from the Ministries of Health, Education, and Agriculture. Ultimately, for reasons of available space and administrative support, MANA was placed in the Ministry of Health. Nevertheless, although the coordinator of MANA was technically under the minister of health, she actually reported directly to the governor. In fact, the director was the only official staff member of MANA. All other staff were on loan from participating institutions. Interestingly, this arrangement contributed both to independence and interdependence. Staff technically still responded to their home institutions, but for the system to work, they had to work together. Having the leadership staff work out of the same program office made this task easier.

Building Multisectoral Collaboration: Weaving the Pieces Together

Although the vision was developed under leadership from the Ministry of Health, the structure that emerged built on and integrated activities from other sectors. Continuous discussion kept all partners on the same page in terms of understanding and action. Participants came to recognize the intrinsic value of each existing program and saw how to integrate their work into MANA's axes of operation. As part of their analysis, partners identified other components that needed to be established or strengthened.

This experience adds an important nuance to the statement that the capacity to carry out obligations is essential to multisectoral collaboration. MANA shows that the type of capacities needed will vary. Participating agencies play different roles and so have distinct capacity requirements. The important thing is that the role be appropriate and the agency understand what it is to do and be capable of carrying out its responsibilities. Organizations do not have to have the same capacities or undertake all roles. But when an ability to fulfill an obligation is weak, the collaboration must find out how to strengthen the participant or work around the problem.

In the case of MANA, in the end no agency had to stop what it was already doing. In fact, participants saw how working with MANA could improve the efficiency of their own programs to more effectively reduce hunger and malnutrition. They would then carry that conviction back to their home institutions. In fact, this synergy was one of the selling points of MANA to ministers outside the home base of the Ministry of Health: working through the MANA structure allowed them to achieve their own program goals at lower cost by integrating their staff into MANA or by coordinating with MANA more closely at the local level. Agricultural extension agents, for example, operated the Productive Agriculture Projects to improve sustainable agriculture and household food security and nutrition under MANA's umbrella, which obtained complementary support from the School Nutrition component.

This focus on results helped shape and, in some sense, limit the conversations. Instead of arguing over the programs themselves, the focus on results kept attention on three main questions: (1) How do we reduce malnutrition in Antioquia? (2) How does my program contribute to that? (3) How can it be modified to improve its ability to help achieve that result? This focus on results then more easily led to conversations across sectors about how they should work together to achieve those results.

Of course, such programmatic articulation is not easy. As the history of multisectoral work in nutrition shows, what makes sense conceptually is difficult to put into practice operationally. This holds true not only at the ministerial level, where most analyses focus, but also at the local level.

Community residents and local partners noted this problem during a feedback exercise. They noted that, despite having mechanisms planned out on paper, in practice the different implementing partners still lacked sufficient articulation and coordination. Partners scheduled training sessions of different components at the same time, for instance. Municipalities did not always fulfill their obligations to the program. Staff would not be available to work with partners, or they would not provide suitable space (such as kitchens) for program operations.

Despite communications efforts, community acceptance of the program could still be weak. Said one participant: "We doubt whether food security is a relevant priority for the school. Boys and girls don't eat salad!" Another, speaking about the educational component, complained: "We get mixed up with the Productive Project. We don't have time to take care of chickens! You really have to get rid of the chickens!" (Gobernación de Antioquia, Plan de Mejoramiento Alimentario y Nutricional de Antioquia 2006b).

Sometimes the issue was operational, a constraint that is just as important to the success of a program as conceptual design or institutional linkages. In Antioquia, for instance, continuing violence in the countryside made program operation difficult. And many housewives, the main target of some of the program components, could hardly find time to travel the long distances for training.

Building up Carefully

By building on existing programs, MANA avoided the wholesale start-up and imposition of a new program, which might have provoked significant resistance from partner organizations. According to Monsalve and Molina (MM17), this approach had a significant political advantage: they could build on what already existed and take advantage of current capacities and legal frameworks. It also followed a principle of lateral leadership—of valuing the contributions of others and of being humble with regard to what we ourselves know.

At the outset, however, some programs were more developed than others. Complementary feeding and the agricultural production and educational projects were already under way, but the introduction to health services and the nutritional surveillance system were weak. And the component having to do with the rights of the child did not exist at all.

MANA leadership, however, made it clear that these last two components were important, and the promotional materials treated each component almost equally. Nevertheless, MANA did not try to get all elements in place and at the same level of operation before introducing the program into the municipalities. MANA was allowed to grow somewhat slowly and to implement components at different rhythms, in accord with resource availability. This approach was partly a result of constraints on human and financial resources, but it nevertheless seems a wise way to deal with the problem of uneven capacity and readiness. The approach allowed MANA to learn and adapt over time and so enhanced its probability of success. The team structure promoted learning, but the team could also decide how and when to implement certain components in specific communities, depending on local capacity and needs and the strengths, capacities, and opportunities of the operating partners.

Paying Attention to Partners: Incentives for Collaboration

An obvious observation, but not one always taken into account, is that effective multisectoral collaboration requires mechanisms to enable it. MANA was innovative in the design of its mechanisms and was careful to establish and maintain the institutional and personal links needed to make them work.

MANA's coordinator, Dora Cecilia Gutiérrez, cared deeply about creating allies. She recognized that personal relationships and incentives were important to creating sustainable links. She considered how to increase benefits to partners while decreasing their costs, a point noted in Chapter 3. She thus tried to create reasons for agencies and partners outside the Ministry of Health to work with MANA. In essence, Gutiérrez constantly asked three strategic questions: (1) What do I need to be done to achieve organizational goals? (2) Who can do it? (3) What can I offer them in exchange for their collaboration?

In interviews, Gutiérrez stressed that MANA "is everyone's program." She considered how partners could advance MANA's interests, and in fact turned down or ended some collaborations where they were not useful. From her perspective, the organizational success of MANA rested on getting ownership and alignment among the partners and having them cooperate in the implementation of the program. "The partners are my children," she said. "I have to take care of them" (GH01).

But how could MANA, located in the Ministry of Health, get other ministries to work in a collaborative structure? One answer was for MANA to manage and implement the programs of client ministries. MANA would function as a service provider. Gutiérrez sat with each minister, explaining to them how working through MANA could help the ministry and the minister achieve institutional objectives.

MANA would carry out a ministry's program, using the available funding, but merge it in a coordinated fashion with the other program components from other ministries. By letting MANA deliver their programs, ministries would profit from synergies both in terms of increased impact of their programs and, through integrative efficiencies, lower delivery costs. MANA would handle program management but still report results and financial accounts to the base ministry. The base ministry would thus continue to get credit and also fulfill its legal, institutional, and political obligations. This last point reduced the potential for conflict over institutional prerogatives and jealousies.

Monsalve and Molina described it this way: "Then the other programs keep going well, because they need MANA. And each institution gets its recognition, according to its institutional interests. A main fear was that we weren't going to give their institution the recognition it deserved. But the other organizations added their own goals, and that increased confidence and also helped to focus on results" (MM17).

In addition to working directly with other government programs, MANA contracted with universities, development associations, and consulting firms to implement program components. Certainly part of the reason organizations wanted to collaborate with MANA was funding. But MANA also allowed each implementing organization to adapt the activities under contract to be consistent with its own goals. Outside of some core principles and activities needed to meet program objectives, MANA and the operating partner adapted the contract to the objectives of the partner and to local needs and strengths. Such flexibility showed institutional respect and also encouraged risk taking and learning.

In one such example, MANA coordinated with the Food Security Network (Red de Seguridad Alimentaria, or ReSA). This national program aimed at providing technical assistance, including education, and some inputs to rural and urban families, so they could produce some of their own food. The target populations of MANA and ReSA overlapped. By working together the two programs could avoid competition, reduce costs, and expand their reach. While the ReSA budget financed some of MANA's activities, ReSA benefited from MANA's infrastructure in delivering assistance and inputs.

> [What we do at ReSA is] within the bounds of what we want. Not to create more lines of action, but to join forces from the social point of view, not duplicate work.
>
> MANA and ReSA give parameters for the work. But it is a process that we are building, taking advantage of the various institutions. No one is the absolute owner. And each operating partner is different. And that is the advantage. They have allowed for a lot of participation. So we are structured to allow for that, and we don't tell people "how" to do something and make them do it, because we don't know how. We know "what" to do, but we don't know "how." (PPFG)

MANA also worked with ICBF, the national program composed of 34 different social protection programs. ICBF had two programs similar to those of MANA in terms of content and target groups: complementary feeding and nutritional rehabilitation, the latter of which is one of the activities under MANA's Introduction to Health Services component. The staff of ICBF realized that they could join forces with MANA and save money, using the savings to expand or intensify their program for beneficiary children. As a result of working with MANA, ICBF was able to more than double its coverage. This occurred partly because the two programs could compare beneficiary lists and uncover duplicate beneficiaries and "ghost children" counted by the municipalities (which managed funds at the local level) (ICBF21).

In another example, MANA looked to the universities for in-depth technical knowledge of food and nutrition security. By working with MANA, the nutrition department at the University of Antioquia gave faculty and students important field experiences. Feedback from those experiences then led to revisions in the curriculum of the school. MANA's target beneficiaries of poor smallholders also overlapped with those of the coffee growers' association and the regional development corporation, yet the coffee growers' extension activities had greater reach and was more effective than the government service. By working together, the three organizations could reach more of the target population more effectively and at lower cost than by working separately.

Fiscal Space

MANA also benefited from disorder at the national level. The national government had designated a special tax to finance activities in health at the departmental level, but did not have a clear plan on how to spend it. MANA was able to make the case that investing some of these funds in MANA would be wise.

The composition of financing, though, shifted over time. In 2002, MANA had funds from Ecopetrol, the state-owned oil company; royalties from petroleum production; and funds from the treasury designated for public health, along with an in-kind contribution from the Ministry of Agriculture. In 2003, the primary funding sources were oil revenues and public health funds. By 2004, however, MANA was beginning to gain its own budget lines, in collaboration with the ministries—but it took years for MANA to gain this fiscal space.

Creating Capacity: Supply and Demand

Those who put MANA together realized that for long-term success, capacity and competence had to exist at all levels of the program. One of the operational partners, for instance, divided this conceptualization into three levels, with administrative, operational, and political components: "The agreement between MANA and the operator is the first level. The decisions on the application of the methodology in collaboration with the community—the operational part—that is the second level. And the third level, to work with the community to strengthen the political actors, that is not administrative or operational but political" (BTFG).

Sufficient capacity needed to exist on both the supply and the demand sides, that is, both among the organizations supplying the program (such as the operating partners) and those demanding it (such as the municipalities). Involving the communities was seen not just as important to implementation but had a political rationale as well, to provide some benefit to local leaders and gain support for the program.

As noted above, MANA's organizational structure had three levels: the overall coordinator, the headquarters' coordinators of each of the program components, and the regional implementing teams. These teams, composed of different partners responsible for implementation of different program components, worked together across a cluster of municipalities. The demand side mainly consisted of the municipal mayors and their staffs, who coordinated the components at the local level.

But MANA not only supplied the program to municipalities, it also aimed to support the demand side in order to strengthen the overall program. A separate team, also part of MANA, worked with each municipality to build local implementation capacity. They worked to strengthen community participation, design local food and nutrition plans, and assist mayors and local staffs to coordinate the components of MANA at the municipal level. This support was important because few municipalities had the knowledge or skills to put together such a plan. By accompanying municipalities in their dealings with MANA, they lessened the risk of failure. MANA and communities were genuine partners.

MANA's approach to linking supply and demand was one of incentives rather than imposition. MANA staff visited each municipality to tell them about the program and offer them a chance to participate in it. The program did not require them to participate, however, in contrast to the usual way a centralized program rolls out or scales up. If the municipality chose to participate, MANA then required each municipality to comply with municipal laws, identify local counterpart staff, and come up with a municipal food and nutrition security plan. This approach encouraged, indeed required, local ownership. But the decision was the municipality's, not MANA's. Although the financing for program components came from MANA, local leaders had to put forth at least a minimum effort to understand the program and integrate it into social policies and programs at the local level.

Each municipality had to have a functioning Social Policy Committee (Comité Municipal de Políticas Sociales, or COMPOS). COMPOS had to be widely representative of the community and to include civil leaders, unions, police, religious organizations, and the private sector. A coordinating committee of COMPOS consisted of various government ministries (Agriculture,

Health, Education, and Environment) and MANA. COMPOS also had a supervisory committee to oversee and assess the activities of MANA and the coordinating committee.

Some municipal leaders still turned down the opportunity to participate in the program. This refusal was likely because of insufficient understanding of the program at first and because participation required time and some local resources. Some municipal staff complained that MANA took up too much staff time. For instance, the municipality usually had only one individual to serve as the contact with all the institutions and MANA staff and to manage delivery of inputs. But soon those municipalities who had chosen not to participate saw MANA activities going on throughout the department, as did their residents. In a few years MANA had expanded to include all municipalities in Antioquia.

Community-Driven Multisectorality?
Involving and Supporting the Community

Staff and operating partners described MANA's strategy with remarkable consistency, suggesting significant, and successful, efforts at developing a common understanding of the program. The program implicitly encouraged institutional articulation at the community level through a continuous process of reflective activities (such as workshops and training courses) and fieldwork.

Cutting across components and regions, operational partners described a similar sequence of activities and a consistent emphasis on community transformation, including community-level empowerment, ownership, and action. The actual process to develop this common understanding across levels took years and included the following stages:

- Year 1. Raising awareness; forming groups for action, advocacy, and implementation; and training trainers (such as local leaders and teachers)
- Year 2. Strengthening the activities of year 1 through continuous action
- Year 3. Improving organization and learning and disseminating lessons

The previous section described how MANA teams worked to create a sense of ownership from the beginning and to build capacity and empower municipal leaders and organizations. Other activities further supported multisectoral action. The local school, in particular, seems to have emerged as the articulating platform for activities, and the influence of educational approaches is evident in MANA's emphasis on learning and capacity building.

Social/Community Mobilization:
Establishing Understanding, Urgency, and Community

To establish understanding, operational partners started by inviting everyone in the community to an informational meeting. This meeting served to introduce the community to the program and to answer any questions. Once the municipality and MANA had reached agreement, operational partners held additional meetings with individuals and community organizations to provide further detail on specific components.

MANA staff and operational partners emphasized the importance of community capacity and involvement as critical to successful implementation. The frustration of the operational partners in municipalities where communities did not fully understand the program and their roles in it or where they did not have the capacity to implement it was palpable:

> Sometimes the community doesn't understand. They say, "You are from Medellín, so we have to do something for you." And so they gather a bunch of people, but they aren't the right people. They don't understand why we're there. And in some communities the officials aren't from there. There's no continuity.
>
> MANA's operational structure is a lot bigger than the operational capacity of the municipality. It is a strength that becomes a problem. Everything is very complex [in MANA, but then it lands in] a structure that is as simple as the municipality's. We have learned it is a problem, but we haven't learned how to solve it.
>
> Although some municipalities are organized, others are not. They don't have very solid internal structures.
>
> The person at the level of the community has to have a lot of experience. They are the ones that make the work happen at the local level. At the rural level, the teacher has a lot of influence. [The teacher is] a key person. (BTFG)

MANA also worked in areas that had been ravaged by violence, especially in battles with the FARC. Part of the government's strategy was to invest in these areas and so address the issues of poverty and social inequity that had historically driven residents to support the FARC. But, according to the focus group members, the presence of so many NGOs and government programs meant that many communities were rather indifferent to MANA. They had no sense of urgency or interest in engaging a new program.

> In some of the municipalities where armed conflict has been the greatest, there are displacements, which have induced passivity, since many organizations now work there. (OrienteFG)

> And so they receive and receive, but they don't even know what they're receiving. So some sectors are not committed. They are saturated with what they have and aren't interested in the project. (BTFG)

Many times a whole lot of people arrive to help, but the municipality doesn't have the ability to coordinate them. We end up fighting for the same beneficiaries. (PedFG)

It has produced paternalism, dependency, because many institutions are working there, and now they wait for something to come to them. (OrienteFG)

Local Capacity Building

The overall objective of the numerous capacity-building activities was to strengthen the community's ability to understand, administer, participate in, and modify MANA as needed. This effort would integrate the program, and capacity, into the municipality's administrative and social fabric and, over time, reduce the possibility of dependency (PedFG). "You have to form the community, so it doesn't depend on us. You have to leave installed capacity," said García and Celis (AGMC). Monsalve and Molina (MM17) noted that such actions not only have to overcome initially low levels of capacity but often also established patterns of behavior. That is, the indifference noted above may be a factor, but communities may not believe in the program or know what to do once they are empowered, because they simply are not used to the government interacting in that way with communities.

Program components built capacity across the municipality, including beneficiaries (children and parents, including fathers); local trainers (teachers and community health workers); and local leaders (mayor and staff of the municipality). As part of the education and health components, staff trained community residents, who then multiplied their effect by training others. A community might have 20-25 such multipliers. Participants in one focus group emphasized the importance of taking this approach from the start:

In this way you maintain multisectorality, because from its beginnings, its structure, its focus is multisectoral. And so from there each municipality develops its own food and nutrition plan. And the consultants that help are interdisciplinary, so that helps to understand the multisectoral focus as well. (BTFG)

The integrated team approach helped resolve any problems with coordination or operation at the municipal level. When any one of the team noticed a problem with another component, they could alert the appropriate team member, or they could connect the municipality with the appropriate institution to resolve the problem (for example, making contracts or getting identification cards for everyone). The team structure itself then supported program operation and increased MANA's potential for personal and institutional transformation of beneficiaries, staff, and local leaders.

Focusing on Results and Accountability.
Of course, MANA also had a traditional incentive for getting agencies to work together: public reporting. And public reporting is tied closely with a theme that runs through the initial conception and subsequent management of MANA: a focus on results. Without a commitment to achieving results, exercises in public accountability are meaningless and usually fall by the wayside.

Mauricio Hernández, one of the governor's chief advisers and a prime mover behind MANA, considered these two elements, when combined with community involvement, as critical for sustained action on social issues. In his opinion, the key to success in social policy is to emphasize accountability, not planning. In some respects this outlook contrasts with commonly held perceptions that social policy failures are the result of lack of capacity and planning.

For Hernández, the key is to elevate the visibility of the problem among stakeholders so that citizens understand the problem and demand action. Government would develop plans collaboratively with partners, including the community, and attach clear indicators to those plans. Accountability structures would be set up so that public officials had to respond openly and periodically to citizens and other stakeholders about what they had or had not achieved. For Hernández, "[you] must measure [the indicators] and make sure society knows about them. If you do not, the problem will become invisible again" (MH).

Municipal leaders and the MANA program coordinator had to provide an accounting of activities and accomplishments to the local community and the legislature, respectively. The governor also valued the program and so continued to press his ministers for progress reports—and MANA had contracts with the operating partners through which it could ensure they met their obligations.

These mechanisms for accountability went beyond simple reporting and promoted continued learning and integration. During start up, the process was intense. At the beginning, public meetings at the municipal level, attended by 40–45 people, lasted for two days each month. Later meetings were held every two months.

These meetings helped to smooth interinstitutional operations and build a common vision, language, toolkit, and framework for analysis and action. The public meetings also brought in ideas about how to improve the program or cooperate with other projects in the municipality. These meetings helped to improve local functioning and achieve goals by (Gobernación de Antioquia, Plan de Mejoramiento Alimentario y Nutricional de Antioquia 2006a)

- requiring public measurement of progress against goals and requiring explanations from public authorities;

- helping to determine what to do by getting help from regional teams or other municipalities who have had similar experiences;
- working together in or across municipalities to solve the problem; and
- promoting the idea that the approach is one of collegiality, not competition.

Summing Up: Working Together

The implementation and operation of MANA reflects many factors identified in the framework presented in Chapter 3, but in practice they are inter-connected and form part of an overall strategy or approach to working together. Note that the actions associated with success have largely to do with management, not with technical aspects of design or interventions, and, as during start-up, together they represent an approach, not an emphasis on one or a few factors with a readily determined hierarchy.

Celis, who was with MANA at the beginning, described what she consid-ered to be the elements of a successful approach to working multisectorally, an approach that MANA's experience seems to reflect:

> You have to have an understanding of institutional inertias that lead you to keep working with [the other sectors] on what they're doing. And you weave them together. You think of incentives, but mostly in terms of their own institutional missions. You develop a shared vision, not a template for doing the same thing everywhere. You need a leader who engenders trust, and who gets results that are shared by everyone. So there is a mutual obligation to succeed. You need clearly defined roles and resources, so you can leverage what others have and no one has to put up everything. There must be a creation of synergies: to make collaborative inertia easy. You must build on the collaborative advantage and share risks, rewards, and responsibilities. Partnerships are not usually created instantly from whole cloth. These are questions of management and leadership. (MC27)

The approach MANA took to working together operationally shares much with the approach to getting started. MANA's director and senior staff con-tinued to appreciate the institutional perspectives of others and to think of ways to provide incentives for them to collaborate. They also drew them into partnership, sharing responsibilities and resources, as Celis notes.

A lateral leadership style continued to predominate. At the same time, the locus of leadership continued to move from politicians to program staff, and the focus on evidence shifted from understanding the problem (concep-tual models and nutrition indicators) to monitoring the program itself for results and lessons learned.

The key actions that seemed to help keep sectors working together during implementation included the following.

Internal Context
- MANA sustained leadership beyond the start-up phase, with managers taking major roles and filling in the political space created by politicians.
- MANA used an intensive strategy of communications and constant dialogue of education and exchange with partners to deepen and spread the vision of MANA beyond its initial partners.
- MANA built capacity for implementation where it was weak (primarily at the municipal level).
- MANA gave implementing partners incentives to participate that outweighed the costs of coordination, providing them funding to, in some sense, do what they were doing already. This approach likely ameliorated turf conflicts and reduced potential disruptions from changes in institutional procedures.
- MANA also gave ministry partners incentives to support the program. As a service provider, MANA integrated their programs into its structure, potentially gaining efficiencies and increasing impact, yet also making sure that participating ministries got recognition for their contributions.
- Previous experiences of multisectoral collaboration by MANA's partners smoothed cooperation.

External Context
- Food and nutrition security remained a development priority.
- Prodded by elections, the political environment supported a continuing sense of urgency, as did management's continued focus on achieving results.
- Funds continued to be available for implementation.
- Legal frameworks appeared to be appropriate to support cross-ministerial work and allow for subcontracting operating partners.
- Legislators also showed an interest in the program, providing oversight as well as funding.
- Accountability structures existed at various levels. Governor, ministers, and legislature had oversight of MANA. MANA had oversight of the execution of program components by operating partners and municipalities. At the same time, municipality agencies, residents, and officials had mechanisms to hold MANA staff and implementing partners accountable.

Institutional Links
- Organizational structures of partner organizations and MANA were sufficiently flexible to permit the provision of incentives for performance.

- Organizational structures were also flexible enough to accommodate the operational model (for example, allowing the subcontracting of implementing partners and incorporation of other ministries' programs under the MANA umbrella).
- Mechanisms were in place to coordinate action among implementing partners at the regional level, although effective articulation was not always achieved.

This list describes MANA's activities with regard to the groupings of factors listed in Chapter 3, but these actions are not easily interpretable as a guideline for action. What elements might be more or less important, for example? If these factors are placed in the context of the narrative, an approach to implementing a multisectoral approach in nutrition begins to emerge, the foundation of which has already been suggested in both this section and the one on start up. In brief, this approach suggests that during implementation, those who want to work multisectorally should consider the following:

- Allow space for technical arguments and give leadership roles to technical staff (civil servants).
- Implement a strong plan of strategic communications to convey understanding about the problem, information about the program, and convincing results.
- Build on existing programs in other institutions, thus reducing the possibility of interinstitutional rifts.
- Keep partners oriented toward working together by focusing on achieving results and clearly defining roles and responsibilities (each one's contribution to the whole).
- Provide incentives for partners, making sure benefits of participating in the program exceed costs of participation and coordination.
- Develop a shared vision but be flexible in execution, taking what others can do well or what they are already doing into account.
- Build up the program over time, allowing space for mistakes and learning how to work together.
- Engender trust by all parties in the leaders, through inclusiveness, respect, and transparency.

These elements might seem obvious, but MANA's own experience and that of others (such as multisectoral nutrition planning) suggest they are not easy to implement in practice. In some sense, success in working multisectorally will most likely occur when programs get the fundamentals right.

In separate interviews, the principals (Celis, García, Gutiérrez, Molina, and Monsalve) largely agreed on the principles that were necessary to make multisectoral collaboration work. Their comments are remarkable because they were given mostly through interviews conducted separately, and they do not pertain specifically to multisectoral programs but to good management practice in general. Developing a common understanding, respecting institutional prerogatives, and making sure benefits exceeded costs for partners seem especially important.

MANA's experience also produced other insights not generally captured by the literature and somewhat beyond our list of factors. These insights have more to do with mindsets and ways of thinking rather than straightforward prescriptive steps.

These observations, mentioned by the main players and by implementing staff and community leaders (who have a view of collaboration from the field or from the bottom up) included the following.

Empower and Create a Sense of Possibility

Operational partners went beyond standard conceptions of capacity building and thought much more about empowerment. "The goal is to empower. You have to modify the plans in light of needs. Some municipalities see a lot they want in the plan. In others they don't pay any attention to it. They haven't empowered their mayors to lead" (IKALA).

Accompany and Respect Partners, Promote Ownership

It is difficult to link the politicians with the social actors. The relationships are very transitory. They meet, but it is difficult to create permanent linkages. They have joint activities, agreements, for example, forums, talking about different themes, trying to find commonalities that are permanent. The actions and the external actors are important in making sure the financing and the projects are there. But when [the external actors in the municipalities] disappear, sometimes they don't stay strong. We try to avoid that. Rather, we try to strengthen what they already have—don't bring in outside things, just let the process be theirs. Obviously we have ideas, and experiences, but we don't impose them on the planning by the municipality. We recognize what the municipality has already done. We want the social actors and the institutions to take it on as theirs. We are trying to transform ourselves into a role as someone who just accompanies a process. We are the support. We can advise, accompany—but the process is theirs. If the process belongs to them, it doesn't matter who comes in later, the process is going to have a life of its own. (BTFG)

We made a map of all the actors (institutions, leaders) in the community, and we located where they can help or how they are important to the project. We try to get them to reach consensus, but we have to respect their area of authority, the competencies of each one. (BTFG)

They need counseling, permanent accompaniment. It's not easy, but it can be done. It's not something that gets done quickly either. It's a long process, but you can do it. (BTFG)

There is no continuity when a new administration comes. People don't share what they know. They don't multiply their learning when new actors come on the scene. They don't do a clear handover. (IKALA)

Be Flexible, Adapt, and Learn

Multisectoral collaborations are fragile. They inevitably depend on making the program work and having it make sense to partners, so they see the value in participation. That is why flexibility of the program to adapt to local conditions and respond to local dynamics is so important, as is opening the program up to empowerment at the local level, including learning from them about how to operate. Staff were committed and aware of the local context, making it easier to adapt to local conditions.

The interventions of MANA should always be planned with the municipalities. It is the only way to make sure MANA's actions are linked with the dynamics of the municipality, its development, its plans, its programs. MANA has to generate a system, and strategies, to plan together, to optimize what MANA has to offer the community. (BTFG)

We have been able to overcome institutional jealousies. In Bogotá, there is a WHO plan. They always say how hard it is, that they can't "multiply." But our objective isn't to have 32 plans of MANA, but rather to apply the idea in each department in accordance with the reality there. (MM17)

Monsalve and Molina argue that this approach does not mean giving up on technical quality. Rather, staff must understand the program well enough to understand how to adapt successfully. "To be successful here you have to have high-quality implementation and open yourself to the ideas of the community. To be able to say 'yes' or 'no,' you have to understand the context" (MM17).

Through supportive alignments of activities and objectives, these adaptations strengthened the partnerships and the program itself. MANA could focus on agreed-on results but also demonstrate flexibility and ability to adapt to partners' needs and strengths, as well as encourage its own staff to learn from trial and error and make changes in accordance with their own judgment (AGMC). The team structure encouraged a systematic exchange of information and learning from experiences, as did upper management. There were team meetings but also meetings for each component and reflective exercises, which included feedback from the community.

Flexibility was possible not only because of organizational values but also because of the organizational structure. First, MANA operated around a set of basic but strategically sound actions. Among these were the following:

- MANA had a clear conceptual framework and core set of activities and organizational principles (including transparency, information sharing, and capacity building) that helped maintain cohesion.
- MANA used open competitions to identify operating partners. Potential partners thus had to show their capacity to carry out the work. This action ensured capacity as well as alignment among partners with MANA's objectives.
- MANA provided incentives to institutions to compete and join by being willing to adapt the operating contract to the objectives, needs, and capacities of the partner.

Show Results and Do What You Say

In some cases, the government's own failure to fulfill previous promises made people skeptical, which complicated community involvement and support.

> In Uraba, there are a lot of interventions. When you get there, the people haven't seen any impact of those programs. They see broken promises, and they don't want to participate. (PedFG)

> The process has ups and downs. When there is a change in the admin-istration, the process falls apart. That may happen in 30 to 40 per-cent of the municipalities. We have to re-do everything. We have to strengthen the decrees and the committees. (BTFG)

Interestingly, this results orientation, along with MANA's own approach to partnerships, means that MANA's director does not worry too much about who is the owner or who gets the credit. Reducing competition and encouraging collaboration facilitate horizontal and vertical integration. Paradoxically, then, sharing the credit has actually increased the visibility and reputation of MANA, together with its partners. Credit-taking need not be a zero-sum game.

Recognize that Multisectoral Collaboration Is Easier at Local and Departmental Levels than at the National Level

At a local or departmental level, personal relations can smooth operation and resolve problems more quickly, and the organization itself is smaller and easier to manage than at the national level. Scarcity of resources and institutional structure encourages a multisectoral approach.

> In the role and construction of the departmental policy they have good multisectorality. [And] decentralization generates multisectorality. Because the municipality can't work alone. It has to look for resources, who can help it govern, and that brings empowerment of inter- and multisectorality as a consequence, to resolve social problems. (BTFG)

The case of MANA reflects these conditions. At the local level one person is in charge of all social programs, rather than there being different heads for each unit, program, or sector. So the municipal person must coordinate all of them. This lack of resources can lead to frustration on both sides. Demands on one person from constituents or outside agencies can become overwhelming as requirements for reporting and action mount. At the same time, local staff may gain insight about problems with coordination among the outside agents or the infeasibility of demands.

Although the small scale of action at the local level may facilitate communication and coordination, Monsalve and Molina argue that it is not the scale itself that improves program functioning. Rather, "you are coordinating at a level where it matters to the functioning of the program and you can do something about it. It is not an issue of scale per se" (MM17). Significantly, this observation implies that multisectoral programming is not necessarily constrained to the local level. This may give rise to a useful truism: multisectoral programming will not work if a multisectoral approach does not matter.

Sustainability: Potential and Challenges

As noted above, multisectoral collaborations are fragile and can bend with the political winds. Successful operation depends a great deal on personal interactions and trust rather than solely on technical design. MANA seems to have done much that is right and set the program up for success. The staff constructed an integrated multisectoral program that has high potential for impact on hunger and malnutrition. They established a flexible organizational structure that values and integrates partner activities while reducing costs and increasing benefits. Most partners have sufficient capacity for design and operation, and MANA has been working to increase capacities where needed. MANA has a public accountability mechanism, including reports in open session on the activities and achievements of MANA.

Over time, the program added allies from other ministries, local government, civil society and the private sector (including universities and private associations), and even from program participants and municipal residents. It has also garnered the support of various parliamentarians, who were formerly part of the governing coalition that began MANA and are now part of the political opposition. But even they maintain a personal interest in the success of MANA, because of their initial affiliation, their personal convictions, and the political and social benefits that MANA's success brought them. Through social marketing; the coordination and involvement of other sectors; and a policy of inclusivity, transparency, and public accounting, MANA has created widespread awareness and built political support across levels, sectors, parties, and government bodies.

These efforts undoubtedly give MANA some political protection, as does the institutional inertia of having now operated for a number of years and established the program in all municipalities. Yet political underpinnings are still fragile. The process of true institutional transformation is slow, and it is unclear how MANA will weather future political change. MANA staff and others spoke, for example, of the need to change the program from a "policy of the administration" to a "policy of the state." This phrase nicely captures the issues of permanent institutionality. If a program is to be sustainable, it must cease being a program affiliated with a specific administration and become a program of the state. Initiating programs in a collective way may contribute to sustainability, but much depends on management's vision and the style of those who follow. Administrative reforms and legal frameworks provide further support for continuity (MM17).

The data to strongly support the underlying rationale for MANA do not exist. At the time of this study, MANA did not have a rigorous impact assessment or specific audits that show how much cost savings it was generating. Of course, dedicating time and resources to documenting actions and results can seem to divert funds from otherwise effective operations. But wise generation and use of information on impact can be important in the long term. A solid management information system will help identify areas where management can improve and gain efficiency, bettering the cost effectiveness and impact of MANA. In this way, MANA can establish its reputation as an effective means to achieve food and nutrition security, widening political support and helping to make the case to a new governor, minister, or director. Continuous education of authorities on concepts, design, and benefits appears to be a rule in guaranteeing the success of multisectoral collaborations. Continuous training is necessary throughout the organization, and not only among the highest authorities. The staff who understand the structure of MANA will leave over time. What will be the understanding of those who take their place?

By the same token, the activities and links with multiple partners have to be well supervised. MANA's use of contracts with private- and public-sector partners was innovative and provides substantial advantages over hiring permanent program staff. Through contract arrangements, MANA can quickly adapt to emerging needs, and it can also end collaborations if the agency does not meet performance standards. But flexibility and collaboration with multiple partners comes at a cost: in the end MANA is partnering with many organizations, each with different terms of reference, contractual obligations, and institutional interests. Each relationship has to be supervised, and this requires significant amounts of time. Many of the administrative tasks are led by only a few people at headquarters. These staff, in particular, have to think about how to coordinate and integrate all the different partners, whose terms of reference and geographic reach varies. The interaction with so many partners means there is a potential for activities to become less coordinated and synergistic. An independent evaluation of the complex organizational structure could be helpful. To date, the various components of MANA seem to be working well. But management must take care that all these demands do not exceed MANA's administrative capacity.

A multisectoral program should also carefully consider what it should not do. For MANA, this delimiting has been difficult, because the boundaries in terms of incorporating food and nutrition activities have not been clearly or completely defined. Overall the comparative advantage of MANA appears to come from the perspective that it should pursue those actions that are helpful to improving food and nutrition security if they can be readily integrated into the rest of MANA's activities. This orientation would exclude programs, for example, that by their nature have a vertical structure. For instance, micronutrients are certainly important to nutrition security—but perhaps the distribution of vitamin A capsules is better made through vertical, direct channels, such as the health clinics.

Achievements

Because the main purpose of this study was to see how MANA operates in a multisectoral way and because no rigorous impact evaluation is available, the study has not detailed the program's impact. Nevertheless, a brief review of MANA's activities to the date of the study indicates that in general MANA is functioning well from an operational point of view.

In its first three years, the program expanded to all 125 municipalities. All have municipal food and nutrition plans. MANA has established 32 nutritional rehabilitation centers and has breastfeeding promotion activities in all municipalities. Although unable to attribute the decline to MANA's work, the infant mortality rate in Antioquia had dropped from 32 per 1,000 live births in 2001 to 8 in 2004.

At that time MANA was reaching 450,000 children in the two lowest income quintiles, about 90 percent of the target, with complementary feeding. Community campaigns about the rights of the child have reached all municipalities and 80,000 parents, and have trained 3,700 multipliers. More than 11,000 production units have been reached through the Productive Agriculture program, and 24,000 individuals have been trained in agricultural production techniques, agribusiness management, and community development. The Educational component has reached 1,400 rural schools, with a new food and nutrition curriculum, some 80 percent of the target, which included 8,500 parents and 6,500 teachers.

Of more importance, MANA has contributed to the foundations of overall social and economic progress in Antioquia. First, MANA created awareness about the importance of nutrition. The programmatic approach and components may change over time, but there is a broad social consensus on the importance of nutrition to economic and social development. But as a participant from the Universidad de Antioquia explained in one of the focus groups,

[w]e are just now recognizing the problem of nutrition as a problem. At first the problem of malnutrition didn't even exist. The governments, the families have to learn. You have to link all the sectors. Can you make these [actors] aware of the issue? I think so. Nutrition wasn't a problem, but now they understand it is. It's an achievement. (BTFG)

MANA has also contributed to changes in thinking about the role of the state and communities and how government programs should interact with municipalities and citizens. It helped to change the future. A participant in a focus group from ICBF said, "It has always been an 'assistentialist' state. It has always been Father State. Only since the constitution of 1990 could we talk of the state as a guarantor, not the one responsible for everything" (ICBF21). MANA goes beyond words to provide an opportunity for the municipalities to lead—it prompts partner programs to change their ways as well. ReSA, for example, has also come to believe that it is more important to leave capacity with families and in communities to do their own work and not just give out inputs. Universities and schools have changed their curricula.

In the end those who created the program are proud of what they have created—even to the extent that they say "now it is easy to work multisectorally" (DCHA). But they want to communicate that the road to "easy" is hard. It takes much effort over a long time and needs to start with people who have minds open to change (DCHA).

For the international nutrition community, perhaps the most important thing about MANA is that it shows that working multisectorally in nutrition is possible. Given the agreed-on importance of a multisectoral approach to reducing malnutrition efficiently and effectively, that, say García and Celis, is the achievement of MANA. "Seeing the reality of the children in Antioquia, [the decisionmakers] made it a flagship program, and they assigned resources to it, and they institutionalized it, and it is now a program of the government, not a political one. When there is complete support, things go very well" (AGMC).

CHAPTER 7

Conclusion: Approaches to Working Multisectorally in Nutrition

JAMES GARRETT AND MARCELA NATALICCHIO

This study aimed to shed light on whether it is possible to work multisectorally in nutrition and if so, how. Despite the importance of this question, we know of no comparative studies in the past 20 years that have looked at this question in depth. Much of the discussion at the international level has revolved around judgments made in an academic debate two decades ago or is based on shared personal experiences. Much in the operational environment has changed, even as the common wisdom has not. Those working at the country level have forged ahead with multisectoral ideas and methods.

The main operational challenge to working multisectorally is how to facilitate cooperation vertically and horizontally across multiple actors and levels. A multisectoral program is a complex system, so success requires achieving alignment and cooperation across ministries, sectors, and levels of government and among a multitude of actors inside and outside the public sector. The literature and debate that are familiar to international nutrition specialists have identified numerous obstacles to such cooperation. Our study resorted to other literature, especially that of political science and public management, for insights.

To develop a conceptual model and a set of hypotheses to guide the study, we reviewed the literature and identified a series of elements and principles that seem to affect the success or failure of multisectoral collaboration. Our conceptual model identifies potential influences that are part of the internal context of the partner organizations and that form the external environment that shapes response. The model also pays careful attention to incentives and the nature of linking mechanisms among institutional partners. The model and corresponding insights from the literature are general and seem to be applicable to other fields than nutrition.

In applying this framework to studies in the field, we have added an element of dynamics and looked at how these contextual factors play out at different times in the life of a collaboration. We have also considered how these factors might affect the sustainability of the collaboration. We examined our hypotheses about how these factors might affect collaboration using case studies of multisectoral nutrition programs in Senegal and Colombia.

Using these examples, we have moved beyond the discussion of barriers to collaboration to identify factors that might encourage success. Many other investigations, especially in nutrition, focus on broad internal forces that inhibit cooperation, such as the defense of institutional prerogatives. These studies rarely consider the potential range of collaborative models or the sorts of incentives that individuals or organizations might have for cooperating. An underlying assumption has been that if there is a need for cross-sectoral collaboration, some agency needs to take the lead and control the participating agencies.

The approaches to working successfully in malnutrition suggested by the case studies considered in Chapters 5 and 6 contrast significantly with these efforts by other investigators. They seem general enough to be applicable to cross-sectoral initiatives in sectors other than nutrition—and indeed many of the insights come from the literature outside nutrition. Perhaps the most important difference between our study and other investigations has been the explicit recognition that an effective coordinating agency cannot merely tell other agencies what to do. Influence over alignment and integration has to come from understanding the perspectives and concerns of the partners and devising incentives for them to cooperate. A formal unit may still need to exist to perform coordinating functions, but as suggested by examples of institutional structures for addressing poverty in Latin America, this unit does not dominate the interests, will, and resources of needed partners (Acuña and Repetto 2006) and force cooperation. We find the difference, then, not so much in the formality or informality of structures as in the nature of the authority that is (at least officially) vested in that structure. The real power for coordination and change comes not from a written mandate but from effective methods of working with others.

In practice, institutional mechanisms for working multisectorally in nutrition generally have meant that either a particular ministry leads the work and tries to coordinate all actions or the coordinating mechanism is located in a higher authority with theoretical control over the participating groups (such as a Prime Minister's Office). The first approach usually runs into difficulty because one ministry has no formal authority over another. The second approach can become problematic over time, because maintaining an interest in coordination on nutrition can depend on the duration of nutrition as a priority for the prime minister. This duration depends on several factors, including understanding of the importance of nutrition to economic development; recognition of the multisectoral nature of nutrition; generation of visible results; and relative priority in economic, political, and social contexts.

The traditional model of coordination can pose a threat to the independence of the partnering institutions. "Being coordinated" implies a change in operating methods and the locus of control, which may not be to the partner's benefit. Whether the leaders of the participating institutions are comfortable with such change—and whether their organizational structures support it—affects the success of the collaboration. Reducing the perception of such threats is one of the primary motivations of lateral leadership.

Leaders involved in the design and management of the programs in both Senegal and Colombia took some time-consuming but ultimately fruitful steps that accounted for the perspectives of the potential partner organizations. They worked to create an integrated program, almost a team. They created ways to reduce the threat perceived by the partner organizations, or at least to reduce the costs of participation and increase the benefits.

In each case they set up processes to let others help construct the vision and the strategy for action. The operational strategies then reflected this input, enhancing a sense of ownership and increasing the likelihood that the operation of the program was more likely to fit with the institutional prerogatives and interests of the partner organizations and those of the individuals who worked in them. Although the conditions and contexts differed, the underlying principles and structure of the approach used in Senegal and Colombia seem to apply to many situations outside nutrition where a multisectoral approach might be beneficial.

Comparison of our two study cases allows some initial exploration of the hypotheses on internal context, external context, and institutional links that we presented in Chapter 4. Table 7.1 summarizes the hypotheses and the evidence. The discussion in the next sections gives more detail. The case studies show that many of the factors we thought might be influential do indeed appear to be associated with an ability to successfully work multisectorally in nutrition.

Assessing Hypotheses on Internal Context

Hypothesis 1: Nutrition is a chosen issue. Champions are needed to put it on the policy agenda. Leaders must develop vision and structures to support action.

Nutrition needs leaders and champions to put it on the policy agenda. Leaders must develop vision and structures to support action. In Colombia, the governor took nutrition on as a priority for his administration. Senegal already had a nutrition program, and government officials do not appear to have been major drivers in formulating Programme de Renforcement Nutritionnel (Nutrition Enhancement Program, or NEP). But an outside catalyst (the World Bank) did choose to engage the issue. Bank staff pushed a revamping of the nutrition project when the previous loan ended.

In both cases, technical staff and organizational structures then filled this opening. The experiences suggest that high-level authorities may need to choose and champion nutrition as a priority. But during design and implementation, the technical staff may lead efforts to fill the space that was created. In our cases, the institutional structures of Plan de Mejoramiento Alimentario y Nutricional de Antioquia (Food and Nutrition Improvement Plan of Antioquia, or MANA) and NEP also filled that space, taking advantage of the window of opportunity.

Thus this hypothesis is supported by the two case studies. Nutrition continues to be a chosen issue, requiring a champion or catalyst to put it on the policy agenda. But leadership need not continue to reside only in high political authority. In a dynamic, multisectoral, multilevel process there is no one leader or champion. The locus of leadership can change over the life of the program. In start-up and implementation, there may be a principal overall leader, but each partner organization can also have its own champions and leaders. On reflection, this is not surprising, but often we think of leadership being embodied in only one person and sitting in one spot, usually at the highest level. The case studies suggest that leadership can exist contemporaneously at different levels and within different organizations. Given the fragility of structures and the need to secure largely voluntary participation, a lateral leadership style may be more productive than a top-down approach. Such leadership is especially persuasive when it promotes co-ownership through creating mutual understanding and mutually beneficial relationships.

We also suggest that the organizations that participate in successful multisectoral collaborations share some common elements.

Hypothesis 2: Advocates work to build a shared vision, through developing a shared language, understanding, and sense of purpose.

Staff in both countries invested a large amount of time in developing a shared understanding of nutrition among stakeholders. Because they focused on multisectoral collaboration, they used UNICEF's multisectoral framework to guide discussion (rather than, say, a more limited "disease model" approach). This choice of framework generated a common understanding and a common language.

Table 7.1 Summary of hypotheses and contexts

Context/Hypothesis	Senegal	Colombia	Conclusion
Internal context			
		Leader or champion	
1. Nutrition is a chosen issue. Champions are needed to put it on the policy agenda. Leaders must develop vision and structures to support action.	World Bank pushed for changes in nutrition program. Prime minister agreed with nutrition as a government priority. Coordination mechanism was placed in the Prime Minister's Office to emphasize the multisectoral nature of the program. The program had operational responsibilities, in addition to its responsibility for coordination.	Governor prioritized nutrition for his administration. Ministry of Health staff were responsible for responding to governor's mandate for action. Coordination mechanism was placed in the Ministry of Health, but with direct report to the governor. The program had operational responsibilities, in addition to its responsibility for coordination.	Nutrition was a chosen issue in both cases. Obtaining high-level authority was critical to creating policy space. Mid-level staff became leaders of follow-up action. They were the ones who involved and coordinated partners and developed structures to fill the opening for action. Organizationally, trade-offs may be made between placing a multisectoral program in a single-issue ministry that nonetheless has implementation experience and funding and placing it in an agency with a multisectoral mandate but no implementing capacity. The characteristic shared in both cases was not location of the program. Rather, both had direct ties to the highest authority and had implementing capacity.
		Vision	
2. Advocates work to build a shared vision, through developing a shared language, understanding, and sense of purpose.	The World Bank and Government of Senegal held meetings with a wide variety of stakeholders, including those outside usual nutrition community, to develop understanding and design the program.	Ministry of Health staff coordinated with high-level advisers and staff in other ministries to undertake a systematic process of analysis and vision creation.	In both cases, creating a vision and shared understanding was a critical underpinning of successful collaboration. This process took time. Heated debate was not uncommon.

Previous program experience and dialogue among the international community meant that potential partners understood the importance of working multisectorally; the main issue was how to do it institutionally. The PROFILES tool was used to create awareness, especially among non-nutritionists.	Data were used to develop a convincing case for action among a wide variety of stakeholders, as was reliance on international frameworks emphasizing multisectorality. Strategic communications were used to spread awareness of the program.	Unless they are part of a broader strategy, high-level consultations or one-off workshops will likely not have much effect. Initial efforts were intensive, but education and communication continued throughout the life of the program. Managers used specific tools and communication techniques to develop consensus and capacity.

Capacity

3. Partner organizations have relatively strong technical, financial, administrative, and managerial capacities, so they can carry out their defined responsibilities.	Ministries were fairly strong but community structures were weaker. Program had sufficient funding for operations. A variety of qualified nongovernmental partners implemented the program at the local level. A contracted agency worked to develop local management capacity. Slower roll-out helped to adapt the program to available capacities.	Strong capacity (in specific ministries) facilitated implementation. Management and leadership skills and sufficient funding to carry out activities were especially important. Not all participating organizations had to be equally proficient across all capacity types. Different players needed different capacities at different times and places. Program directors identified comparative advantages of participants and, as part of the program, built capacity where needed through specific support or an extended timeline.
	Ministries were fairly strong but community structures were weaker. Qualified NGOs assisted implementation at the local level. Finances were able to support operations and provide some incentives for collaboration. NEP was intended to last 15 years. It was intended to learn, change, and build capacities as it progressed. The director paid attention to building the capacities of his team.	

(continued)

Table 7.1   Continued

Context/Hypothesis	Senegal	Colombia	Conclusion
Internal context	*Organizational structures, values, cultures, and experiences*		
4. Organizations have values that promote collaboration, including respect for the organizational routines and missions of others, an openness to learning from them, and an orientation toward results. These values encourage participation, transparency, accountability, and institutional flexibility.	New structures were created (NEP, CLM, and BEN) that facilitated cooperation and alignment among a wide range of actors. Consultations with ministries reduced resistance and prevented establishment of parallel structures. Awareness of nutrition through a previous program meant that understanding the multisectoral nature of nutrition, rather than understanding the institutional arrangements, were the biggest sticking point. Use of NGOs provided structural flexibility. Manager had a reputation for effectiveness, transparency, technical knowledge, and professionalism.	Use of a variety of nongovernment operating partners provided operational flexibility. Managers based action on respect for others, including other organizations and community residents. Director accounted for spending to ministries. Previous experiences eased the integration of ministerial programs.	Organizational flexibility proved crucial in both cases. It allowed the programs to adapt to local needs and to the abilities of operating partners. Managers built bridges with partners based on a reputation for respect, truthfulness, transparency, participation, and competence. Partners, helped by the further advantages of understanding and vision, then collaborated closely and effectively with leadership. Previous exposure to ideas about the multisectoral nature of nutrition or work on nutrition in a multisectoral way helped advance discussion or, in the case of Colombia, meant that partners had already addressed some obstacles to working together.
5. Organizations provide incentives for action, including personal and financial incentives, and have established accountability structures.	The program had standard accountability mechanisms, such as routine monthly monitoring of output data and before/after project surveys, with reporting to donors. The initial design team had personal and institutional interests in promoting nutrition.	The program had several accountability mechanisms for each level and actor (departmental, municipal; governmental, nongovernmental). Ministries and other partners implemented programs with greater efficiency.	Accountability mechanisms were not essential to the creation or operation of multisectoral collaboration but may, over time, contribute to building support among decisionmakers and donors and may help sustainability.

6. Partner organizations perceive that the benefits of participation outweigh the costs.	The manager instituted a performance assessment system for his own staff. Standard financial support of program partners in implementation, but budget support of various activities of partner ministries. Success in implementation brought interest from donors. NEP provided incentives for change to actors (AGETIP, urban youth) who were left out of new plans. The manager nurtured partners and provided incentives for participation.	Operating partners received funding. They were able to share credit for MANA's successes. They also learned and made organizational changes as a result of the collaboration. The director consistently focused on identifying where organizations might work more effectively and on what benefits collaboration would bring to both.	Personal incentives (including being held responsible for certain tasks) tended to be important for initiating the collaboration. Financial support for activities was important for operation, but beyond that, finances did not seem to be a major incentive for multisectoral collaboration. Participation in a program that is successful and builds the capacities of partners can be an important incentive. A benefit-cost mindset can help managers and policymakers with decisions about design, implementation, and partnering structures.

External context

Nutrition as a development priority

7. Promoting nutrition as a development priority among a wide range of stakeholders creates openings for action and sustained attention to nutrition.	A nutrition program already existed, but combined interest from the prime minister and the World Bank created an opening for continuing investment. Involvement of other stakeholders may increase support for nutrition action in the long run.	Although not initially from an external source, the social marketing by MANA staff helped to create widespread awareness of the importance of nutrition, thus building support for MANA in the short term and potentially in the long run.	Claiming nutrition as a policy priority was key in both cases, although this did not happen by itself. Having evidence at hand helped to make the case—but leaders first took up the issue.

Sense of urgency

8. Advocates create a sense of urgency to promote action.	Nutrition was chosen as an area for continued investment. The prime minister was convinced of its importance, but motivation for action came from institutional or operational timelines, especially those imposed by the World Bank.	After the Ministry of Health was tasked with formulating a nutrition program, the sense of urgency came from timetables imposed by the need to respond to the governor or ministers, who were themselves driven by election timelines.	Creating a sense of urgency motivated actors. This motivation consequently provided them with a sense of progress and accomplishment. But no sense of crisis drove the action. Rather, the urgency came from operational timelines, including accountability mechanisms.

(continued)

Table 7.1 Continued

Context/Hypothesis	Senegal	Colombia	Conclusion
External context			
	Environmental context: Economic, social, cultural, political, and legal		
9. General economic, political, and social conditions do not bring attention to nutrition, although specific events may.	Senegal has high rates of malnutrition and a low Human Development Index score. Some space was made for human development under a new party, but aside from the previous program (which was partly a response to economic crisis), nutrition had not yet become an investment priority. Interest by the prime minister and First Lady, and continued efforts by the World Bank, ensured attention to nutrition. The World Bank changed staff as the previous nutrition project came to an end, opening the possibility for change. This was furthered by criticism of the previous program that allowed for the possibility of thorough reform.	Rural areas in Antioquia have long lagged behind urban areas or the general level of human development in Colombia, which is high. Despite the seriousness of the problem, until Governor Gaviria put food and nutrition on the policy agenda, few policymakers considered addressing hunger and malnutrition as a development priority.	In both cases, socioeconomic conditions had long been poor—but nutrition had not emerged as a priority for investment. Specific events (changes in administration or in donor staff) tend to drive the issue.
Institutional links			
	Shared understanding, roles and accountability, participation, and partner relations		
10. Multisectoral collaboration requires institutional change, say in budgeting structures or modalities of implementation.	New coordinating and implementing structures were created. World Bank oversight may have contributed to relatively effective functioning of CLM.	The umbrella organization MANA integrated existing programs, strengthened some, and established others.	Although difficult, integration, (rather than mere coordination) seems to best support genuine multisectoral collaboration.

11. Successful multisectoral collaboration involves establishing linking structures that • promote shared understanding; • are inclusive and participatory; • promote accountability to the public and stakeholders, including partners and program management;	Management of the program did focus on implementing these values. CLM allowed for continuous involvement of ministries. World Bank insistence on having a country nutrition strategy provided a framework; clear interest in the selection of NEP director favored technical competence. A decree established a strategy to provide an institutional framework.	Operational connections became much tighter; NGOs assisted with implementation at the local level. The overall coordinating structure had less effect on integrating ministerial programs.	Adopting a novel approach, ministries arranged to have MANA serve as a service provider, and MANA contracted with firms to implement operations. Support structures, including programmatically integrated teams and specific support to develop municipal capacity, were created. Managers and policymakers promoted these values throughout the organization, as also expressed in program operation and coordination. The governor's cabinet was a way to keep contact among ministers, and the legislature periodically called for progress reports. The Government of Antioquia did not have a food and nutrition strategy, but the process of program development essentially created one.	Reliance on coordinating structures at the ministerial level ran into the standard problems noted years ago with multisectoral planning.	These characteristics have much to do with leadership and management. They appear to be shared by the programs in Senegal and Colombia. Although the institutional arrangements are undoubtedly important, these values appear to be critical to success and essential for making any collaborative structure work. Legal frameworks or strategies can help guide work but do not appear to be essential. A common understanding among actors of what needs to happen matters more than having a formal framework or broad national strategy for nutrition. If formulation of the strategy helps with that, perhaps through a participatory process, it could be helpful.

(continued)

Table 7.1   Continued

Context/Hypothesis	Senegal	Colombia	Conclusion
Institutional links			
11 (cont.). Successful multisectoral collaboration involves establishing linking structures that • value the contributions of all partners; and • make the roles and responsibilities of all partners clear.	Vertical relations were as relevant as horizontal ones. Partners included a wide range of organization types, including public and private sector and civil society. Relations tended to be cooperative rather than coercive or competitive among horizontal partners. Relations were supervisory—with the potential for mutual gain—in vertical relations.	Vertical relations were as relevant as horizontal ones. Partners included a wide range of organization types, including public and private sector and civil society. Relations tended to be cooperative rather than coercive or competitive among horizontal partners. Relations were supervisory—with the potential for mutual gain—in vertical relations.	No arrangement or partnership type is best in all situations. MANA and NEP used a range of partnership structures. More importantly, a program should have flexibility to meet needs and capacities using different types of partnerships. The human elements associated with good management and leadership (including understanding which partnership types will work best) remain the foundation for success.

Notes: AGETIP means Agence d'Exécution des Travaux d'Intérêt Public Contre le Sous-Emploi (Executing Agency for Works of Public Interest against Unemployment); BEN means Bureau Exécutif National (National Executive Bureau); CLM means Cellule de Lutte contre la Malnutrition (Coordination Unit for the Reduction of Malnutrition); MANA means Plan de Mejoramiento Alimentario y Nutricional de Antioquia (Food and Nutrition Improvement Plan of Antioquia); NEP means Nutrition Enhancement Program (Programme de Renforcement Nutritionnel); NGO means nongovernmental organization.

Interestingly, actors in both Senegal and Colombia had similar approaches to developing this common purpose and vision. They both initiated their efforts with a small core group of individuals who were interested in nutrition and then reached out to include other stakeholders and interested parties over time. They were ready to expand only once the main actors had a shared understanding of the problem and solution and had worked through their principal disagreements.

Development of vision and understanding is crucial, but the process takes time. This stage appears to be essential. Actions at this stage are critical to overcoming cognitive barriers to cooperation. Lead institutions can employ systematic processes, such as Situational Strategic Planning (Planificación Estratégica Situacional, or PES), to help partner organizations think more deeply, or think in alternate ways, about the problem and determine how to shape their own institutional missions, cultures, and procedures to support multisectoral initiatives and work more synergistically with others.

Vision and commitment are symbiotic. Working to achieve a vision can create commitment, and having commitment can express itself in a vision. More practically, working together to create a strategy or plan brings partners together. If structured appropriately (as in Rapid Results Initiatives), it imposes a time limit and creates a sense of urgency (and thus focus). It also results in a product (so that people see concrete outcomes of their efforts) and helps uncover obstacles to collaboration and suggest ways to overcome them.

In the beginning, a mandate to create or establish a program drives action. In some sense partners had to collaborate, based on orders from others. There was no guarantee that beyond these initial efforts anything would happen. But the task of creating something together, of developing vision and a strategy to execute it jointly, seems to enhance understanding and dedication to the program. Partners may even become convinced that achieving results requires working together.

The case studies show that the creators and managers of the programs did work to build a sense of common purpose. Through continuous exchanges with partners, they developed a common vision and a shared understanding of the problem and proposed solutions. Such exchanges also help partners understand one another. Tools to guide this process exist. And information plays a crucial role in this situation: actors need conceptual models to structure thinking. To avoid unfounded rigidity in positions (perhaps resulting from limited personal experience or misguided institutional perceptions), they need evidence about the nature of the problem and potential solutions (especially about what others have done). Actors also need to have an open mind and be able to consider evidence and new ways of doing things. We return to this point below.

Hypothesis 3: Partner organizations have relatively strong technical, financial, administrative, and managerial capacities, so they can carry out their defined responsibilities.

Logic suggests that coordination and implementation are more difficult when agencies are institutionally weak and are not prepared to carry out their responsibilities as part of the partnership. In Colombia, technical capacity in the Ministries of Agriculture and of Education gave those based in the Ministry of Health capable colleagues with whom to interact and plan. The relatively strong programs those ministries already had in place also gave MANA a foundation of administrative and managerial support. The program itself had sufficient financial resources to operate and, importantly, had start-up funding that allowed it to take time to design and plan the program. In Senegal, the financial solidity of NEP and the strong skills of its manager Ndiaye were important to successful implementation and provision of partnering incentives.

Although the case studies support the general thrust of this hypothesis, they suggest several modifications. First, a low level of interest in the program, rather than capacity, posed the greatest challenge to implementation, at least for MANA. Institutional strength did not guarantee successful collaboration. In fact, as with the interministerial component of NEP, such strength meant that ministries had less incentive to join in collaboration to achieve their goals. If agencies do not have common vision when they are institutionally strong, they can also make collaboration more difficult. Perversely, institutional strength may sometimes be a barrier. Collaboration may in fact prove easier at a local level, which does not have separate institutional structures for each partner and where an integrating office or agency (a mayor or a social programs coordinator, for example) serves as an operational focal point.

Second, multisectoral collaboration can work even when some of the partners are weak, because programs can create ways to overcome or circumvent weaknesses. In Colombia and Senegal, implementation depended to a large extent on nongovernmental organizations (NGOs) or private-sector firms that had the necessary skills to support implementation. In Colombia, MANA contracted a firm specifically to strengthen the municipality's ability to develop a food and a nutrition plan and to manage interactions with MANA. In Senegal, NGOs monitored operations at the local level. Subcontracting to outside firms allowed each program to tailor the support to needs (to build capacity or ensure effective implementation by going outside government) and allowed them to monitor performance and get rid of nonperforming agents.

Third, given the nature of multisectoral collaboration, not all partners have to be strong in all areas. Needs will differ over time and by objective, and so different sorts of capacities are relevant at different stages. The case studies do not allow us to say whether a particular capability trumps any other, or which are essential and which are not. But in some environments, some capacities may be strong and others weak or nonexistent. Different contexts and capacities can generate different optimal structures, even if programs aim to achieve the same goal. In Senegal, for instance, relatively weak capacities throughout the system meant that the central organization initially had to take on more responsibilities. In Colombia, ministerial-level agencies and even some municipalities were fairly strong. This strength allowed the implementation structure to be more decentralized from the beginning.

We have so far discussed differences in relative capacities. Operating structures can be modified to take advantage of institutional strengths and can also address certain weaknesses. But to achieve results, some minimal level of capacity may be necessary. There requirements can include convening authority as well as technical, financial, and managerial capacities.

Good management seems to be one of these required capacities. Programs in both Colombia and Senegal had an outstanding manager as program leader. It is hard to see how these programs could have been operationally successful without such individuals. These individuals paid close attention to managing day-to-day relationships with partners, political authorities, and donors. Their decisions shaped the operational processes (including planning and internal and external communications) and infused them with particular values and principles.

We often think of capacity in terms of ability to support implementation, in the form of technical, financial, and administrative (bureaucratic) capacities. But obviously capacities are needed for starting up and sustaining the collaboration as well. Efforts in those stages seem to require relatively more talent in management and leadership. Leaders of MANA and NEP, for instance, needed not just administrative talents to keep the machine running but also personal abilities of negotiation and persuasion. They had a capacity to develop and enable vision, engender trust, align efforts across sectors and agencies, and achieve results. Such skills seem especially pertinent to success when leading laterally.

These observations on leadership suggest it is possible to work multisectorally even when local capacities are weak. Donors sometimes try to circumvent weaknesses in institutional capacities by creating new organizations. The case studies suggest that, although potentially very difficult and certainly time consuming, effective collaboration may be possible even in capacity-constrained environments. Creators of programs must identify at least one strong node of capacity and leadership and be willing either to provide additional support to develop capacity in other organizations (as MANA did for the municipalities) or to counter constraints by relying on the capacities of other partners (using NGOs for implementation, for example, as NEP did). The threshold for what is sufficient institutional capacity for effective collaboration may thus be lower than one might think. Further, such collaboration can lead to substantial benefits, through much-improved institutional capacities, in the long term.[1]

Hypothesis 4: Organizations have values that promote collaboration, including respect for the organizational routines and missions of others, an openness to learning from them, and an orientation toward results. These values encourage participation, transparency, accountability, and institutional flexibility.

This hypothesis is based on reasonable inferences from the literature. It is somewhat unusual, however, in that it focuses on the softer, more personal aspects of multisectoral collaboration and not on the structure of coordination that other researchers have emphasized. Yet experiences in both study countries suggest that these values are instrumental to success. On reflection, that these personal qualities emerge as being important is not surprising, given that powers of coercion are weak and success requires convincing others to cooperate voluntarily. Few organizations and individual like being told what to do with minimal regard for what they are doing already or for what they might do.

Inclusion and Respect. In both cases, program managers worked hard at start up and implementation to be inclusive. They incorporated partners from inside and outside government and from various sectors and levels of government into program design and operation.

MANA built on existing programs in counterpart ministries in a way that NEP did not. By respecting institutional missions and inertia, MANA was able to include existing programs under an umbrella coordinating unit. Although NEP's actions were multisectoral and involved various ministries, NEP did not have as much success in being inclusive horizontally. That is, the secretariat, located at the central level, largely implemented this program through NGOs and governments at the local level. Operational integration among ministries at the national level was still weak, although ministries were involved in national-level coordination and did receive benefits from NEP, mostly funding for specific activities. NEP's operation and management, nevertheless, reflects attempts to keep other ministries connected and informed, with the hope that operational links will strengthen over time.

The experiences highlight a common question that comes up when starting up a program: Do we build on what exists, or do we build a parallel structure? In Colombia, MANA built on what existed—and it is difficult to see how a truly

---

[1] We are grateful to an anonymous reviewer for highlighting this point.

multisectoral collaboration could have been done any differently, given the existence of relevant food and nutrition programs. That is, the Ministry of Health could have chosen to go it alone, but that probably would not have resulted in integrated multisectoral action.

In Senegal, program designers tried to learn from the Community Nutrition Program (Programme de Nutrition Communautaire, or PNC) experience. Ministries participated in the initiation, design, and operation of NEP. This inclusion may have helped to build support for the program, or at least stalled bureaucratic animosity or indifference. In the end, however, most ministries apparently saw NEP as a structure apart and considered that they would have only limited integration in operations. The various ministries in Senegal also appear to have had fewer programs that could be sensibly folded into an integrated program compared to the situation in Colombia. Under these conditions, establishing a new structure seemed reasonable. It also may imply that a new structure had limited competition for operational turf.

Establishing structures outside the sectoral ministries, however, undermines the very idea of a multisectoral integration. If such an organization is truly independent and self-reliant, it may be able to achieve some success. But by its very nature it is highly vulnerable to political change, as it is not tied to any permanent body. Such structures frequently emerge from the frustration of international agencies in working with government. They may be effective, but only so long as the donor agency prioritizes and funds the program. Although it takes more time and will certainly run up against challenges faced by any other government program, having the ministries and other stakeholders develop understanding and take ownership is likely more sustainable in the long term.

We argue that respect for institutional missions and routines is essential when putting a program together. Challenging these fundamental qualities can create inter- and intra-institutional conflict that a new program may not be able to survive. Although not confirmed by a controlled experiment, MANA's approach and success fit well with findings from the literature and insights from management experts. The resultant relative operational harmony compares favorably to the multiple failures of other attempts to work multisectorally in nutrition.

NEP's emphasis on securing ownership by the implementing partners is consistent with these observations. That partners quickly agreed on the concepts but struggled over institutional arrangements confirms how critical this point is. It also suggests that developing the operational structure jointly with partners, so they have ownership and understanding, is essential. In fact, when this is not done (as in the case of PNC), the potential partners may simply create another, parallel structure.

Operational and Transactional Flexibility. The internal characteristics of the agency itself (openness to learning, capacities, and so forth) can be just as critical to success as the agency's relationships with other institutions, which is often the focus of explanations about why collaboration fails.

For instance, bureaucratic organizations have set ways of doing things. These standard operating procedures are a requirement for a large organization to function reasonably well. Internal coordination of effort and the ability to respond to the external environment would be impossible without them. But there is nothing that says those operating procedures are optimal or that they cannot be changed.

Each agency involved in collaboration likely has its own operating procedures and organizational culture. As corporate mergers have demonstrated countless times, one of the fears of integrating operations of differing entities is that these organizations will have to accommodate other ways of doing and being. Yet such accommodation would seem essential if multisectoral collaboration is to work.

Some procedures may be appropriate for one organization, context, or need—but not another. To apply the same set of procedures to all organizations in a collaboration is likely to lead to cultural and operational conflicts. Rigid rules and procedures may make interagency cooperation collapse rather quickly. This observation suggests that procedural flexibility is an important characteristic for cooperating organizations (Serrano-Berthet 2003). These organizations may need to be flexible both with internal procedures (for example, when and how to produce audits) and with transactional procedures among partners (financial accounting between partners, for example).

In addition, rigid procedures may also inhibit staff from performing needed experimentation with ways of working. If staff are reprimanded for not following rules, instead of being rewarded for innovation, they are likely to focus on rules rather than results. They are less likely to try to find creative solutions to overcome obstacles to collaboration.

The variety in modalities of operation shows that both MANA and NEP were adaptive organizations. They seem to have guided operations based on a focus on results rather than on rules, thus placing a premium on flexibility. One of the strategies used by both programs to gain operational flexibility was to contract NGOs to carry out program activities. These partners could essentially do what they felt was needed to achieve the results specified in the contract. This gave the NGOs significant flexibility in implementation. In theory, it also enhanced the ability to achieve results. The practice did not lead to random outputs or implementation strategies, because the purpose and strategy of the program was made clear, as were the principles of operation. Furthermore, the agreement on expected results set operational boundaries. The programs had a good chance of success, because selection of the NGO was competitive and depended on proven capacity. Performance measures were incorporated into the contract. Success in implementation determined whether the contract was renewed. In principle this model allowed for maximum flexibility while also ensuring results. A future evaluation should determine whether this innovation had a significant impact on program outcomes.

In another instance of flexibility, the structure of MANA was allowed to emerge organically from discussions among potential partners. In Senegal, the structure tended to be imposed, but NEP's management nevertheless also valued results and organizational flexibility in implementation. Because of the diversity in context, capacities, and interests of the partners, it is not surprising that they did not arrive at the same blueprint for action. But both programs seem to do well by being flexible and results oriented.

Flexibility in operating strategy and operating procedures is likely a key factor in success in bringing agencies to work together. Trying to coordinate or cooperate may uncover problems with organizational integration, and organizations may need to change their own standard operating structures and procedures to be able to work better in a given environment or with a particular partner. But the operating environment of each agency must allow modifications. Keeping a focus on results and on the benefits to all partners may help make the case for flexibility to overcome procedural obstacles to collaboration or political resistance to change.

Results Orientation. The results orientation of both MANA and NEP appears to be particularly important. A results orientation helps reduce institutional territoriality by focusing actors on defining and solving the problem. Combined with efforts to create a vision, such an orientation encourages participants to work as a team and defend the program (and their institution's role in achieving goals) rather than protect their respective institutions.

Monitoring, Learning, and Accountability. Although we have argued above that information plays an important role in successful collaborations, it is less certain whether information from monitoring and evaluation makes any difference to operation or impact. Both MANA and NEP instituted mechanisms to monitor program performance and hold staff accountable. Public accountability encourages managerial transparency and, if handled correctly, can promote a learning organization. In MANA, citizens and legislators held municipal mayors and staff accountable through regular public presentations.

The governor and ministries monitored the performance of the program, particularly the director. And MANA staff oversaw the performance of operating partners through the use of contracts.

NEP had no public accountability mechanism but did have to provide regular progress reports to the World Bank. In addition, staff knew the World Bank would finance evaluations and an end-of-project report, which may have provided some incentive for good performance. These are standard monitoring and evaluation mechanisms, however, and are shared with many poorly performing projects. Thus the evidence suggests that these mechanisms by themselves are unlikely to have improved overall performance of NEP.

Monitoring and evaluation are likely to have more effect when they are an intrinsic part of the program, they are public, there are consequences for failure to perform, and they are shared by various actors across operational levels. MANA had stronger structures in place for learning than did NEP, with significant input from their partners in education, but no evidence was uncovered that this information changed the program.

Experience and History of Working across Sectors. A history of working with others and being open to learning and to new ideas (which can also be considered a capacity) can encourage collaboration. As noted, the literature and experience with Rapid Results Initiatives suggest that previous experiences working with partners in other sectors can help organizations smooth out working relationships in new undertakings. Previous experiences can be especially helpful in making potential partners aware of landmines in developing relationships and in grasping how to arrive at jointly owned solutions.

The case studies suggest that the optimal operational and coordinating structures depend on context. Yet the two programs do share some principles: both worked to be inclusive and keep stakeholders informed (even if they were not a significant part of operations). This approach may assuage fears of change that stakeholders may feel if they do not know what is going on. Being inclusive and sharing information widely are probably good politics, because they can reduce the possibility that actors who feel left out will critique or try to sabotage the program.

Organizational flexibility also seems important. Allowing collaborating organizations to bend standard operating procedures to adapt organizational structures to a particular context can lead to better results, as long as this is done within the framework of guiding principles and is results oriented. Having previous experience in working cross-sectorally seems like a logical advantage, but, given that several partners had no such experience, it does not seem essential.

Hypothesis 5: Organizations provide incentives for action, including personal and financial incentives, and have established accountability structures.

These incentives may be intrinsic, stemming from personal goals and values, or extrinsic, stemming from external incentives and pressures to perform (Heaver 2005b). MANA and NEP, for example, provided incentives for co-operation among partners, but these were not only financial, as the litera-ture on interagency collaboration in the United States might suggest. Both programs offered an opportunity for organizations and individuals to achieve their goals. MANA and NEP offered assistance or arrangements that would help partner organizations fulfill institutional missions or obligations. This was particularly true in the case of MANA.

In both cases, however, personal interests and passions tended to be the initial forces that brought people together (once a higher authority had established a space for the initiative to develop). Participants then saw how to promote their own programs or interests within the emerging frame-works of the programs. The primary movers behind MANA also expressed a personal dedication to the issues around which they structured the program (namely, health and nutrition, agriculture, and education). Having suffi-cient funding available made the mechanics of the collaboration possible, but the drivers of the collaboration nevertheless tended to be of a more personal nature.

The difficulty of support and integration at the ministerial level in Senegal, where NEP provided small amounts of money to finance a variety of activi-ties simply to maintain interest among national ministries, shows the limits of using financial incentives to establish effective multisectoral collaboration. When funding runs out for its particular activity of interest, if the institution has no other stake in the success of the collaboration, its engagement will most likely decline.

One of the major selling points for collaboration with MANA was, in fact, institutional efficiency and synergy. Development associations, national programs, or departmental ministries could implement their own programs more efficiently by integrating them into MANA. These organizations real-ized that their programs could be more effective or could expand coverage by collaborating with MANA—yet they were able to keep their institutional structures and reap the credit. MANA's strategic communications solidified this incentive. The multiple opportunities for establishing a presence (as in putting a logo on the side of a truck) gave the collaborating partner, includ-ing ministries, ways to publicize their own agencies and take credit through association with a successful program.

Thus sharing in success was an additional incentive to collaborate. Success bred success. Both MANA and NEP found that if they achieved results, they acquired a positive reputation, which encouraged others to want to work with them. Success could also draw further resources. Donors in Senegal actively courted NEP once they realized the NEP structure and management were solid, and they could be confident in achieving results by going through NEP. Program feedback and sharing of this success (letting partners know results and identifying and valuing their contribution in achieving them) was important to keeping partners interested in cooperation.

Hypothesis 6: Partner organizations perceive that the benefits of participation outweigh the costs.

Leaders of efforts to work multisectorally may find the benefit-cost framework useful for developing a partnership strategy. Considering how potential partners view the opportunity to collaborate may be particularly useful for providing them with the incentives to work together. Understanding the potential benefits and threats to personal and institutional positions can help them devise approaches to motivate partner participation and commitment. A partnership strategy seeks to provide incentives, enhance benefits, and reduce costs for each partner.

The start-up costs were relatively high in both cases, involving a significant investment of staff time in attending meetings and workshops and designing the operational structure. But the effort seems worth the long-term benefits to each organization. Furthermore, the inclusive approach adopted in both programs actually reduced risks and operational costs (including financial costs as well as time costs of staff and the emotional costs involved in dealing with partners) by working out a common vision and a mutually owned strategy.

The lead partners will need to structure the collaborative arrangements to make sure the benefits of participation are clear. Otherwise the partner organizations have little incentive to collaborate. Understanding this calculation of benefits and costs was most visible in the case of MANA. There the director's inclusive style made benefits clear (and may have enhanced them) and further reduced costs and risks associated with participation. Each partner organization could easily tell that the benefits to them outweighed the costs of participation.

The experiences did not suggest any particular partnership structure or archetype would guarantee this outcome. Rather, they illustrated that context is indeed important to determining optimal structure. They also show that many different types of partnerships can exist within the collaborative structure because there are many different partners. NEP and MANA established partnerships horizontally and vertically with a wide range of institutions, including different layers of government, private- and public-sector entities, universities, and civil society.

Our study did not further analyze partnership types by characteristics (for example, by intensity or autonomy of partnership; structure of the relationship; or structure, size, or style of partners), but a stylized observation would suggest that fitting each partnership to needs is more important than any particular characteristic. It strongly suggests that initiators and managers of multisectoral collaborations should pay attention to vertical as well as horizontal relationships. The horizontal relationships, which tend to be cross-sectoral, are often the primary focus of concern. But the case studies also showed that NEP and MANA needed to work vertically as well to reach the community level where service provision actually took place. In fact, the experiences suggest that working multisectorally comes easiest at the local level, even if the impetus for the program is at the national or departmental level.

Chapter 3 listed different modalities of collaborative interaction along a continuum from less to more engaged, and more to less coercive. In Colombia and Senegal, the principal relations between partners were not supervisory, coercive, or competitive. The experiences emphasized that multisectoral collaborations are, by their nature, largely voluntary. Relations involving direct oversight or following rules laid down by another agency are not very attractive for a potential partner. And competitive relations undermine the reason for the collaboration in the first place, which is to reduce duplication and promote cooperation. Relations among agencies, therefore, tend to revolve around generating mutual gains from collaboration, such as trading services or planning or cooperating on joint work. In both cases, however, operational funding and managerial oversight came from the base organization.

Although the internal structures of the partner organization may influence how well it performs, the main consideration should be how well the organizations fit with one another to achieve the collaboration's goals. The needs of the collaboration and thus the fit of the organizations may vary over time, depending on particular program needs and the environment. This dynamic institutionality precludes having a single template for partnership arrangements.

From a strategic management point of view, we should remember that a multisectoral collaboration is really a set of relationships with specific people inside institutions, not simply connections with impersonal monolithic organizations. These personalities and institutions have their own interests and ways of working. The links should therefore be strategically determined.

There will probably be some principal actors and then a constellation of other partners around them. One core set of partners may be specific ministries or the municipal administration. They may themselves have different arrangements during different phases of the program (initiation, operation, and so forth), or may be distinguished by type, such as decisionmakers and operators or implementers. Other partnerships may be temporary, with organizations coming and going, depending on requirements and performance (the operating partners in MANA, for instance).

In sum, the costs of participating in a multisectoral collaboration are likely to be high. Collaboration requires adaptation of organizational procedures; it requires time for the partners to understand the program and each other; it may pose risks of failure. But building a sense of common purpose, being explicit about valuing partners, and helping them to achieve their own personal and institutional goals can be sufficient incentives to make the collaboration worthwhile from their perspective.

Assessing Hypotheses on External Context

Hypothesis 7: Promoting nutrition as a development priority among a wide range of stakeholders creates openings for action and sustained attention to nutrition.

In both study countries top decisionmakers agreed that nutrition was a priority for development. The attention given to nutrition by the governor and the prime minister helped create space for action in their respective countries. Leadership from high political authorities put nutrition on the policy agenda. Interestingly, in both Senegal and Colombia those who developed and managed the initiative paid attention to actors outside nutrition, especially in the beginning. This broader, more inclusive approach provided important support and operational links later in project development and may ultimately contribute to sustainability.

The role of information at the initial stage appears to be very important. The Ministry of Health staff starting up MANA first had to break through a wall of incredulity among other experts that malnutrition was a problem. The statistics they provided still may not have convinced others to prioritize nutrition in their own actions, but the numbers backed up the governor's decision to act based on what he had heard in community consultations. The information solidified the position of nutrition in public discourse and may have at least neutralized potential opponents, allowing action to proceed even if others only went along begrudgingly.

Some analysts argue that nutrition is a less politically divisive issue than other topics (such as subsidies for agricultural producers), because who would be against nutrition? But in practice, the issue is not one of being for or against malnourished children. Rather, (1) many policymakers view nutrition as a noncritical investment and so rank it below other priorities they consider more urgent; (2) many issues in nutrition (such as technical recommendations or operational approaches) are contentious, especially among nutritionists; and (3) when programs change, decisionmakers encounter the same problem of group interest as with any other program. The Senegal experience with transitioning out of Executing Agency for Works of Public Interest against Unemployment (Agence d'Exécution des Travaux d'Intéret Public Contre le Sous-Emploi, or AGETIP) illustrates the typical problem of how to install "winners" and compensate, co-opt, or control "losers" during change.

The conflict inherent in the second and third points above may cause politicians and decisionmakers to think that nutrition is too complex an issue to deal with. They may withdraw nutrition from the policy arena. It is important to generate solid evidence and have an effective social marketing plan to present the problem and its solution to a wide range of stakeholders, many of them untraditional.

Benson (2008) argues it is important to have a policy narrative relevant to country conditions about the importance of nutrition that can be presented to policymakers. A policy narrative is a tool, but advocates must carry it beyond the usual audiences of those directly involved with nutrition activities. Advocates must work beyond their usual social network to integrate these ideas into the fabric of society. The creation of a broad social consensus in support of action on nutrition—one that will continue in spite of political change—requires that advocacy go beyond one narrow constituency, such as the technical nutritionists who are already convinced and who are just one of many threads in that fabric. The goal is to inculcate the notion that nutrition is central to development to all who may influence action on nutrition, to those in and out of government, and in and out of nutrition. When political change occurs, those who are coming into government, as well as those who are leaving, will understand the importance of nutrition. Nutrition will remain as a priority.

Encouraging widespread understanding of the key role nutrition plays in development would logically lead to greater support throughout society. But in the case of MANA and NEP this broad social understanding does not seem to have existed initially. Broadened understanding of the importance of nutrition emerged, for the most part, after decisions were made to take action on nutrition. These decisions resulted from specific initiating catalysts (for example, the governor or the World Bank).

These catalysts outside the program may have put nutrition on the agenda, as this hypothesis suggests. But the prioritization of nutrition in development did not imply a decision to design a multisectoral nutrition program. Rather, program design was largely a decision left to technicians and nutrition experts.

Perhaps a deeper understanding by politicians and other stakeholders of the reasons for working multisectorally could lead them to support the idea and could sustain the program through political transitions. So rather than asserting that broad acceptance of nutrition as a development priority leads to multisectoral action, a different hypothesis is perhaps more appropriate. Future work could more closely examine the hypothesis that engagement with a broad range of stakeholders (especially nonexperts in nutrition) is helpful for supporting multisectoral action and improves the chances for sustainability. The communications and continuous-education strategy of leaders of both MANA and NEP suggest that they felt this was important, but we do not as yet have evidence to show what effect their strategy of engagement had on the ability to work multisectorally or to sustain the programs.

Hypothesis 8: Advocates create a sense of urgency to promote action.
Experts on leadership and change management argue that along with vision, change processes are more likely to be successful when leaders create a sense of urgency to force focus and action (Kotter 1996). We, however, posited that nutrition is most often not a pressing issue. Policymakers hardly ever see it as an issue demanding their immediate attention. Parents as well as government officials may consider a certain level of malnutrition normal. They do not consider acting on nutrition to be urgent. Except perhaps during economic crises or famines, society sees malnutrition more as a chronic social condition, not an emergency. Creating a sense of urgency about nutrition is thus a challenge.

Indeed, these case studies imply that attention to nutrition normally comes from political priorities or bureaucratic deadlines. Some initial sense of urgency can be important at the initiation of a program. A politician favoring action on nutrition might give dire warnings about the levels of malnutrition and frame the issue as urgent. Policymakers and bureaucrats may then feel a need to act because the issue has been defined as a political priority and the administration knows it has limited time to deal with the problem. A sense of urgency may thus reflect organizational time clocks, including time frames set out by standard operating procedures or political calendars. The deadlines faced by other players become factors determining urgency.

In Colombia, the governor prioritized the issue during and after his election. By pushing for progress, he created a necessary sense of urgency. The interim governor who followed Gaviria also placed a priority on nutrition. The staff members who put together and then led MANA (principally Monsalve, Molina, and Gutiérrez) also imposed their own sense of urgency, if only by leading the project and making sure that they completed assigned tasks. Of course, although Monsalve and Molina were civil servants, they nevertheless had to work under the political clock of the elected administration. And Gutiérrez, an appointed official, was certainly aware of how the electoral calendar would affect the amount of time she had to consolidate achievements—an electoral calendar that was interspersed with other dates for accountability, including reporting to the municipality, the governors and ministers, and the legislature.

In Senegal, the need to design a follow-on program and loan when PNC ended drove the action calendar. The internal clocks of the World Bank and of the Government of Senegal determined the urgency for closing PNC and initiating NEP. Once initiated, the agreement with the World Bank largely determined the schedule. The 15-year time frame was laudable in its understanding of how long it takes to construct vision, build capacity, and align action—but, given the unlikelihood that the same Senegalese administration would be in place for the entire period, it essentially placed the responsibility for maintaining momentum on the World Bank. The deadlines in negotiated agreements for reporting, monitoring, and evaluation provided the urgency to get things done. Again, however, beyond what was written on paper, the personal investments of the director and other stakeholders in NEP were even more important drivers of success. The leaders needed to use the conceptual framework to create a sense of commitment and urgency in their partners and their own staff to make sure they did their jobs.

Although we expect staff to do their jobs, we should perhaps pay closer attention to this issue. We should ask: Are staff doing what they should be doing? Are they responding to expectations of their bosses? Are they establishing and keeping to deadlines for action and outputs? If so, they can potentially create their own sense of urgency—because they will have agreed to carry out certain tasks by specific deadlines. It is not surprising, then, that they can devise ways to make collaboration work.

Once a program has been fully implemented, however, and becomes integrated into the administrative apparatus, the sense of urgency may disappear. The time limits that push action dissolve. A program becomes part of the bureaucratic routine and attention falters. If so, it is important that the program transition from a program of an administration to a program of the state. A sense of urgency may drive efforts to initiate a program. But ensuring sustainability of program operation may require institutionalizing the program to weather future political change.

A sense of urgency seems helpful but not essential to putting nutrition on the policy agenda. In practical terms, creating a sense of urgency did seem to push efforts forward in both Colombia and Senegal. Both outside leaders and organizational timelines drove the urgency rather than any factors from the broader political or economic environment. Thus the pressure for change will likely be generated internally (in line with the view of nutrition as a chosen issue), and so the pressure for continued attention is subsequently more fragile than if strong external pressures existed.

This observation, however, has to do with the promotion of action on nutrition. "Urgency," in the context of leadership or change management, requires simply that *something*—sometimes almost anything—be done. Urgency does not necessarily shape what that something looks like. Decisions about program design—about whether to have a multisectoral program—seem to have been left to the technical experts.

Hypothesis 9: General economic, political, and social conditions do not bring attention to nutrition, although specific events may.

Despite high levels of undernutrition, in neither country did everyday economic, political, or social conditions put nutrition on the policy agenda; nor did those conditions result in a push for a multisectoral solution. Some progress had been made in reducing malnutrition (certainly more in Colombia than in Senegal), but broader society was not pushing government to act. This was partially because the hungriest and most malnourished had hardly any voice in the few mechanisms to pressure government, although Gaviria's walks showed that rural communities did, in fact, recognize that hunger and malnutrition were serious problems. In both countries more influential actors in the broader environment (the governor, the prime minister, and World Bank staff) gave voice to these concerns and chose to put nutrition on the policy agenda.

Windows of opportunity to act, therefore, did arise, but not from moments of crisis, which is frequently how an issue is placed on the policy agenda. Rather, these windows occurred as a result of particular moments in the normal timelines of political or institutional change, such as elections. Such change can often wreck the stability of current programs, but it can also be used to put new ideas and new programs on the agenda.

As a chosen issue, nutrition must take advantage of these moments. Nutrition advocates must make choosing easy. Choosing becomes less desirable for politicians when technical advocates bicker over how to understand or solve the problem. Advocates must use evidence to make clear the seriousness of the situation and what to do about it, including showing how to make multisectoral collaboration work. In addition, advocates have to respond to the specific concerns of influential actors who do not usually deal with nutrition policies and programs, including ministers of finance or ordinary citizens. They may particularly want to emphasize the political as well as the economic and social gains from reducing hunger and malnutrition.

We contend that the issue of moments of change cuts two ways. From one perspective, nutrition must be aware of and ready to take advantage of those moments of change. But once a program is under way or nutrition is on the policy agenda, then advocates must guard against such change. In Senegal, for instance, NEP became the principal nutrition program because the World Bank pushed for it. Likewise, loss of continued World Bank funding, a genuine possibility, may effectively abandon NEP as a program and nutrition as a priority issue in Senegal.

In brief, the danger of being a chosen issue is that attention to nutrition becomes a much more personal issue, one associated with a particular administration or individual. Advocates must therefore work to (1) prioritize nutrition in a broad fabric of society so that nutrition is always chosen, and (2) institutionalize attention to nutrition (convert it from a policy of the administration to a policy of the state).

Finally, although the case studies generally track this hypothesis, the considerations raised here do not specifically relate to working multisectorally in nutrition. In general, however, the studies support the notion expressed in discussions of the previous two hypotheses: the external context influences attention to nutrition. It seems to have less effect on whether policymakers push for a multisectoral solution. That decision seems to have been left to technical experts in the government bureaucracy or with the funders. However, this situation at least made a multisectoral approach feasible. Those who led the design and implementation considered how to persuade policymakers to support a multisectoral program, knowing that the players in the external context, if not forcing a multisectoral solution, could impede it if they desired.

Assessing Hypotheses on Institutional Links

Hypothesis 10: Multisectoral collaboration requires institutional change, in budgeting structures or modalities of implementation, for example.

In Colombia, institutional change involved creation of a unit to coordinate operations and integrate programs from different ministries into the umbrella structure of MANA. Staff from other ministries kept their affiliations but moved to an office in the Ministry of Health. Other institutional changes included partnering with and piggybacking on existing programs operated by the national government, NGOs, or regional development associations. The contracting of NGOs, universities, and private firms for implementation was also a new way of working, as was the structure of multiskilled regional teams that covered specific geographic areas. Increased involvement and the requirement of significant ownership by municipalities were also novel.

NEP in Senegal actually established several new administrative structures to oversee and guide the work (Coordination Unit for the Reduction of Malnutrition [Cellule de Lutte contre la Malnutrition, or CLM] and National Executive Bureau [Bureau Exécutif National, or BEN], respectively). NEP itself also developed work along two lines of action, at the national level with ministries and at the local level with communities and NGOs. Ministries affiliated with the ministerial arm of action actually did not change much about the way they worked, indicating limited programmatic integration at this level. When viewed from the perspective of NEP, this arm of action was far less successful at working multisectorally and achieving impact than the community-based arm.

Proposing that working multisectorally implies institutional change may seem a truism. However, past efforts at working multisectorally have tended to ignore the deeper implications of this statement, and we felt it deserved closer examination as a hypothesis about how to work more effectively. Indeed, attempts to work across sectors need not require operational integration or force significant institutional change. In fact, the structure of the ministerial arm of action of NEP and many other attempts at multisectorality did not make this assumption. Rather, they implicitly assumed that by establishing a coordinating superstructure the programs or ministries would simply work together. Our analysis, however, suggests more significant change is needed. Previous experience with multisectoral nutrition planning, interministerial coordinating committees, and NEP itself suggest that different structures and incentives are needed to support multisectoral work. The case studies show how these changes (and particularly the integrative and linking mechanisms) can be developed organically through participatory processes.

Most of those who have tried to work across sectors appear to not have fully appreciated the profound changes in institutional arrangements and organizational behaviors that are needed. Decisionmakers for nutrition recognized a need for coordination in these earlier efforts, but they somehow expected that a fairly simplistic realignment of policies or priorities—say, through the establishment of a coordinating body—would accomplish the task. They almost expected those in charge of multisectoral work, often based in a small coordinating unit with little power and few options to offer incentives, would force the needed changes on their home institution or those of others. When these approaches did not work, analysts and practitioners then concluded that the task of working multisectorally was hopelessly complex. They did not look deeper to consider how to resolve problems they had identified—problems with institutional arrangements, political context, leadership, and incentives.

These case studies show that individuals and institutions can work across agencies and sectors in a multisectoral fashion. They also show that working multisectorally was associated with fairly profound organizational change. Those who want to work multisectorally, therefore, must understand the nature of the institutions involved and think clearly about how to set up and manage multisectoral programs. This effort goes beyond simple coordination. It implies that the institutions involved will change their ways of operating and linking with others, and individuals will change the ways they think and work together.

Hypothesis 11: Successful multisectoral collaboration involves establishing linking structures that
- **promote shared understanding;**
- **are inclusive and participatory;**
- **promote accountability to the public and stakeholders, including partners and program management;**
- **value the contributions of all partners; and**
- **make the roles and responsibilities of all partners clear.**

This hypothesis describes the general characteristics of interaction in multisectoral collaboration. It proposes in a stylistic way that these elements compose one successful approach to working multisectorally. Not each element mentioned may be present in the collaboration to the same degree, and some elements may not be present at all.

In fact, the planning, managerial, and operational structures of MANA and NEP did include many of these characteristics. This is in large part because the leadership of these programs appears to have taken similar approaches that incorporated many of these values and ways of working. These values seem to have undergirded the way Monsalve and Molina, along with García and Celis, led the process of developing MANA. The actions of the directors of MANA and NEP also reflected these principles. Ndiaye, for example, consistently talked about how much he valued each partner and was in continuous contact with them. Gutiérrez also talked about the need to nurture partner relationships. Their statements suggest that attention to relationships with partners and authorities at all levels (and not just to institutional structures) is critical and must be continuous.

Shared Understanding

We have already discussed the importance of vision and shared understanding. One element that links institutions in this way is a national nutrition plan or policy. Is such a framework necessary to promote multisectoral collaboration? The case studies suggest it is not necessary, but logic suggests it may be helpful for supporting understanding and subsequently linking institutional structures and programs. The Government of Senegal implemented PNC without a plan and could have proceeded in the same manner with NEP but for the World Bank's insistence. The Government of Antioquia also did not have a strategic food and nutrition policy, although through the establishment of MANA (especially the PES process), it essentially established one.

The generation of an overall policy, however, can be a useful process that brings stakeholders together and develops guides for action. The resulting framework focuses efforts, helping to determine which actions fit and which do not. If such a policy becomes a policy of the state, and not just of the administration, the plan may also be able to help to protect the program from political turbulence.

Inclusive, Participatory Structures

The case studies do, however, support an association of success with valuing the contributions of partners, as explored in detailed above. Both MANA and NEP did this. Linking structures should therefore also be participatory and operationally flexible.

Public Accountability

The idea behind this hypothesis is that public accountability can help to make the program better and, in the best of cases, provide documentation that a multisectoral approach is preferable to one that does not integrate across sectors. But we have little evidence to judge one way or the other.

As noted in the section assessing the hypotheses on internal context, MANA and NEP did keep in touch with communities. And they did sponsor sessions for feedback and continuous learning. MANA had to respond to legislative oversight committees, and NEP had to respond, primarily, to World Bank evaluators. But whether these activities had much impact on program operations is unclear. On a daily basis, such monitoring may be sufficient to maintain program operation.

Despite being results oriented, neither program instituted a rigorous impact evaluation. MANA had expanded to all municipalities, and malnutrition was indeed decreasing in Antioquia. But we cannot state with certainty that this result is attributable to MANA. In Senegal, the World Bank's Implementation Completion Report noted that NEP was an outstanding program, but it based this conclusion largely on operational criteria, including coverage, along with a small-scale study of the impact on nutrition.

The public accountability mechanisms appear to have been used more for reporting purposes and not for determining the effectiveness of a multisectoral approach. Such mechanisms may in fact be more important for sustaining the program over time. In both countries, for instance, when new officials have come to power, they have considered moving or modifying the programs in ways that would cause them to lose their multisectoral character. Not having solid documentation of impact may weaken their case for working multisectorally.

Clear Roles and Responsibilities

Without knowing their roles and responsibilities, participating agencies will likely have little knowledge of how to proceed. In large bureaucracies, standard operating procedures help define actions. The same may be true in working multisectorally in nutrition because of multiple actors doing various things at different levels. If they do not understand their roles or responsibilities, lack of coordination will diminish the impact of the program and may result in organizational chaos.

The case studies indicate that defining roles and responsibilities is associated with success. NEP's and MANA's proposals were developed over time by means of multiple meetings with partners. This process created an understanding among partners at the strategic level. The need for integration, coordination, and understanding roles and responsibilities does not undermine the argument that the successful program also requires flexibility. Operational partners of MANA and NEP had significant operational flexibility, but the programs spelled out roles and responsibilities in contracts. Accountability mechanisms also provided bounds to this flexibility and kept the focus on results.

New Thoughts on Working Multisectorally

The above assessment details how the experiences square with the hypotheses, but the experiences in Senegal and Colombia also brought to the fore some aspects of working multisectorally not present or fully captured in the initial hypotheses. These new thoughts are discussed in this section.

Leadership across Levels Is Important to Success

Leadership was displayed not only at a high political level, but also at different levels of the government structure, especially by the director and managers (civil servants) of the program. Our initial framework and hypotheses emphasized organizational characteristics, so the emergence of leadership as an essential factor came as something of a surprise—less so after recalling that multisectoral programs represent complex systems. Leadership is clearly essential for the individual elements to work as a whole.

In analyzing the case studies, we found that management style and personal relationships among the players seemed absolutely critical to interagency collaboration. Thus succeeding in working in a complex system may owe much to not only institutional but also personal factors. For example, in both NEP and MANA, management decisions about how to bring others to the collaboration and keep them there served to animate the processes of reaching consensus and the building of coordinating structures. These were personal choices made by managers, not results of institutional arrangements or processes.

Another unexpected result was that the locus of leadership varies over time as the collaboration develops. We can categorize the type of leadership that corresponds to each phase: initiators, who envision the collaboration, create policy space, and start up the collaboration; creators, who take the initiative to fill the policy space and gather potential partners to bring the collaboration into being; and, finally, managers, who further operationalize the collaboration. Potentially, a separate leadership type will emerge to deal with the challenge of sustainability.

Note that these moments and the emergence of these leaders happen not on their own but because the process itself is dynamic. The individuals holding particular posts need not change: the locus of action itself moves. Different agencies or levels of agencies come into play, and so their leaders become more prominent. What is striking, however, is that the leaders, across time and loci, shared a similar approach to working with others (encouraging participation by stakeholders, developing understanding and vision, and thinking of interinstitutional incentives), suggesting that the approach itself is of great importance and should be applied at each stage in the process.

The Main Actors Shared an Approach to Collaboration and Management

This approach is focused on people rather than on institutional relations and coordinating mechanisms. The observation brings us back to a point made earlier, that regardless of the appropriateness of institutional arrangements, we must never forget that these institutions are populated by individuals with their own perspectives, ideas, talents, and interests. The same structure can operate very differently when the people within it are different and are making different choices. The creators and managers of NEP and MANA seemed to have realized this and used a management approach that took advantage of it to the benefit of their programs.

The specifics obviously varied in each case, but the outlines of a general approach emerge from the two cases. The approach involves employing a strategy, that is, a bundle of actions taken together. Employing an overall strategy with multiple actions may be more important to success than focusing on ensuring the presence or absence of any individual factor. Developing a strategy involves an inclusive process of bringing potential partners together to build consensus around the problem and its solutions. It respects their institutional missions and procedures, helping them see how they can contribute to achieving the common vision, providing incentives, and using evidence and reason to support the discussion in designing and implementing the program.

This process was not ad hoc. Each program had specific activities to guide the process. For example, NEP and MANA both held small meetings over time, bringing actors together to share information and perspectives, address controversial issues, build vision and understanding, and work out ways to work together despite differences. MANA used a particular technique, PES, to structure the process.

It is important that these elements not be seen as separate activities but as parts of a holistic process to bring a multisectoral nutrition program into being. In practical terms, we do not think any one element can be singled out as "the key" to successful collaboration, although we have indicated based on our observations which elements may matter more than others.

These sorts of elements are largely present in lateral leadership, a style that is particularly well suited to managing complex systems like multisectoral programs, where the leader has little direct line authority and so must rely more on persuasion and incentives to create alliances for working collaboratively.

The Role of Information Was More Influential than Expected

Survey data in Antioquia helped to establish the severity of the problem of hunger and malnutrition. Staff used the UNICEF conceptual model and used PES to develop a systematic process of analysis and to encourage working multisectorally. The governor insisted on measuring results. Mauricio Hernández, one of the governor's advisers and closely linked to the development of MANA, also emphasized the role of information, not only for tracking operational performance but also for making the issue of nutrition politically viable, promoting widespread understanding and ownership, creating calls for action, and keeping nutrition on the development agenda. He made these points clearly in an interview:

Interviewer: Did MANA staff or leaders do something to make nutrition more politically viable or attractive?

MH: They made it visible to the governor and society. They began to mobilize people. They brought together all the institutions, people, and organizations that had to do with nutrition. They brought together the ministers, they focused

on results, had the same language. We invited business-
men, to say "this catastrophe that we have is also your
responsibility. Make sure what you sell is done with an
eye to your social responsibility."

Interviewer: Yes, but how do you make that sustainable?

MH: By emphasizing public accountability, not planning. Use
            indicators. Measure them and make sure society knows
            about them. If you don't, the problem will just become
            invisible again. And let everyone participate and make
            sure decisions are taken by everyone. We gave them
            resources, not just financial resources but also organiza-
            tional resources. Knowledge, political resources. We used
            conversations, not a dialogue or a forum. (MH)

Establishing Multisectorality Can Take Years

Given experience with designing and institutionalizing other development
programs, the 15-year period established for NEP was in line with good practice in development. But not even that decision adequately captured how
development of the program was actually part of a process.

To be able to succeed at working multisectorally requires a long, multiactivity process, not a one-off workshop. It requires extensive consultation,
particularly with other mid- and upper-level civil servants and with the entire
range of operating partners, to develop understanding, vision, and strategy,
not simply agreement at the ministerial level.

Unprompted, the leaders in both cases used similar language to say that
the process was difficult and littered with contention. They worked through
setbacks and failures of consensus. They seemed surprised at how difficult
it was to achieve the collaboration and at their ultimate success. The
principals as well as the operating partners are now quite proud of their
accomplishment.

Strains can and will develop over institutionality. But the experiences of
NEP and MANA show ways to overcome these strains to reach an agreement
and achieve widespread ownership by stakeholders. Most critically, leaders
paid constant attention to partners, a form of maintenance management
revolving around continuous education of stakeholders (beyond those directly
involved in the program to those who could affect or support it). The leaders
showed potential partners and other stakeholders the severity of the problem
and the importance of addressing malnutrition, and they showed the political
and organizational benefits of cooperation. They kept partners informed but

also produced verifiable results for them, which partners could promote to their own constituencies as evidence of a good return on investment.

The Extent and Significance of Community-Level Action Was Unexpected

Both NEP and MANA relied to a large degree on engagement with community actors, particularly local officials. This seemed surprising for what are effectively national- and departmental-level programs. Although community capacity was sometimes a constraint, NEP and MANA found ways around this problem. Both relied on contracts with NGOs to implement the program and strengthen community capacity for implementation and oversight. These experiences provide empirical evidence that multisectoral coordination takes place more easily at the local level than at the national or regional level. Partly this is a result of the dissolution of sectoral silos at that level.

Decentralization thus seems to provide an opportunity to improve implementation and generate citizen demand. Greater local integration can give operators a better sense of local conditions. If they have operational flexibility, they can make changes to improve impact. Still, government would have to ensure that decentralized, participatory programs do not overload community structures. Capacity building and solid accountability mechanisms probably need to accompany decentralization.

Success at the community level provides a foundation for higher level success, which is not too surprising but is often overlooked in discussions of interagency collaboration. There may not have been extensive collaboration and integration with the community across all levels, but certainly community structures were involved. Community actors helped to design and implement the program, and they were linked to higher levels. As with other partners, this inclusion provided them with further incentive to cooperate, as they understood the importance of what they were doing and how they fit into the larger picture of the program.

Mauricio Hernández was a strong proponent of community participation, arguing that "the people participated but they weren't deciding, and that's not good. Value added [of programs] wasn't being left with the communities. The communities had little motivation to participate effectively" (MH). And as these case studies demonstrate, participation—giving everyone a sense of understanding and ownership—is critical.

Both NEP and MANA Created a Mystique around Their Operations

The mystique of success seems to permeate all levels and all those who participate in the program. There is a certain pride of accomplishment, of being part of a larger whole that is achieving something important in perhaps new and unique ways. Staff and stakeholders of NEP and MANA both exhibit this mystique, this confidence and pride in their programs. Other successful programs also have this mystique (Garrett 2001), although it is uncertain whether it is a result of or a contributor to success, or both.

Findings in the Broader Context

These case studies exhibit two examples of approaches taken to working multisectorally in nutrition that reflect some of this new understanding. Despite different country conditions and operational contexts, close analysis showed that the initiators, creators, and managers of the programs shared certain values and methods. We avoid sweeping generalizations for how to do things on the basis of two successful cases and do not claim to have drawn causal links. But we have shown an association between the nature of these approaches and operational success. The case studies confirm that working multisectorally in nutrition is possible, although it may take a change in routinized actions, behaviors, and ways of thinking and may involve a process that develops a strategy for action that is more reflective of partner needs, conditions, and context than is traditionally the case.

These strategies differ from the usual conceptions about how to work multisectorally, but they represent new knowledge and a new context for undertaking multisectoral action. And they may represent a new, second chance for success in working multisectorally. Traditionally nutrition actions are project focused, which implies a timeline and a bounded institutional framework. Addressing complex social problems, however, will need to go beyond these concepts and will require an inclusive process (of institutions and actors) with a strong focus on results (McLachlan and Garrett 2008). The focus on process emerges from an understanding that many problems, such as nutrition, result from the operation of complex systems, and so understanding how to devise and manage dynamic, multiagent, multi-institutional processes is an emerging facet of modern management. These case studies help us begin to understand how to better manage complexity in nutrition. They outline some of the strategies that might be useful and the conditions that are necessary to support such strategies. Such conditions include the importance of shared vision, the need for institutional incentives, and an understanding of how others gauge the costs and benefits of participation.

Research has led to a deeper understanding of problems, and we know that a problem does not generally have a single cause. Rather, causes are multiple and often interrelated. This complexity means that a single organization cannot generally solve a public policy problem by itself. And it cannot generally pull only one lever to do so.

But institutional and political constraints have largely conspired in the past to frustrate efforts to work multisectorally in nutrition. The approach, however, retains its attractiveness. We argue not only that a multisectoral approach is going to become more important with time, but also that our understanding and the operating environment have changed to increase its probabilities of success.

For example, we now know more about how to promote interagency collaboration. The approach to planning and implementation has changed in recent decades to favor less top-down direction and more local-level engagement. In the past, planning ministries did indeed take responsibility for planning and controlling program investment for others. Ministries of Health, Agriculture, and Education were also primarily directed from the top, with little input from other ministries or from citizens or lower levels of government. And, although still valuing indigenous and local knowledge, there often was a lack of capacity and broader knowledge at the local level. Those conditions and that structure implied an approach that relied on management from the national level.

Advocates, scientists, and policymakers are now quite familiar with other ways of working in nutrition. Almost everyone now appreciates that the causes of malnutrition are multisectoral. Donor agencies have pushed others to think more multisectorally. Multistakeholder and participatory processes are more familiar as well, so asking policymakers to think and work vertically and horizontally is not such a novelty. Along with a more educated populace and economic growth, institutional capacities have also grown.

More practically, we have a better idea of how different sectors or programs can contribute to improved nutrition. Without a clear idea of what piece fits where or how, multisectoral collaboration was more difficult. Thirty years ago the idea of integrating agriculture and nutrition, for example, was fairly new. We now know that some programs, such as vitamin A supplementation, lend themselves to a vertical approach; others, such as growth promotion, require community involvement; and still others, such as food fortification, require interaction with the private sector. We now have a better idea of which components might make sense as part of a multisectoral program.

So the context is different today. We found that two programs have operated fruitfully in that new context to work multisectorally in nutrition. And we have examined them in depth to shine some real-world light on the coordination problem specified at the beginning of this volume: how to facilitate collaboration vertically and horizontally across interrelated sectors, ministries, and actors inside and outside government.

The solutions in Senegal and Colombia involve a long-term participatory process that developed understanding of the problem and solutions in partnership with others. The solutions tended to be multi-institutional and took the needs, concerns, and contributions of potential partners into account. The process largely respected organizational missions, routines, and procedures, and looked for ways to provide incentives for cooperation. The collaborations focused on results and used evidence to guide discussion and decisions, two factors that helped reduce interinstitutional friction.

At the same time, we found that the observations of what makes working multisectorally difficult still largely hold. Although previous analyses brought out the problems then viewed as caused by institutions, much of the difficulty actually has to do with problems of capacity and management. We now have tools and techniques—and lessons learned—to address many of the constraints in capacity. And we now have some ideas about how to lead and manage intersectoral cooperation successfully, both from these studies and from new knowledge about leadership and change processes. The types of people, or more specifically, their management styles and approaches, appear to play a large role in success. Not surprisingly, the same system in the hands of different people will behave differently. So to understand success in working multisectorally in nutrition, we must emphasize the role of leaders and managers and not just the institutional arrangements themselves.

Although we started with a history that looked at the problem largely through an institutional lens, it is individuals who populate those institutions. In both countries, the same institutions and collaborative mechanisms could have existed—but the results could have been very different with different individuals in charge. The less-than-transformative experience with the first director of MANA and with the previous task manager of NEP shows that, in fact, changing people did change outcomes. That is, when someone with a different approach to making the multisectoral approach work arrived, someone who emphasized collaboration and lateral leadership over direction and top-down leadership, the program worked. Earlier assessments of failure in working multisectorally overemphasized the institutional difficulties and underrated the personal aspects of management. Of course, coordinating mechanisms and institutions must exist, but people grease them and make them go—or not.

This study shows that working multisectorally is not easy, but it is possible, even under limited and trying conditions. It does not mean that every nutrition intervention should be multisectoral. Sometimes a vertically run intervention that stays within sectoral boundaries may be most effective. In other cases, a multisectoral understanding is enough, with each sector doing its part. An integrated multisectoral program would not be necessary and could be institutionally unstable and duplicative. But in some cases just leaving it up to the sectors to coordinate is not sufficient either: significant interagency collaboration is required. Tackling complex problems, dealing with decentralization, and taking advantage of community-driven develop- ment—all are instances where understanding how to work in interagency col- laborations can produce significant benefits.

Our study also disproves the notion that successfully working multi- sectorally is possible only at small scales. The argument that this approach only works when managers can pay attention is specious. Of course, programs only work when managers pay attention! Managers should be attentive, and they should manage. Program management cannot be put on autopilot. These programs illustrate that the management skills needed for working success- fully and multisectorally in nutrition exist. One can argue that developing the necessary attitudes, skills, and supportive operational context takes time and is not easy—and that these are in short supply in many developing countries. One cannot argue, however, that it cannot be done.

Multisectoral structures are inherently fragile. Our study set out some principles for working multisectorally in a fragile environment. It did not, however, go further to understand how to institutionalize and sustain multi- sectoral programs. That is a question both MANA and NEP now confront. An initial hypothesis is that advocates and analysts must build widespread under- standing and political commitment, so that a wide range of actors supports the prioritization of action on nutrition over time. Most essentially, those who initiate, create, and manage programs must carry with them an awareness of the multisectoral nature of nutrition and of the advantages they can get from working multisectorally. Now that we know working multisectorally in nutrition is possible, we should build on these lessons to learn more about how to do so even more effectively and understand what to do to make sure these good efforts are sustained.

References

Acuña, C., and F. Repetto. 2006. Institutionality of poverty reduction policies and programs in Latin America. Executive summary, Inter-American Development Bank, Washington, D.C. <http://idbdocs.iadb.org/wsdocs/getdocument.aspx?docnum=723037>. Accessed July 28, 2008.

Agranoff, R., and M. McGuire. 2003. *Collaborative public management: New strategies for local governments.* Washington, D.C.: Georgetown University Press.

Alcaldía de Medellín. 2006. Medellín y su Población. In Documento técnico de soporte: Plan de ordenamiento territorial: Acuerdo 46/32006. <http://www.medellin.gov.co/alcaldia/jsp/modulos/P_ciudad/pot/Acuerdo%2046/4%20MEDELLIN%20Y%20SU%20POBLACION.pdf>. Accessed February 9, 2010.

Alderman, H., B. Ndiaye, S. Linnemayr, A. Ka, C. Rokx, K. Dieng, and M. Mulder-Sibanda. 2009. Effectiveness of a community-based intervention to improve nutrition in young children in Senegal: A difference in difference analysis. *Public Health Nutrition* 12 (5): 667–673.

Alesin, A., ed. 2005. *Institutional reforms: The case of Colombia.* Cambridge, Mass., U.S.A.: MIT Press.

Alexander, E. 1995. *How organizations act together: Interorganizational coordination in theory and practice.* Amsterdam, Netherlands: Gordon and Breach.

Álvarez, M., M. Benjumea, P. Roldan, M. Martínez, M. Maya, and E. Montoya. 2004. *Perfil alimentario y nutricional de los hogares de Antioquia.* Medellín, Colombia: Divergráficas.

Ambert, A., P. A. Adler, P. Adler, and D. F. Detzner. 1995. Understanding and evaluating qualitative research. *Journal of Marriage and the Family* 57 (4): 879–893.

Austin, J. 2000. *The collaborator challenge.* San Francisco: Jossey-Bass.

Bardach, E. 1998. *Getting agencies to work together: The practice and theory of managerial craftmanship.* Washington, D.C.: Brookings Institution Press.

Bassett, L., J. Levinson, and J. Garrett. 2007. Multisectoral approaches in nutrition: Lessons emerging from a review of processes and mechanisms. World Bank, Washington, D.C. Photocopy.

Bennis, W. 2009. *On becoming a leader.* New York: Basic Books.

Benson, T. 2008. *Improving nutrition as a development priority: Addressing undernutrition within national policy processes in Sub-Saharan Africa.* Research Report 156. Washington, D.C.: International Food Policy Research Institute.

Berg, A. 1973. *The nutrition factor in national development.* Washington, D.C.: Brookings Institution.

———. 1987. Nutrition planning is alive and well, thank you. *Food Policy* 12 (4): 365–375.

Berg, A., N. S. Scrimshaw, and D. L. Call, eds. 1975. *Nutrition, national development, and planning: Proceedings of an international conference.* Cambridge, Mass., U.S.A.: MIT Press.

Berger, A. M. 1996. Leadership in strategic partnerships: The case of a multi-sectoral collaboration. Ph.D. dissertation, University of Minnesota, Minneapolis-St. Paul, U.S.A.

Boogaerde, P., and C. Tsangarides. 2005. *Ten years after the CFA franc devaluation: Progress toward regional integration in the WAEMU.* Working Paper 145. Washington, D.C.: International Monetary Fund.

Britannica. 2009. Dakar. <http://www.britannica.com/EBchecked/topic/150012/Dakar#>. Accessed November 24, 2009.

Byrne, D. S. 1998. *Complexity theory and the social sciences.* New York: Routledge.

Carney, D., with M. Drinkwater, T. Rusinow, K. Neefjes, S. Wanmali, and N. Singh. 1999. *Livelihoods approaches compared.* London: Department for International Development.

Chisholm, D. 1989. *Coordination without hierarchy: Informal structures in multi-organizational systems.* Berkeley, Calif., U.S.A.: University of California Press.

CIA (Central Intelligence Agency). 2005. *CIA world factbook.* Washington, D.C.

Colombia, Departamento Administrativo Nacional de Estadística. 2005. Censo 2005. <http://www.dane.gov.co/censo/>. Accessed January 17, 2008.

Colombia, Ministerio de Comercio, Industria, y Turismo. 2004. Perfil de comercio exterior Antioquia. <http://www.mincomercio.gov.co/eContent/documentos/carces/perfiles/2004/Antioquia.pdf>. Accessed February 10, 2010.

Colombia, Ministry of National Defense. 2009. The FARC at their worst moment in history. <http://web.presidencia.gov.co/english/publicaciones/farc_peor_momento.pdf>. Accessed February 10, 2010.

Cropper, S. 1996. Collective working and the issue of sustainability. In *Creating collaborative advantage,* ed. C. Huxham. London: Sage.

Dillinger, W., and S. Webb. 2001. *Decentralization and fiscal management in Colombia,* Vol. 1. Policy Research Working Paper WPS 2122. Washington, D.C.: World Bank.

Dolan, C., and F. J. Levinson. 2000. *Will we ever get back? The derailing of Tanzanian nutrition in the 1990s.* Food Policy and Applied Nutrition Program Discussion Paper 17. Boston: Tufts University, Gerald J. and Dorothy R. Friedman School of Nutrition Science and Policy.

EIU (Economist Intelligence Unit). 2005. *Country profile: Senegal.* London: The Economist.

Field, J. O. 1985. Implementing nutrition programs: Lessons from an unheeded literature. *Annual Review of Nutrition* 5 (July): 143-172.

———. 1987. Multi-sectoral nutrition planning: A post-mortem. *Food Policy* 12 (1): 15-28.

———. 2006. Email to Lucy Bassett, June 15.

Fischer, F. 1998. Policy inquiry in postpositivist perspective. *Policy Studies Journal* 26 (1): 129-146.

Fisher, R., and A. Sharp. 2004. *Lateral leadership: Getting it done when you are not the boss.* 2nd ed. London: Profile Books.

GADM (Global Administrative Areas). 2010. GADM database. <http://www.gadm.org>. Accessed February 23, 2010.

Galasso, E., and N. Umpathi. 2009. Improving nutritional status through behavioural change: Lessons from Madagascar. *Journal of Development Effectiveness* 1 (1): 60–85.

Garrett, J. 2001. Comedores Populares: Lessons from urban programming from Peruvian community kitchens. CARE-USA, Atlanta and CARE-Peru, Lima.

———. 2008. Improving results for nutrition: A commentary on an agenda and the need for implementation research. *Journal of Nutrition* 138 (3): 646–650.

Geddes, B. 1990. How the cases you choose affect the answers you get: Selection bias in comparative politics. *Political Analysis* 2 (1): 131–150.

Gentilini, U., and P. Webb. 2008. How are we doing on poverty and hunger reduction? A new measure of country performance. *Food Policy* 33 (6): 521–532.

Gillespie, S., and L. Haddad. 2003. *The relationship between nutrition and the Millennium Development Goals: A strategic review of the scope for DFID's influencing role*. London: Department for International Development.

Gillespie, S., M. McLachlan, and R. Shrimpton. 2003. *Accelerating nutrition improvement: Time to act*. Washington, D.C.: World Bank.

Gobernación de Antioquia. 2006. *Anuario estadístico de Antioquia*. Medellín, Colombia: Gobernación de Antioquia. Available online at <http://planeacion.gobant.gov.co/anuario2006/historia/indice-1.htm> and <http://planeacion.gobant.gov.co/anuario2006/historia/indice-9.htm>. Accessed February 9, 2010.

Gobernación de Antioquia, Plan de Mejoramiento Alimentario y Nutricional de Antioquia. 2006a. MANA Eje 6 Contratos, 2006. Medellín, Colombia. PowerPoint presentation.

———. 2006b. MANA Sistematización Final, 2006. Medellín, Colombia. PowerPoint presentation.

———. 2006c. Plan de mejoramiento alimentario y nutricional de Antioquia. Medellín, Colombia. PowerPoint presentation.

———. n.d. *Plan de mejoramiento alimentario y nutricional de Antioquia (MANA)*. Brochure. Medellín, Colombia: Gobernación de Antioquia.

Grindle, M., and J. Thomas. 1991. *Public choices and policy change: The political economy of reform*. Baltimore: Johns Hopkins University Press.

Gubser, M. 2006. *Time's visible surface: Alois Riegl and the discourse on history and temporality in fin-de-siècle Vienna*. Kritik: German Literary Theory and Cultural Studies Series. Detroit, Mich., U.S.A.: Wayne State University Press.

Haddad, L., H. Alderman, S. Appleton, L. Song, and Y. Yohannes. 2003. Reducing child malnutrition: How far does income growth take us? *World Bank Economic Review* 17 (1): 107–131.

Heaver, R. 2002. *Improving nutrition: Issues in management and capacity development*. Health, Nutrition, and Population Discussion Paper, January 2002. Washington, D.C.: World Bank.

———. 2005a. *Strengthening country commitment to human development*. Washington, D.C.: World Bank.

———. 2005b. *Good work but not enough of it: A review of the World Bank's experience in nutrition*. Washington, D.C.: World Bank.

Heaver, R., and Y. Kachondam. 2002. *Thailand's national nutrition program: Lessons in management and capacity development*. Health, Nutrition, and Population Discussion Paper, January 2002. Washington, D.C.: World Bank.

Himmelman, A. 2002. Collaboration for a change: Definitions, decision-making models, roles, and collaboration process guide. <http://depts.washington.edu/ccph/pdf_files/4achange.pdf>. Accessed July 2, 2008.

Himmelman, R. 1996. On the theory and practice of transformational collaboration: From social service to social justice. In *Creating collaborative advantage*, ed. C. Huxham. London: Sage.

Hirschman, A. 1975. Policymaking and policy analysis in Latin America—A return journey. *Policy Sciences* 6 (4): 385–402.

Huxham, C. 1996. *Creating collaborative advantage*. London: Sage.

Hylton, F. 2002. The occupied territories of Medellín. Colombia Journal Online, October. <http://web.archive.org/web/20070610075101/http://www.colombiajournal.org/occupied_medellin.htm>. Accessed November 15, 2011.

———. 2006. *Evil hour in Colombia*. London: Verso.

Jarvis, A., H. I. Reuter, A. Nelson, and E. Guevara. 2008. Hole-filled seamless SRTM data V4, International Center for Tropical Agriculture (CIAT). <http://srtm.csi.cgiar.org>. Accessed June 30, 2011.

Jennings, E. T., Jr., and D. Krane. 1994. Coordination and welfare reform: The quest for the philosopher's stone. *Public Administration Review* 54 (4): 341–348.

Kabeer, N. 2003. *Gender mainstreaming in poverty eradication and the Millennium Development Goals: A handbook for policymakers and other stakeholders*. Ottawa: International Development Research Centre.

Kamensky, J. M., T. J. Burlin, and M. Abramson. 2004. Collaborating to achieve results no one can achieve alone. In *Collaboration: Using networks and partnerships*, ed. J. M. Kamensky and T. J. Burlin. Lanham, Md., U.S.A.: Rowman and Littlefield.

Katz, J. 1982. *Poor people's lawyers in transition*. New Brunswick, N.J., U.S.A.: Rutgers University Press.

Kotter, J. 1996. *Leading change*. Boston: Harvard Business School Press.

Kouzes, J., and B. Posner. 2007. *The leadership challenge*. 4th ed. San Francisco: John Wiley and Sons.

Kühl, S., T. Schnelle, and F.-J. Tillmann. 2005. Lateral leadership: An organizational approach to change. *Journal of Change Management* 5 (2): 177–189.

Kurtz-Phelan, D. 2007. Colombia's city on a hill: Medellín goes from murder capital to model city. *Newsweek*, November 10. Available online at http://www.thedailybeast.com/newsweek/2007/11/10/colombia-s-city-on-a-hill.html. Accessed October 13, 2011.

Leroy, J., and P. Menon. 2008. From efficacy to public health impact: A call for research on program delivery and utilization in nutrition. *Journal of Nutrition* 138 (3): 628–629.

Levinson, F. J. 1995. Multi-sectoral nutrition planning: A synthesis of experience. In *Child growth and nutrition in developing countries: Priorities for action*, ed. P. Pinstrup-Andersen, D. Pelletier, and H. Alderman. Ithaca, N.Y., U.S.A.: Cornell University Press.

——. 2000. International nutrition: Searching for an institutional home. Summary statement, World Bank-UNICEF Nutrition Assessment Project, Washington, D.C., and New York.

——. 2006. Meeting with Lucy Bassett, June 5.

Loevinsohn, M., and S. Gillespie. 2003. *HIV/AIDS, food security and rural livelihoods: Understanding and responding.* RENEWAL Working Paper 2. Washington, D.C.: International Food Policy Research Institute and International Service for National Agricultural Research.

McLachlan, M., and J. Garrett. 2008. Nutrition change strategies: The new frontier. *Public Health Nutrition* 11 (10): 1063-1075.

McLaren, D. 1977. Nutrition planning: The poverty of holism. *Nature* 1267 (5614): 742. Quoted in Field, J. O., Multi-sectoral nutrition planning: A post-mortem, *Food Policy* 12 no. 1 (1987): 15-28.

Natalicchio, M., J. Garrett, M. Mulder-Sibanda, S. Ndegwa, and D. Voorbraak. 2009. *Carrots and sticks: The political economy of nutrition policy reforms.* Washington, D.C.: World Bank.

Ndiaye, A. 2007. Making nutrition policy central to development: Understanding the political and institutional factors for policy change: Senegal case study. World Bank, Dakar, Senegal. Photocopy.

Neustadt, R., and E. May. 1986. *Thinking in time: The uses of history for decisionmakers.* New York: Free Press.

Oliver, C. 1990. Determinants of interorganizational relationships: Integration and future directions. *Academy of Management Review* 15 (2): 241-265.

Partington, D. 2002. *Essential skills for management research.* London: Sage.

PBS Online News Hour. 2003. Colombian president seeks support after rebels kill ten hostages. <http://www.pbs.org/newshour/updates/colombia_05-06-03.html>. Accessed February 10, 2010.

Pelletier, D. 2002. *Toward a common understanding of malnutrition: Assessing the contributions of the UNICEF framework.* World Bank-UNICEF Nutrition Assessment Background Paper. UNICEF and World Bank, Washington, D.C., and New York. Mimeo.

Pines, J. M. 1982. National nutrition planning: Lessons of experience. *Food Policy* 7 (4): 273-301.

Porter, T. M., and D. Ross, eds. 2003. *The Cambridge history of science: The modern social sciences.* Vol. 7. Cambridge, Mass., U.S.A.: Cambridge University Press.

Ranson, S., and J. Stewart. 1994. *Management for the public domain: Enabling the learning society.* Hong Kong: St. Martin's Press.

Rapid Results Institute and Micronutrient Initiative. 2009. Accelerating food fortification: A rapid results initiative in Kenya. <http://www.rapidresults.org/evaluations/kenya.php?top=318>. Accessed July 24, 2009.

Republic of Senegal. 2000. *Multiple indicator cluster survey.* Dakar.

——. 2004. *Deuxieme enquete Senegalaise aupres des ménages.* Dakar.

——. 2006. *Nutrition Enhancement Program: Phase II strategic plan 2007-2011.* Dakar.

Republic of Senegal, Nutrition Enhancement Program. n.d. Towards the MDG of reducing malnutrition by half by 2015 in Senegal: The Nutrition Enhancement Program (NEP). Dakar. PowerPoint presentation.

Richardson, K. 2008. Managing complex organizations: Complexity thinking and the science and art of management. *Emergence: Complexity & Organization* 10 (2): 13–26.

Rokx, C. 2000. *Who should implement nutrition interventions?* Health, Nutrition, and Population Discussion Paper, December 2000. Washington, D.C.: World Bank.

Ruel, M. T., J. L. Garrett, S. S. Morris, D. Maxwell, A. Oshaug, P. Engle, P. Menon, A. Slack, and L. Haddad. 1998. *Urban challenges to food and nutrition security: A review of food security, health, and caregiving in the cities.* FCND Discussion Paper 51. Washington, D.C.: International Food Policy Research Institute.

Schlager, E. 1999. A comparison of frameworks, theories, and models of policy processess. In *Theories of the policy process*, ed. P. Sabatier. Boulder, Colo., U.S.A.: Westview.

Seawright, J., and J. Gerring. 2008. Case selection techniques in case study research. *Political Research Quarterly* 61 (2): 294–308.

Seidman, H., and R. Gilmour. 1986. *Politics, position, and power: From the positive to the regulatory state.* 4th ed. New York: Oxford University Press.

Serrano-Berthet, R. 2003. What makes inter-agency coordination work? Insights from literature and two case studies. Inter-American Development Bank, Washington, D.C. Photocopy.

Shekar, M., on behalf of 17 other signatories. 2008. Letter to the editor. *Lancet* 371 (9626): 1751.

Snyder, W., and X. Briggs. 2004. Communities of practice: A new tool for government managers. In *Collaboration: Using networks and partnerships*, ed. J. M. Kamensky and T. J. Burlin. Lanham, Md., U.S.A.: Rowman and Littlefield.

Tucker, R. 1995. *Politics as leadership.* Rev. ed. Columbia, Mo., U.S.A.: University of Missouri Press.

UNDP (United Nations Development Programme). 2008. Human development report. <http://hdr.undp.org/en/statistics/>. Accessed August 19, 2008.

UNECA (United Nations Economic Commission for Africa). 2009. Senegal. <http://www.uneca.org/aisi/nici/country_profiles/Senegal/senegab.htm>. Accessed December 6, 2009.

UNESCO (United Nations Educational, Scientific, and Cultural Organization). 2008. UIS statistics in brief. <http://stats.uis.unesco.org/unesco/TableViewer/document.aspx?ReportId=121&IF_Language=eng&BR_Country=6860&BR_Region=40540>. Accessed August 19, 2008.

UNFPA (United Nations Population Fund). 2006. *The state of the world population.* New York: United Nations.

UNICEF (United Nations Children's Fund). 1990. *Strategy for improved nutrition of children and women in developing countries.* New York.

U.S. Department of State. 2008. Background note: Senegal. <http://www.state.gov/r/pa/ei/bgn/2862.htm>. Accessed January 18, 2008.

———. 2009. Background note: Colombia. <http://www.state.gov/r/pa/ei/bgn/35754.htm>. Accessed August 1, 2009.

Waddell, S. 2005. *Societal learning and change.* Sheffield, U.K.: Greenleaf Publishing.

Waldrop, M. M. 1993. *Complexity: The emerging science at the edge of order and chaos.* London: Viking.

WHO (World Health Organization). 2006. *World health report 2006.* Geneva.

———. 2008. WHO global data. <http://www.who.int/whosis/database/core/core_select_process.cfm>. Accessed June 18, 2008.

Wikipedia. 2008. Guillermo Gaviria Correa. <http://es.wikipedia.org/wiki/Guillermo_Gaviria_Correa>. Accessed January 8, 2008.

———. 2009. Historia de Antioquia. <http://es.wikipedia.org/wiki/Historia_de_Antioquia>. Accessed July 30, 2009.

World Bank. 2001. Implementation completion report (IDA-27230; PPFI-P8900) on a credit in the amount of SDR 11.7 million (US$ 18.2 million equivalent) to the Republic of Senegal for a community nutrition project. <http://www-wds.world bank.org/external/default/WDSContentServer/WDSP/IB/2001/09/18/000094946_01083004024820/Rendered/PDF/multi0page.pdf>. Accessed July 13, 2010.

———. 2006a. *Madagascar—Second community nutrition project additional financing.* Report 37718. <http://www-wds.worldbank.org/external/default/WDSContent Server/WDSP/IB/2006/11/02/000090341_20061102092910/Rendered/PDF/37718.pdf>. Accessed October 14, 2011.

———. 2006b. *Country assistance strategy: Senegal 2006-2011.* Washington, D.C.

———. 2007. Implementation completion and results report on a credit in the amount of SDR11.8 million (US$14.7 million equivalent) to the Republic of Senegal in support of the first phase nutrition enhancement program. <http://www-wds.world bank.org/external/default/WDSContentServer/WDSP/IB/2007/02/15/000020953_20070215115249/Rendered/PDF/ICR000107.pdf>. Accessed October 14, 2011.

Yin, R. 2009. *Case study research: Design and methods.* 4th ed. Thousand Oaks, Calif., U.S.A.: Sage.

Yin, R., and D. Campbell. 2003. *Case study research: Design and methods.* 3rd ed. Thousand Oaks, Calif., U.S.A.: Sage.

Yukl, G. 2001. *Leadership in organizations.* 7th ed. Upper Saddle River, N.J., U.S.A.: Prentice-Hall.

Interview References

AGMC	Alírio García and Marta Celis, June 27, 2006
BN	Biram Ndiaye, October 2007
BTFG	Buen Trato focus group, June 20, 2006
CR	Claudia Rokx, November 2007
DCHA	Dora Cecilia Gutiérrez Hernández, June 16, 2006
GH01	Dora Cecilia Gutiérrez Hernández, June 24, 2006
GHFV	Dora Cecilia Gutiérrez Hernández, June 19, 2006

GS   Galaye Sall, October 2007

ICBF21   Key informant, Colombian Institute for Family Welfare (Instituto Colombiano de Bienestar Familiar, or ICBF), June 21, 2006

IKALA   IKALA Consulting Firm focus group, June 26, 2006

JNG   Jean-Noel Gentile, October 2007

MC27   Marta Celis, June 27, 2006

MH   Mauricio Hernández, June 21, 2006

MM17   Patricia Monsalve and Angela Molina, June 17 and 24, 2006

MMS29   Menno Mulder-Sibanda, May 29, 2008

OrienteFG   Oriente regional team focus group, June 27, 2006

PedFG   Pedagogical Projects focus group, June 20, 2006

PPFG   Productive Projects focus groups, June 20 and 26, 2006

About the Authors

Lucy Bassett is a social protection specialist in the Latin America and Caribbean region of the World Bank, Washington, D.C.

James Garrett was a research fellow in the Poverty, Health, and Nutrition Division of the International Food Policy Research Institute, Washington, D.C., and a senior research fellow in the Institute's Development Strategy and Governance Division, where he served as leader of the Mozambique Strategic Analysis and Knowledge Support System, based in Maputo. He is currently working for the Food and Agriculture Organization of the United Nations, Rome, to strengthen its organizational strategy in the areas of nutrition and the promotion of a nutrition-aware food and agricultural system.

F. James Levinson was director of the International Food and Nutrition Center at the Friedman School of Nutrition Science and Policy at Tufts University, Boston, at the time he contributed to this work. He currently teaches at the Boston University School of Public Health.

Marcela Natalicchio is a consultant in political economy and governance for the World Bank, Washington, D.C.

Index

Page numbers for entries occurring in figures are suffixed by *f*; those for entries in notes by *n*; and those for entries in tables by *t*.